written,

tirely the great concept of Liberal Edu
cation with which Newman has endur

During the troublous years that Newman spent as the Rector of the ill-
starred Catholic University of Ireland
no work of his has had more lasting
significance than his brilliant series of
lectures that became *The Idea of a
University*. Composed in great haste
and under considerable difficulties it
suffers under certain defects of composition which may tend to confuse the
reader and certain omissions which
have to be supplied from Newman's
other writings in order that his thought
may be more fully understood. These
lectures from the pen of Father Mc-
Grath, whose *Newman's University:
Idea and Reality* placed him in the
forefront of interpreters of Newman's
thought, bring to light the intellectual
context in which they were originally

tional though
ept is insepara-
ristian concept
e urbanity and
's style brings
1en and move-
he germination
seen.

*

IOR

an Irish Jesuit
il. at Oxford;
attached to the
in Dublin and
of the Jesuit
nham Castle,
ar 1949-50 as

Visiting Professor at Fordham University where he is remembered for his
charm and deep learning.

THE CONSECRATION OF LEARNING

THE
CONSECRATION
OF
LEARNING

Lectures on Newman's
Idea of a University

WITHDRAWN

FERGAL McGRATH, S.J., D.Phil. (Oxon.)

FORDHAM UNIVERSITY PRESS · NEW YORK

FIRST PUBLISHED NOVEMBER 1962

CUM PERMISSU SUPERIORUM. NIHIL OBSTAT: JOSEPHUS A. CARROLL, CENSOR THEOL.
DEPUT. IMPRIMATUR: ✠ IOANNES CAROLUS, ARCHIEP. DUBLINEN., HIBERNIÆ PRIMAS.
18° OCTOBRIS 1962.
PRINTED AND BOUND IN THE REPUBLIC OF IRELAND AT THE PRESS OF THE PUBLISHERS

"... IN THE MEDIAEVAL UNIVERSITY
... THE OLD MONASTIC IDEAL OF THE
CONSECRATION OF LEARNING TO THE CHRISTIAN
WAY OF LIFE WAS RENEWED AND RAISED
TO A HIGHER INTELLECTUAL PLANE."

CHRISTOPHER DAWSON,
The Crisis of Western Education

CONTENTS

FOREWORD

THESE LECTURES were delivered in 1952 at the Summer
School of the Newman Association of England, held by
courtesy of the Provost and Fellows at Oriel College,
Oxford. They seemed to some of those present to merit
publication, but pressure of other work has made it impossible for me until now to find time for the necessary
revision. However, on re-reading the manuscript the themes
treated appeared to me to be just as actual as they were a
decade ago, so I am not without hope that they will of be
interest to those now engaged in or concerned with higher
education.

It was unavoidable that I should in the lectures cover
some of the same ground as in my *Newman's University: Idea
and Reality*, published in 1951, but I consider that there is
ample room for a second work based on the four years of
research which I devoted to the first. There is a considerable
difference of emphasis between the two. *Newman's University:
Idea and Reality* was mainly a history of how Newman came
to write his great *Discourses on the Idea of a University*, and
of his efforts to realise in the Catholic University of Ireland
the principles they enunciated. The present work is mainly
an analysis of the *Discourses*, and an examination of the
manner in which their principles may be applied to the
solution of modern problems.

Such an analysis is, of course, to be found in many of
the biographies of Newman, beginning with that of Wilfrid

Ward,[1] but I venture to hope that mine may prove to be of
value, if only for the fact that it is more detailed than most
of those which have already appeared.[2] As I point out in
several of the lectures, *The Idea of a University* is not an easy
book to read. It was composed in great haste and ·under
great difficulties and—if it is not presumptuous to speak thus
of so great a work—it has certain defects in composition
which tend to confuse the reader, and certain omissions
which have to be supplied from Newman's other writings
in order that his thought may be fully understood. For the
reading of *The Idea*, therefore, the average student will need
a fairly detailed analysis and commentary, and these I have
endeavoured to provide in the lectures at the risk of giving
them a certain prosaic character. I trust that my work may
succeed in a twofold aim; to present accurately and entirely
the great concept of Liberal Education with which Newman
has enduringly endowed educational thought, and to show
that this concept is inseparably linked with the Christian
concept of human destiny.

ACADEMIC FERMENT

I

AT THE OUTSET of this course of lectures some apology may seem to be needed for the fact that an Irishman should address you in completely English surroundings on the subject of an English classic.[1] There is, however, a certain fittingness in his so doing. By a strange train of circumstances it was in Ireland exactly a hundred years ago that this great book was almost entirely written. The main incentive to write it was to help an Irish project, and the principles laid down in it were, at least to some extent, put into practice by the author himself in Ireland. On the other hand, the book has its roots in England. It was here in this university, mainly here in this college, that its principles were evolved and clarified, and it was the cultural formation of this university, fostering a great native genius, that enabled Newman to set them down in such memorable form. Both countries, therefore, have a claim to be the cradle of this great contribution to human thought, and hence an Irishman, though conscious that it is a privilege to be invited to speak here about it, may be absolved from any accusation of presumption in accepting that invitation.

Indeed, he may welcome this opportunity of paying a

tribute of gratitude and reverence to the great Englishman
who laboured so earnestly for the cause of higher education
in Ireland, who sought so sincerely to unravel and understand
the tangled skein of the history of that troubled country, and
who paid such generous tributes to the virtues of her people.
It is to be regretted that Newman was, to some extent at
least, not understood or appreciated in the Ireland of his
day, as indeed in his own country also. But the passage of
time has vindicated him, and today his own people and the
people of the country to which he lent his genius for seven
years are at one in recognising that his contribution to
educational thought ranks among the great intellectual
heritages of all time.

The plan of these lectures is as follows. We shall first
consider the main events and trends of thought which
influenced the composition of Newman's *Discourses on the
Idea of a University*. We shall then endeavour to determine
exactly what Newman taught concerning that Liberal
Knowledge whose cultivation he held to be the main
function of a university. Finally we shall consider some
later major writings on the same subject, comparing their
treatment of it with that of Newman, and thus establishing
both the perennial nature of the problems which he raised
and the perennial value of the solutions which he offered.

2

In sketching the background to Newman's *Discourses*
our first task must be to take a rapid glance at the condition
of university education in England during the half century
preceding their composition. Not only was it antecedently

likely that Newman would be influenced in his ideas by his long years of residence at Oxford as an undergraduate at Trinity College from 1816 to 1820, and as Fellow of Oriel from 1822 to 1845; but in his introductory *Discourse* he states his definite intention to base his arguments largely upon his past experience. This intention was prompted mainly by the desire to rely upon reasoning which would not be linked with the tenets of Catholic theology, but would be acceptable to Christians of all denominations. It may be remarked, however, in passing that for reasons which we shall see later, Newman slightly modified this plan during the composition of the *Discourses*, and devoted the last two, more particularly the last, to the consideration or the relations between the Catholic Church, as the custodian of Catholic theology, and secular knowledge.

When we approach the subject of university education in England in the first half of the nineteenth century, we are at once struck by two contrasting facts: on the one hand, the very restricted extent of that education, and on the other, its great influence on the life of the nation. Up to 1826 there were but two universities in existence, the mediæval foundations of Oxford and Cambridge. In that year came the foundation of London University. Its influence, as we shall see, was destined to be very great both in itself and as a model for the future provincial universities; but at the date of the composition of Newman's *Discourses* its fortunes were still fluctuating, and it had not yet taken a definite place in the life of the nation.

We have said that the extent of the education offered by the older universities was restricted. The student body indeed was very limited in numbers. The average yearly enrolment in Oxford, for instance, in the first half of the century was about 200, and of these a good proportion did not persevere to the taking of a degree. There were two causes for this restriction. By tradition and owing to the expense of residence the undergraduates were drawn almost exclusively from the ranks of the wealthy landed aristocracy, and by statute they were drawn exclusively from the ranks of professing Anglicans, Nonconformists being excluded by the regulation which demanded the acceptance of the 39 Articles, in Oxford at matriculation, in Cambridge on the taking of a degree.

Nevertheless, the influence of the universities was undoubtedly very great in the intellectual and political life of the country. The great political leaders, the dignitaries of the Established Church, and the masters in the great public schools were preponderatingly Oxford and Cambridge men.

This fact is all the more remarkable when it is realised that the eighteenth century had witnessed a woeful decay in the level of studies of both great seats of learning.[2] At the end of that century the only recognised course in Oxford, that for the B.A., had degenerated into a classical course of the most narrowly literary type, with a smattering of Aristotelian philosophy. In Cambridge matters were somewhat better, but far from satisfactory. During the eighteenth century a formal examination, the Senate House examination, had been instituted for the degree, but it was almost purely mathematical. There was no entrance examination, and, incredible as it may seem to the modern mind, peers could get their degree without examination.

At the beginning of the nineteenth century movements for reform took place in both universities. In Oxford the leading figures in this reform were John Eveleigh, Provost of Oriel; Cyril Jackson, Dean of Christ Church; and John Parsons, Master of Balliol. In 1800 a new Examination Statute prescribed a formal examination in place of the old disputations for both Bachelor's and Master's degree, and also a separate examination for Honours. The examination for Masters, however, was dropped after a five years' trial, and has never been restored. In 1808 another examination, Responsions, was added in the second year, consisting of Latin, Greek, Logic and Geometry. By 1830 the classical degree had been restored to something of its proper fullness, and included history, rhetoric, poetry, moral philosophy and political economy, thus approximating to the Greats degree of today. In 1833 a formal examination in medicine was introduced, and in 1850 a third examination, Moderations, was brought into the classical course between Responsions and the final degree. New schools were instituted for law and modern history. But for all students, even those of medicine, the classics remained the fundamental part of the degree.

These details may seem somewhat tedious, but they are essential for an understanding of the famous controversy between the Edinburgh Reviewers and the Oxford Fellows, with which we are about to deal, and which on Newman's own avowal was the starting-point for his *Discourses on the Idea of a University*.[3]

In Cambridge the reform took a somewhat different course. As we have seen, already in the eighteenth century there had been introduced the Senate House examination for a degree. Early in the nineteenth century this was divided into two sections, the Mathematical Tripos and the ordinary B.A. By 1848 the Mathematical Tripos had become a reasonably satisfactory examination, and in 1822 a Classical Tripos was instituted. However, candidates for it were obliged to take honours mathematics also. In 1829 a formal examination was introduced for the degree in medicine, and in 1848 triposes in natural science and moral science. There had, therefore, been considerable advance in Cambridge, both in scope and thoroughness, up to 1850; but the whole curriculum was still excessively dominated by mathematics, there was little encouragement given to science except for the degree in medicine, there was still no entrance examination, and the level of the pass degree was low.

One other feature of the two universities deserves mention. It is constantly alluded to in Newman's correspondence, and in his provisions for the government of the Catholic University of Ireland, but finds no specific mention in his *Discourses*. In Oxford ever since the Code of Archbishop Laud (1636), who had become Chancellor of the University in 1629, the government had been in the hands of the Hebdomadal Board, which was chiefly composed of the Heads of Colleges. Similarly in Cambridge the government was in the hands of the Caput, on which the Heads of Colleges were represented together with the Doctors of Divinity, Law and Medicine, and which by the vote of one member could veto any Grace proposed to the Senate. This concentration of power in the hands of the resident Heads of Colleges had had a twofold effect. The professorial body was virtually excluded from government, and as a result of its loss of prestige the teaching authority of both universities had largely passed into the hands of tutors.

3

It was the irony of fate that at the very time when Oxford and Cambridge were commencing to set their houses in order, a memorable attack should have been made on them for the very defects they were trying to remedy. One stormy night in March, 1802, three young men had met in Edinburgh, and with an assurance that was justified by after events, had decided to found a quarterly journal for the furtherance of liberal ideas. The first of the trio was Francis Jeffrey, a Scottish graduate of Queen's College, Oxford, an unsuccessful barrister, later to be a successful editor, a judge of the Scottish Court of Sessions, and a peer. The second was Henry Brougham, a rising barrister, who eventually rose as high as the Lord Chancellorship of England. The third was Sydney Smith, graduate of New College, Oxford, a parson of some six years' standing, at the moment tutor to a young English squire, and destined to be the greatest wit, and perhaps the most unconventional clergyman who ever adorned—and slightly embarrassed—the Anglican establishment. The journal they founded was the *Edinburgh Review*, which was to play such a vital part in the rise of the Liberal Party and in the promotion of most of the great reforms associated with its name. They found willing and able helpers amongst the lawyers and university men of Edinburgh, amongst whom may be mentioned John Playfair, professor of mathematics, and they proceeded to disturb the British conscience by a new form of journalism, of which humour, sarcasm and invective were the outstanding characteristics.

In 1809 they began their attack on the old universities of England. According to Newman, Playfair, Jeffrey and Sydney Smith joined forces in the production of the anonymous articles.[4] It is probable that Playfair and Jeffrey supplied some of the ammunition, but the style and method of the articles leave no doubt that Sydney Smith was the active combatant. The contest had more than a purely academic interest. It was, in fact, a vital episode in the growth of the liberal ideal. In spite of the reforms that had been initiated, Oxford and Cambridge were still strongholds of the landed gentry, who mostly represented the Tory spirit in its most extreme form. The attacks of the Edinburgh reviewers did not aim merely at educational reform within the old universities, but had also the obvious purpose of shaking their prestige, and fostering the creation of a new type of university man, whether within their gates or without.

The battle opened with a review of a work entitled *Essays on Professional Education*, by Richard Lovel Edgeworth, the father of Maria Edgeworth the novelist. It occupies pp. 40-53 of the *Edinburgh Review* for October 1809 (No. XXIX), and after a few brief remarks on Edgeworth's book proceeds to the real business of criticism of higher studies in England. The reviewer commences by warning the reader that he is about to tackle a rather thorny subject.

> To almost every educated Englishman, up to the age of three or four-and-twenty classical learning has been the great object of existence; and no man is very apt to suspect, or very much pleased to hear, that what he has done for so long a time was not worth doing. His classical literature, too, reminds every man of the scenes of his

childhood, and brings to his fancy several of the most pleasing associations which we are capable of forming. A certain sort of vanity also very naturally grows among men occupied in a common pursuit. Classical quotations are the watchwords of scholars, by which they distinguish each other from the ignorant and illiterate; and Greek and Latin are insensibly become almost the only test of a cultivated mind.

All these considerations make it extremely difficult to procure a candid hearing on this question; and to refer this branch of education to the only proper criterion of every branch of education—its utility in future life.[5]

We will emphasise here in passing this claim that utility is the criterion of true education, and note that in making it the usually sagacious Smith made at the very outset a false step. Later he was to make it more definitely, so we may reserve our criticism for the present.

Before proceeding to his main attack on the English university system of classical education Smith clears the ground by making an important concession to the study of the classics in general, namely that they are the best models of style. He rightly claims that style is a result of and a manifestation of the activity of both intellect and imagination.

The cultivation of style is very justly made a part of education. Everything which is written is meant either to please or to interest. The second object it is difficult to effect without attending to the first; and the cultivation of style is the acquisition of those rules and literary habits which sagacity anticipates, or experience shows to be the most effectual means of pleasing. Those works are the best which have longest stood the test of time, and pleased the greatest number of exercised minds. Whatever, therefore, our conjectures may be, we cannot be so sure that the best modern writers can afford us as good models as the antients; we cannot be certain that they will live through the revolutions of the world, and continue to please in every climate—under every species of government —through every stage of civilisation. The moderns have been well taught by their masters, but the time is hardly yet come when the necessity for such instruction no longer exists. We may still borrow descriptive power from Tacitus; dignified perspicuity from Livy; simplicity from Caesar; and from Horace some portion of that light and heat which, dispersed into ten thousand channels, has filled the world with bright images and illustrious thoughts. Let the cultivator of modern literature addict himself to the purest models of taste which France, Italy and England could supply, he might still learn from Virgil to be majestic, and from Tibullus to be tender; he might not yet look upon the face of nature as Theocritus saw it; nor might he reach those springs of pathos with which Euripides softened the hearts of his audiences. In short, it appears to us, that there are so many excellent reasons why a certain number of scholars should be kept up in this and every civilized country, that we should consider every system of education from which classical education was excluded, as radically erroneous, and completely absurd.[6]

This important concession being made, Smith proceeds to his criticism of the type of classical education given by the English universities. His first ground of complaint is that there is too much of the classics, to the exclusion of other subjects.

The bias given to men's minds is so strong that it is no uncommon thing to meet with Englishmen, whom, but for their grey hair and wrinkles, we might easily mistake for school-boys. Their talk is of Latin verses; and it is quite clear, if men's ages are to be dated from the state of their mental progress, that such men are eighteen years of age and not a day older . . . Attend, too, to the public feelings—look to all the terms of applause. A learned man; —a scholar; —a man of erudition; are they given to men acquainted with the sciences of government? thoroughly masters of the geographical and commercial relations of Europe? to such men who know the properties of bodies, and their action upon one another? No: this is not learning: it is chemistry or political economy—not learning.[7]

Secondly, the classical education given at the universities fosters the imagination rather than the intellect.

The present state of classical education cultivates the imagination a great deal too much, and other habits of mind a great deal too little; and trains up many young men in a style of elegant imbecility, utterly unworthy of the talents with which nature has endowed them.[8]

Smith here forestalls a very natural and valid answer which the universities might be expected to make, especially in view of the reforms of the early nineteenth century, which as we have seen, had restored much of its intellectual content to the classical degree.

It may be said there are profound investigations, and subjects quite powerful enough for any understanding, to be met with in classical literature. So there are; but no man likes to add the difficulties of a language to the difficulties of a subject; and to study metaphysics, morals and politics in Greek, when the Greek alone is study enough without them. In all foreign languages, the most popular works are works of imagination. Even in the French language, which we know so well, for one serious work which has any currency in this country, we have twenty which are mere works of imagination. This is still more true in classical literature; because what their poets and orators have left us, is of infinitely greater value than the remains of their philosophy; for as society advances, men think more accurately and deeply, and imagine more tamely; works of reason advance, and works of fancy decay.

So that the fact of the matter is, that a classical scholar of twenty-three or twenty-four years of age, is a man principally conversant with works of imagination. His feelings are quick, his fancy lively, and his taste good. Talents for speculation and original inquiry he has none; nor has he formed the invaluable habit of pushing things up to their first principles, or of collecting dry and unamusing facts as the materials of reasoning. All the solid and masculine parts of his understanding are left wholly without cultivation; he hates the pain of thinking, and suspects every man whose boldness and originality call upon him to defend his opinions and to prove his assertions.[9]

The practical conclusions to which Smith comes are such

as we should all probably approve of. He would certainly encourage the training of classical scholars, as of scholars in any other fields. He sees a particular advantage in classical training for those destined for the Church. Even for the young man going into what he describes as Public Life, he admits the value of a classical foundation, but he would demand something more.

He should know what the constitution of his country really was,—how it had grown into its present state,—the perils that had threatened it,—the malignity that had attacked it,— the courage that had fought for it, and the wisdom that had made it great . . . (He should understand also) the mischief caused by bad laws, and the perplexity which arises from numerous laws,—the causes of national wealth, the relations of foreign trade, the encouragement of manufactures and agriculture,—the fictitious wealth occasioned by paper credit,—the laws of population,—the management of poverty and mendicity, —the use and abuse of monopoly,—the theory of taxation, —the consequences of the public debt . . . After the first period of life had been given up to the classics, and the reasoning powers were now beginning to evolve themselves,—these are some of the propensities in study which we would endeavour to inspire.[10]

4

So far it may be granted that Smith's views are reasonable and moderate. His accusation against the university classical course of training the imagination rather than the intellect was perhaps somewhat out of date at the time when he wrote, and, as we shall see, it was indignantly repudiated by the champions of Oxford. But his concessions to classical education are generous, more so, probably, than ours would be today. He appears to envisage the study of the classics as the invariable foundation for all other studies. Whether we admit or not that it is the best foundation in itself, modern circumstances have made such a classical foundation in practice impossible. For one thing the numbers embarking on secondary education have enormously increased, so that there is a correspondingly larger number of pupils with no natural ability for languages, who could never reach the degree of facility where the classics bear their full fruit. Again, the study of history and of modern foreign languages has increased in content and improved in method, so that these subjects now offer good alternatives. The level of mathematical and scientific studies has also been so raised that early specialisation, however it may be regretted, and however far we may try to postpone it, is forced to some degree even on secondary schools.

But in his desire to bring out the defects, as he saw them, in the universities of his day Smith went on to elaborate the theory of utility in education, to which he had made allusion at the beginning of his review. This is a subject over which much heat has been generated, and the heat has usually been the result of misunderstanding.

Pedants, said the late Dr Whitehead, Fellow of Trinity College, Cambridge, and Professor of Philosophy in Harvard, sneer at an education which is useful. But if it

is not useful, what is it? Is it a talent to be hidden away
in a napkin? Of course education should be useful,
whatever your aim in life. It was useful to St Augustine
and it was useful to Napoleon.[11]

Whatever pedants may do, no true educationist will sneer
at an education which is useful. But he will make an important distinction, which is not noticed by Dr Whitehead.
Some education is immediately useful, that is, it imparts to
the mind knowledge which is capable of being used for the
immediate betterment of the human race. But some education is not immediately useful. The knowledge it imparts
cannot be immediately used for the betterment of the human
race. However, it is ultimately useful, because it gives to
the mind certain qualities which enable it to use better
whatever immediately useful knowledge it may gain, either
previously, concurrently, or subsequently. We shall observe
in a later lecture that education cannot be divided into
water-tight compartments of the immediately and ultimately
useful. Knowledge which tends to the cultivation of the
mind can in unusual circumstances be of immediate use,
and almost all knowledge which is of immediate use gives
to the mind some cultivation. But the two types of knowledge are quite sufficiently differentiated by their preponder-
ant immediate or remote utility.

It seems clear that Sydney Smith also ignored this distinction, and had only immediate utility in mind when he
spoke of utility as being " the only proper criterion of every
branch of education." He explained this view in two later
passages, to which his Oxford opponents and, at a later date,

Newman rightly took exception. One of these we may quote:

> Classical Literature is the great object at Oxford. Many minds, so employed, have produced many works and much fame in that department; but if all liberal arts and sciences useful to human life had been taught there, if some had dedicated themselves to chemistry, some to mathematics, some to experimental philosophy, and if every attainment had been honoured in the mixt ratio of its difficulty and utility, the system of such a University would have been much more valuable . . .
>
> When a University has been doing *useless* things for a long time, it appears at first degrading to them to be *useful*. A set of Lectures on Political Economy would be discouraged in Oxford, probably despised, probably not permitted. To discuss the inclosure of Commons, and to dwell upon imports and exports, to come so near to common life, would seem to be undignified and contemptible. In the same manner, the Parr or the Bentley of the day would be scandalized, in a University, to be put on a level with the discoverer of a neutral salt; and yet, what other measure is there of dignity in intellectual labour but usefulness? And what ought the term University to mean, but a place where every science is taught which is liberal, and at the same time useful to mankind? Nothing would so much tend to bring classical literature within proper bounds as a steady and invariable appeal to utility in our appreciation of all human knowledge . . . Looking always to real utility, as our guide, we should see, with equal pleasure, a studious and inquisitive mind arranging

the productions of nature, investigating the qualities of bodies, or mastering the difficulties of the learned languages. We should not care whether he was chemist, naturalist, or scholar, because we know it to be as necessary that matter should be studied and subdued to the use of man, as that taste should be gratified and imagination inflamed.[12]

We may note for the sake of clearness that, when Smith speaks of utility, the examples he gives are all taken from the field of material welfare, and this would further narrow down the scope of education. However, we need not urge that point. Let us grant that utility covers the entire welfare of man, spiritual, intellectual and material. The ground taken up by Smith is that unless education immediately fits man to improve the condition of his fellowmen, it is not true education, and that the studies of the universities of his day had not that effect.

5

This challenge was read in copies of the Blue and Buff, as the *Edinburgh Review* was popularly called, propped up against coffee-pots on every don's breakfast-table in Oxford, and it was not surprising that champions spurred forthwith into the lists to defend the honour of England's oldest seat of learning. It is of peculiar interest to us to recall that they were found amongst the ranks of the Fellows of the College whose hospitality we are now enjoying, and which some twelve years after the events we are now recording, was to be the academic home of John Henry Newman. We may fittingly recall here the feeling words with which in the *Seventh Discourse* of his *Idea of a University* he speaks of Oriel.[13]

In the heart of Oxford there is a small plot of ground hemmed in by public thoroughfares, which has been the possession and the home of one Society for above five hundred years. In the old time of Boniface the Eighth and John the Twenty-second, in the age of Scotus and Occam and Dante, before Wiclif or Huss had kindled those miserable fires which are still raging to the ruin of the highest interests of man, an unfortunate king of England, Edward the Second, flying from the field of Bannockburn, is said to have made a vow to the Blessed Virgin to found a religious house in her honour, if he got back in safety. Prompted and aided by his Almoner, he decided on placing this house in the city of Alfred; and the Image of Our Lady, which is opposite its entrance-gate, is to this day the token of the vow and its fulfilment. King and Almoner have long been in the dust, and strangers have entered into their inheritance, and their creed has been forgotten, and their holy rites disowned; but day by day a memento is still made in the Holy Sacrifice by at least one Catholic Priest, once a member of that College, for the souls of those Catholic benefactors who fed him there for so many years.

Newman here goes on to recall the prominent part played by the Fellows of Oriel in the reforms to which we have already alluded; how, in particular, they had thrown their Fellowships open to candidates of the greatest merit, and hence how it was natural that when the storms broke upon the University from the North, their Alma Mater, whom they loved, should have found her first defenders within the walls of that small College, which had first put itself into a condition to be her champion.

It is as well that we should emphasise the earnest tone in which Newman chronicles this intellectual battle. As we shall see, it had its lighter, not to say comic side, but we must be careful not to regard it as a mere academic sham fight between " remote and ineffectual dons." There were real and deep issues at stake, issues which are still undecided, and which concern the welfare, indeed the very life of higher education.

It was, perhaps, unfortunate for Oriel and Oxford that the first champion who emerged into the lists was the less able Edward Copleston, a Devonshire man, graduate of Corpus, later to be Provost of Oriel and Bishop of Llandaff. Newman pays a tribute to " the good sense, the spirit, the scholar-like taste, and the purity of style " by which his replies to the *Edinburgh Review* were distinguished, but acknowledges that those of his successor in the fray, John Davison, were marked by " more of method and distinctness."[14] We may add also by more caution in approaching such a dangerous adversary as Sydney Smith.

Copleston's reply was published as a pamphlet of 187 pages entitled " A Reply to the Calumnies of the *Edinburgh Review* against Oxford containing an account of the Studies pursued in that University." It defends in great detail the curriculum of Oxford at that day, but we need concern ourselves only with those passages which deal with the value of classical studies.

Copleston points out [15] that there must be a division of labour in the acquiring of knowledge, the different subjects covering their various fields. There is an advantage in this concentration, namely that the study of each subject becomes more detailed and perfect. There is a disadvantage, namely that what the mind gains by concentration, it loses in breadth of vision. Copleston claims that the study of literature helps to counteract the narrowing effect of specialisation. It will be seen from what he has to say about the content of classical literature, that he was not using the word literature in the narrower sense of polite or elegant literature, or belles-lettres, but in the wider sense of the whole body of literary composition (except those works relating to positive sciences and art), and thus including history, philosophy and even theology. We may note too that for the moment he is envisaging literature in any language, not necessarily in Latin or Greek.

In the cultivation of literature is found that common link, which among the higher and middle departments of life, unites the jarring sects and subdivisions in one interest, which supplies common topics, and kindles common feelings, unmixed with those narrow prejudices with which all professions are more or less infected. The knowledge, too, which is thus acquired, expands and enlarges the mind, excites its faculties, and calls those limbs and muscles into freer exercise, which, by too constant use in one direction, not only acquire an illiberal air, but are apt also to lose somewhat of their native play and energy. And thus, without directly qualifying a man for any of the employments of life, it enriches and

ennobles all. Without teaching him the particular business
of any one office or calling, it enables him to act his part
in each one of them with better grace and more elevated
carriage; and, if happily planned and conducted, is a
main ingredient in that complete and generous education,
which fits a man ' to perform justly, skilfully, and mag-
nanimously, all the offices, both private and public, of
peace and war '. [16]

It may be noted that Copleston does not deal in any
detail with the question of utility in education, but in a
passing sentence he takes it for granted that literary studies
have a certain utility. " Thus far," he says, " we have considered the utility of those liberal pursuits . . . " It is that
" enlargement " of the mind which constitutes their utility,
and we see at once that he is speaking of what we have called
" ultimate utility."

Copleston then goes on to claim that classical literature
" answers this purpose most effectively." Smith had allowed
that the classical authors provide unrivalled models in style.
Copleston furthermore claims that their intellectual content
is of the highest order.

That the relics of Grecian and Roman literature contain
some of the choicest fruits of human genius; that the
poets, the historians, the orators, and the philosophers
of Greece especially, have each in their several lines
brought home and laid at our feet the richest treasures
of invention; that the history of those early times presents
us with a view of things ' nobly done and worthily
spoken '; that the mind and spirit which breathed them,
lives still, and will for ever live in the writings which

remain to us; that, according as taste, and genius, and learning have been valued among men, those precious remains have been held still dearer and more sacred; are all positions which it is better to assume as indisputable, than to embarrass the present argument with any new attempt to prove them.[17]

This argument has been better put by other writers, but its validity is indisputable. It need not, and it cannot, be defended in the extreme form sometimes heard, that the ancients said everything worth saying on every subject, but it certainly can be defended in the sense that almost everything they said is still of value.

Copleston then deals with an objection not specifically raised by Smith, namely that the content of the classical writings can be equally or better studied in translations. This is a difficult and somewhat subtle question, but there is much to be said for Copleston's arguments that only the original can fully convey the thought. Translated thought, he says, is often cold in another language. It affects the reader in the original, but leaves him untouched in the translation. The simplest languages have wholly characteristic phrases and constructions; the more perfect, amongst which must be reckoned Latin and Greek, abound in them. Simple facts may be adequately translated, but, asks Copleston,

> how shall even the ordinary phraseology of moral reasoning, of sentiment, of opinion, preserve its native colouring, and exact features? How shall the language of varied passion, of tender feeling, of glowing description, find, in the distant region to which it is transported, the precise measure of its value?[18]

His concluding argument is a weighty one.

But all that constitutes the grace, the beauty, the charm, the dignity of composition, all that tends to awaken the fancy, or to affect the heart, like the finer and more volatile parts of substance, is lost during the experiment; or if these qualities be partially retained, they are, in a manner, the invention of the translator; and serve rather to tell us, that the original was excellent, than to present us with a view of that excellence itself.[19]

6

Having established the value of classical education in general, Copleston proceeds to consider the specific charges of Smith against the actual classical education given by the English universities. And here the future bishop of Llandaff made the fatal mistake of losing his temper with an adversary who loved to provoke, and of waxing sarcastic at the expense of one of the greatest masters of sarcasm of all times.

The writer of an article in the *Edinburgh Review*, on *Edgeworth's Professional Education*, whose petulant sarcasms alternately provoke our spleen and our laughter, endeavours to convince the world that, notwithstanding the advantage of Classical learning, the ascendancy it has acquired in English education is preposterous, and the mode of teaching it in English schools and universities, utterly absurd. I confess it was the reading of that article which drew forth the present remarks, and I had designed a formal discussion of the false opinions and accusations contained in it. The bulk of this work, however, swelling imperceptibly beyond my first intention (he had already got to page 115), induces me to contract the plan; and the truly meagre and flimsy text of the article itself is hardly deserving of any solid criticism. There is a sprightliness, however, and vivacity, which takes with the world at first reading, and raises a transient admiration, which perhaps was the sole ambition of the writer; for, upon comparing one page with another, he seems wholly regardless of the dull virtue of consistency, and, like some popular divines (Copleston here surely is giving a hint that he has no doubt about the identity of the reviewer) thinks only how he may keep up the requisite smartness for his fifteen minutes to amuse his audience.[20]

Copleston then summarises the Reviewer's accusations against Oxford:

Firstly, that classical learning forms the sole business of English education;

Secondly, that hence the taste and imagination only of the student are cultivated;

Thirdly, that the instruction of public schools and universities, even in classical literature, is of a limited and mistaken kind;

Fourthly, that in Oxford particularly every manly exercise of the reasoning powers is discouraged.[21]

Copleston's reply to the first charge is given in a separate chapter, in which he gives details of the courses and examinations introduced by the recent reforms. It cannot be said that the syllabus is very impressive, and Copleston makes the damaging admission that a degree is rarely refused. " Nothing but extreme incapacity, extraordinary want of school education, or gross idleness at the University, will absolutely exclude a student from his degree at the regular time." We may recall that it was not until 1830 that the classical degree was restored to its proper amplitude, and a formal examination in medicine instituted, and not until the middle of the century that special schools for history and law were established. However, this domestic. issue need not detain us here.

In answer to the second charge he denies that languages are studied at the universities for the sake of the sound or form of the letters, not for the stores of taste and knowledge which they contain. As so often happens in controversy, Copleston here exaggerates his adversary's charges, in order the more easily to refute them. However, it was true that the precise aim of the reforms initiated by Eveleigh, Jackson and Parsons had been to stress the value of the context of the classics rather than their form, and Copleston was entitled to feel some indignation that Smith should attribute to Oxford an evil which Oxford men themselves had set about eliminating.

But once again Copleston gave Smith just the assurance he wanted that the barbs of his satire had gone home.

The third charge (namely, that English classical instruction is limited to mere exercises of style) is worked up with all the smirking pleasantry and pert playfulness peculiar to a certain school, whether consisting of Divines, or Lecturers, or Letter-writers, or Reviewers whose main object seems to be to have their laugh out, whatever truth or justice or decency or right reason may say to the contrary.[22]

In the main what Copleston has to say about the value of prose and verse composition in Greek and Latin is sound enough, but it is somewhat beside the point, as Smith had merely said that there was too much of it in English education. We may pass on to Copleston's reply to Smith's claim that utility is the criterion of good education, and that classical studies are largely useless. Copleston does not make our distinction between immediate and ultimate utility, but contents himself with pointing out that there is even immediate utility in the knowledge of human nature and human thought which the study of the classics gives.

> Never let us believe that the improvement of chemical arts, however much it may tend to the augmentation of national riches, can supersede the use of that intellectual laboratory, where the sages of Greece explored the hidden elements of which man consists, and faithfully recorded all their discussions.[23]

We shall see that this very cogent argument was to be more ably developed by Copleston's colleague Davison, and by Newman and later writers.

Copleston has one more tilt, in the fifth chapter of his voluminous pamphlet, at what he calls the Reviewer's " plausible affectation of zeal for what is called utility." [24] We have noted that Smith's examples of utility are all taken from the field of material welfare, and that this made his claim for utility as the criterion of education more obviously false. Copleston enlarges on this point for some fifteen pages, and finds it easy enough to demonstrate that the useful is " that which conduces to some good end," [25] but that that end is not necessarily material welfare. He grants that

" cultivation of mind must not be permitted to *interfere* with bodily well-being, nor to unfit men for producing it,"[26] but rightly denies that this is any proof " that the highest intellectual labour is that which helps to satisfy bodily wants."[27]

7

Let us now sum up the result of the first two rounds of the contest between these academic champions. The outstanding points made by Smith are as follows:

1 The classics will always remain the best models of style.
2 There is excessive study of the classics in English education.
3 There is too much study of imaginative works.
4 It is too difficult to study the intellectual context of the classics in the original.
5 The general run of student should add to classics the study of politics and economics.
6 Utility is the criterion of education. Smith implies that immediate utility is the only utility. He stresses material utility as the most important.

Copleston's main contentions are these:

1 Literature gives a general culture to the mind which more specific studies do not.
2 Classical studies are peculiarly fitted to this end because of their intellectual content.
3 This can be studied accurately only in the originals.
4 It is untrue that the Oxford curriculum gives excessive attention to classics.
5 It is untrue that only works of imagination are studied.

6 Granting that utility is the criterion of good education, the knowledge of human nature which the classics give is of greater utility than the knowledge of natural phenomena which physical science gives.

7 It is untrue to say that studies which conduce to material welfare are higher than those which cultivate the mind.

We may save ourselves trouble by ignoring the views expressed by both opponents on the state of Oxford studies. That is an issue that belongs to the past and has no permanent value.

The views of lasting significance that emerge are these:

1 All education conduces to some good. This is agreed on by both.

2 This good may be the immediate improvement of the human race, either materially, intellectually or spiritually. Smith implies that this is the only good to be aimed at, and perhaps unwittingly stresses the value of material good.

3 Or it may be the training of the mind to produce such good ultimately. This is the aim stressed by Copleston.

4 Literature has a peculiar value in this training of the mind.

5 Classical literature above all others is fitted for this task.

It may be noted that whilst these two last points are the main basis of Copleston's defence of the classics, they are to some extent conceded by Smith by the very fact that he does not deny the value of the intellectual content of the classics, but urges that the mastery of it is too difficult for the ordinary student.

8

In 1806 Sydney Smith at the age of thirty-five had been presented, through the influence of his Whig friends in the " Ministry of All the Talents," with the living of Foston-le-Clay in Yorkshire. His early life had been a struggle against poverty, and though he hated the country, he was glad to accept a secure livelihood, and settled down in the village of Heslington, near York, driving a dozen miles to Foston with his wife every Sunday. Though, as he said, he did not know a turnip from a carrot, he threw himself with energy into the farming of three hundred acres, took to baking, brewing, churning, fattening poultry, started allotments for the poor, experimented with smoking chimneys, tried his hand at candle-making, and made all kinds of curious agricultural experiments. Once he fed his pigs on fermented grain, and reported that they were quite happy in their sty, grunting the National Anthem. It must have been a refreshing intellectual change for him to turn to the castigation of his Oriel critic, which he inflicted in the *Edinburgh Review* for April 1810.[28]

We may pass rapidly over what he has to say about Copleston's defence of the Oxford curriculum. He grants that he had not known much of the recent reforms, but holds that they have been short-lived, and that their introduction proved the existence of previous abuses.

Turning to the more fundamental issues, Smith put his finger on a lacuna in Copleston's reply. Copleston had emphasised the value of the intellectual content of the classics, but had ignored Smith's objection that the task of mastering it in the original was beyond the power of the ordinary student. Smith returned to the attack on this issue.

If a man reads a book in a difficult language, copious in its words and licentious in its variations, it is not possible that he should attend as much to the meaning of what he reads, as if that meaning were conveyed to him in his native tongue. The attention which should be given to things, is inevitably distracted by words.[29]

Another weakness in Copleston's reply was that he had not given credit to Smith for his concessions to the value of classical studies.

Our objection is not, that classical knowledge is not a good, but that it is not the only good. We contend, that all young men need not be classical scholars; that some may be allowed to deviate into mathematical knowledge, some into chemistry, some into natural philosophy, some into political economy, some into modern languages; that all these occupations, though not, perhaps, superior in importance to classical erudition, are not inferior to it.[30]

As we shall see later, the last words cannot be accepted without reservation. The subjects enumerated by Smith have all their special value in the total mental equipment of the human race, but they are of varying value in enabling man to attain happiness even in this life, and much more so in helping him to attain his final end.

So far Smith had been courteous enough, but he had not forgotten Copleston's ill-advised reference to " the smirking pleasantry and pert playfulness " of the popular divine. The fault he found in his adversary was pompous obviousness.

This Oxford gentleman is always burning candles by daylight, proving what no human being ever called in question, and making the most pompous display of the most trite and insignificant truths . . . And all this is not done carelessly, or despatched in a few words, as a man gets rid of a commonplace which is a necessary passport to an important truth; but our tutor gets warm and cackling; and when he has laid his little truism, makes such an intolerable riot, that we might suppose he had produced a diamond instead of an egg.[31]

It was possibly Smith's own hens at Heslington that had suggested this polemical metaphor. He was now warming to his favourite task of making his opponent seem ridiculous.

One who passes for a great man in a little place, generally makes himself ridiculous when he ventures out of it. Nothing can exceed the pomp and trash of this gentleman's observations; they can only proceed from the habit of living with third-rate persons; from possessing the right of compelling boys to listen to him; and from making a very cruel use of this privilege . . .

Here possibly a cackling from his hen-yard brought Smith back to the poultry metaphor.

He who has seen a barn-door fowl flying—and only he —can form some idea of this tutor's eloquence. With his neck and hinder parts brought into line,—with loud screams and all the agony of feathers and fatness,—the ponderous little glutton flaps himself up into the air, and, soaring four feet above the level of our earth, falls dull and breathless on his native dunghill.[32]

Amusing as this tirade is, it cannot be said to have any bearing on the issues under discussion. It is merely a clever example of the historic technique of belittling one's adversary. Indeed, in the whole of the rest of Smith's reply there is only one other passage worthy of serious consideration, in which he endeavours to defend his criterion of utility. He thus replies to Copleston's denial of its validity.

> The objections which he makes to the science of chemistry are really curious—that it raises and multiples the means of existence, and terminates merely in the bodily wants of man . . . And what, we should be glad to know, is the main object of most branches of human knowledge, if it be not to minister to the bodily wants of man? What is the utility of mathematics, but as they are brought to bear upon navigation, upon astronomy, mechanics, and so upon bodily wants? What have law and politics in view, but to consult our bodily wants—to protect those who minister to them—and to arrange the conflicting interests and pretensions which these wants occasion? [33]

9

Summing up now the third round of the contest, and prescinding from minor issues and irrelevant abuse, we see that the kernel of the dispute is the meaning to be given to the word utility. Smith had laid down the indisputable principle that all education must be useful in the sense of conducing to good, but had falsified it by assuming, or at any rate suggesting that the only good to be considered was the immediate material welfare of mankind. Copleston had rightly denied this, and had correctly emphasised the fact that the culture given to the mind by literary studies in the wide sense, has also its use, and a higher use than material amelioration. It may, perhaps, be conceded that he would have strengthened his case had he on the one hand expounded more fully the benefits that culture of mind can confer on the human race, and how the mastery of physical science can be of benefit to man only when it is controlled and utilised by properly trained minds; and had he on the other hand been somewhat more liberal in his concessions to the value of physical science when properly controlled and utilised. He would thus have safeguarded himself against the obvious misrepresentation of his arguments made by Smith.

We may note here in passing that there were two fundamental considerations which neither contestant thought of, or at any rate formulated: firstly, that the most essential part of intellectual training is in the realm of philosophy and theology, and secondly, that it is impossible to come to any satisfactory definition of utility or of its various degrees, unless one has a definite conviction as to whether the end of man is temporal happiness or something beyond it. We shall revert to these two considerations later.

10

Copleston returned to the fray in two shorter replies, which do not throw any further light on the subject, and need not delay us here. He was not, however, left alone in his combat with the redoubtable Smith. Four months later, in August 1810, there appeared in the *Quarterly Review* a critique of his first and second replies. It is unsigned, but may possibly have been from the pen of John Davison, the second Oxford champion, a north-countryman who had been an undergraduate at Christ Church, was Fellow of Oriel from 1800 to 1817, later attained a moderate reputation as a theological writer of the conservative school, and died in 1834 as Prebendary of Worcester. The critique certainly contains one passage enunciating a theme which Davison was later to develop more fully.

We may add that the appropriate subject of almost all that is commonly called classical learning is nothing else than man's moral nature—his passions, his plans of action —their springs and various movements—and whatever humanity or moral speculation is concerned with. All that deserves the name of wisdom, all the common sense of life in its most improved state, is drawn from this source. The fruit of other studies is learning or science. Men may range over the whole compass of nature and art; but their best researches will be those which are most intimately connected with some point of moral character in its diversified relations.[34]

The reviewer does not make any absolutely exclusive claim for these studies.

Contracted and exclusive systems must, indeed be wrong; but if any one part of learning were to be set high above the rest, we know of none which could fill the station of pre-eminence with less disadvantage than those studies which engage men in the contemplation of themselves and their common nature; in the knowledge of which they must always have a greater interest than in

any combination of matter which the chemist can analyse
or the astronomer survey.[35]

We may note that this reviewer, whether he be Davison
or not, is more precise than Copleston in his description
of the special merit of literary studies. Copleston had
alluded in a passing way to " that intellectual laboratory,
where the sages of Greece explored the hidden elements
of which man consists." Our new writer specifies these
" hidden elements " as being " man's moral nature . . .
whatever humanity or moral speculation is concerned with."
Over a year later, in October 1811, there appeared in the
Quarterly a review of Edgeworth's Essays on Professional
Education, the work on which Sydney Smith had based his
initial attack on Oxford studies. We have it on Newman's
authority that it was from the pen of Davison. It contains
a much more balanced defence of classical studies than
Copleston's, and the writer, perhaps out of caution, deals
with Smith's animadversions in a completely serious vein.
Much of it is quoted in Newman's Seventh Discourse, so
that we need not delay long on it. We may note, however,
that Davison clearly states the scope of the so-called literary
studies. According to him they include " religion (in its
evidences and interpretations), ethics, history, eloquence,
poetry, theories of general speculation, the fine arts and
works of wit."[36] Whether or not he was the author of the
preceding review in the Quarterly, he gives the same description of the common nature of these seemingly diversified
subjects, but is more specific. " They are all," he says,
" quarried out of one and the same great subject of man's
moral, social and feeling nature."[37] It is, however, curious

that Davison does not enlarge further on the value of this study of man in itself, but devotes himself at length to the consideration of the peculiar value it has in the training of the intellect. These subjects of study, he asserts, " are all under the control (more or less strict) of the same power of moral reason; there is a balancing, an option, and a doubt in judging of them." [38]

It is obvious that Davison does not use the term " moral reason " in the sense of reasoning on moral problems alone, but rather in the sense of the exercise of the intellect in forming comparative judgments, whether on moral or other subjects. Curiously enough the words " balancing, option and doubt in judging," which make Davison's meaning clear, are omitted in quotation by Newman, but he gives several other passages from Davison which clearly attribute to " moral reason " the sense we have accepted. The power of the mind which exercises this moral reason is called by Davison " judgment." He describes it as " that master-principle of business, literature and talent, which gives him (man) strength in any subject he chooses to grapple with, and enables him to seize the strong point in it," and he states that " Judgment lives as it were by comparison and discrimination." [39]

Davison's view then is that the study of the physical sciences does not give the same scope for the exercise of comparative judgments as the study of literature in the wide sense.

Physical science treating of the properties of matter, whether in the form of plants, minerals or planets, is no more than a number of well-authenticated facts, addressed to our admiration rather than to our judgment. The wisdom of contrivance displayed in them is vast; but it is a wisdom we cannot transplant into our minds. It is even too perfect for us to deliberate upon. We can neither imitate nor question it. As subservient to the arts—chemistry, botany and astronomy may be among the most *useful* studies, and as the food of ingenious curiosity, they are amongst the most liberal. But these are their proper attributes. They will not interest us in our own nature, nor furnish us with any of the talents, by which that nature is governed in society, or fashioned within ourselves.[40]

He finds the same inferiority in mathematical studies.

In works of demonstration there is so simple and uniform a process of the mind that, without much violence of expression, we may affirm the first page of Euclid to be just like the last page of Archimedes. The value and amount of the series may be increasing, but the component parts of it are a succession of conclusions, each obtained by a monotonous style of proof all issuing out of the simple relation of greater and less. How different are the sameness and simplicity of these diagrams of thought from the full and varied picture produced by the mixed relations and contending principles that subsist in taste, morals, literature, law and policy.[41]

It may, perhaps, have been remarked that there is a certain slight confusion in the enunciation of these views of Davison, though their substantial correctness will hardly be questioned. Davison is really attributing two virtues to the study of literature, but lays all the stress on one. That which he only indicates in passing is the fact that their subject matter is the intellectual, ethical and aesthetic nature of man. That which he stresses is that the study of this subject-matter demands constant exercise in recognising the good and the bad, whether intellectual, ethical or aesthetic, an exercise which produces in the mind a power of analysis, of synthesis and of appreciation of values, which give a balance not produced by other studies.

These issues will come up for consideration later, and we may leave them for the moment. Before we take leave of our Oxford and Edinburgh controversialists, we may note that Davison closed on a note of moderation with regard to classical studies in the strict sense. The claims he had made were for literary studies in general. Whether these are to be in the classical languages or in others, he rightly declares to be a secondary question.

> The established system of the universities of England has given a declared preference to the ancient languages. As compositions of speech we are not solicitous about those languages in the present argument. But so far as they afford the right modes of study, within the scope of that range of literature we have been describing, so far they are the proper *Lares* to be set up in an English university . . . If their intrinsic value will stand a comparison with the works of any age or country, they are at least on a par with those of any other language.[42]

He freely grants that if, for instance, a course in the English classics were proposed, he " should be inclined to enter into parley with the proposed reform, and deliberate upon the exchange." [43]

II

Some twenty years later the *Edinburgh Review* returned to the attack upon Oxford. This time the critic was a much more able one than Sydney Smith, Sir William Hamilton,[44] a Balliol man, professor of logic and metaphysics in Edinburgh and one of the greatest philosophers of the day. Though we are anticipating somewhat, we may here briefly review his strictures, of which Newman must certainly have been cognisant, though he makes only a vague and passing reference to them in his *Discourses*.[45] The first two articles, which appeared in 1831, we need merely mention.[46] They deal with the usurpation of both the teaching office and the governing power in Oxford by the collegiate bodies. This was a matter which Newman always had in mind, and we shall see later that, when he came to draw up the constitutions of the Catholic University in Dublin, he took care to safeguard the powers of the professoriate. But this question of authority in the university has no direct bearing on our subject.

The third and fourth articles, which appeared respectively in 1834 and 1835,[47] are of greater interest to us, since they raise the issue of undenominational education, which was to be the partial and more fundamental theme of Newman's *Discourses*. Hamilton found his occasion in the Bill of 1834 to enable Nonconformists to be admitted to the universities. He held it to be beyond argument that Dissenters should have this right, since the university is " the necessary national establishment for general education." [48] He takes it for granted that the religious observances of the colleges would continue to be those of the Church of England. In his first article he went so far as to say that " it would be an un-warrantable exercise of legislative interference either on the one hand to compel them to accommodate these observ-ances to the taste of those intruded into their society; or, on the other to subvert the discipline of the house, by emancipating any part of its inmates from the rules estab-lished for the conduct of the whole." [49] He would not favour the establishment of nonconformist colleges, which he believed would foster religious bigotry by creating a spirit of rivalry, but thought that the best solution would be " the establishment of Halls where no religious observances would be imposed." [50] In his second article, however, he went further, and suggested that, though the present constitution of the colleges entitled them to confine their membership to those of the Anglican faith, that constitution could and should be altered by the statutory power of the university. [51]

All along Hamilton considers the question mainly from the legal aspect. He makes, however, a brief reference to the more fundamental question of the effect on religion of the abandonment of the denominational character of the university.

> But again it is clamoured: By the removal of academic tests the most influential situations in the universities may be filled with men, enemies not only of the estab-lished religion, but of religion altogether. [52]

To this he has three answers. Firstly, the example which is commonly adduced to support this argument is that of the German universities. Hamilton holds that the heterodox character of their theology was due not to the abandonment of religious tests, but to the general heterodoxy of German theology. Secondly, he avers, without very specific proof, that in many universities in other countries professors of all faiths are admitted without injury to religion. Thirdly, he adduces an *argumentum ad hominem* in the fact that even in the English universities, where tests are imposed, heterodox views on theology are common.

When these articles were re-published with other essays in 1852, Hamilton added a further essay entitled *On a Reform of the English Universities with special reference to Oxford: and limited to the Faculty of Arts.* It is much abler and more interesting than any of his *Edinburgh Review* articles. We can only deal with it briefly, but I can recommend the reading of it to students of education and in particular to young university teachers who are looking for guidance as to the aims and methods of university lecturing.

It is most unlikely that Newman had read this essay before the composition of his *Discourses*, which were delivered in the same year that it was published. It touches, however, on several of the themes which Newman dealt with. Hamilton establishes very clearly the twofold function of a university as an institution for liberal education and as a training ground for the professions, and his views on the difference between the kinds of knowledge imparted by each function agree in the main with those which we shall see to be held by Newman.

In the former respect, the student *is considered as an end unto himself*; his perfection, as a man simply, being the aim of his education. This is the end proposed in what is academically known as the Faculty of Arts or of Philosophy. In the latter respect, the learner *is not viewed as himself an end*, that end being now something out of himself; for not his perfection as a man, but his dexterity as a professional man—in a word, his usefulness as an instrument, has become the aim of his scientific preparation. This end is that proposed in what are academically known as the Faculties of Theology, Law, Medicine etc.; and in this relation, a University is, in fact, only a supplemental and contingent aggregation of special schools, the only connection that these have with each other, or with the University, being, that they all hold out to be *liberal*, that is, they all hold out to educate to professions, which presupposes always a liberal accomplishment, if not always an education in the liberal faculty, or faculty of arts.[53]

Among the subjects of the curriculum for the Arts course Hamilton makes a division based on a principle which we shall find also enunciated by Newman. He would have two departments, one of Humane Letters, the other of Philosophy. He does not, however, use these titles in their ordinarily accepted sense, but gives them a special meaning of his own, which he thus explains:

The former (Humane Letters) is of *empirical*, the latter (Philosophy) of rational knowledge.

Empirical knowledge is a knowledge of the *fact*. Humane Letters would thus comprehend all dexterity at language, all familiarity with literary products, all acquaintance with historical record. This department, by the conditions stated, should in a great measure be limited to the domain of Greek and Roman letters.

Rational knowledge is a knowledge of the *cause* or *reason*. Philosophy would thus comprehend—in a proximate sphere, the science of mind in its *faculties*, its *laws*, and its relations (Psychology, Logic, Morals, Politics etc.); in a less proximate sphere, the science of the instrument of mind (Grammar, Rhetoric, Poetic etc.); in a remote sphere, the science of the *objects* of mind (Mathematics, Physics etc.).[54]

We shall see later that Newman also made this distinction between studies of particular facts and studies which concern themselves with the inner nature of these facts, and that Newman also gave to the latter the title " Philosophy," using the term in a very special sense. Hamilton, however, makes two reservations which Newman obviously does not admit. Though he grants that Physical Sciences and History belong to the " philosophical " group of subjects, he does not think them to be worthy of the highest examination honours. The former he holds to be " subjectively too unimproving, and objectively too eccentric, too vast and withal too easy." [55] The latter he grants to be " of great importance in itself," but avers that " it does not necessarily call forth, exercise, and develop the higher powers of thought." [56]

As we would expect, Hamilton lays great stress on the fact that among the " philosophical " subjects Philosophy, in the strict sense, is the most fundamental. (He takes it for granted that some theological knowledge should be required of all candidates for a degree, but that it should not be a subject in which academical distinction should be awarded.) On the value of philosophy he has a passage which strikes a note which we shall find often echoed in Newman's *Discourses*:

Nor is the omission of philosophy from an academical curriculum equivalent to an arrest on the philosophising activity of the student. This stupor, however deplorable in itself, might still be a minor evil; for it is better, assuredly, to be without opinions, than to have them not only speculatively untrue, but practically corruptive. Yet, even this paralysis, I say, is not accomplished. Right or wrong, a man must philosophise, for he philosophises as he thinks; and the only effect, in the present day especially, of a University denying to its alumni the invigorating exercise of a right philosophy, is their abandonment, not only without precaution, but even prepared by debilitation, to the pernicious effect of a wrong: *Sine vindice praeda.*[57]

At the close of this lecture I should like to repeat a note of warning, which was sounded earlier, against the possible impression that the issues we have been dealing with are somewhat academic and unpractical. We are approaching a very great and difficult subject, and we must proceed gradually. Not only are these remote and almost forgotten controversies between the *Edinburgh Review* and Oxford University of interest as being the historical starting point of Newman's *Idea of a University*; but as we shall see from our later lectures, they raised most fundamental issues which are academic only in the sense of being philosophical and not at all in the sense of being unpractical. We shall see indeed that these issues continue to the present day to be hotly contested, that divergent views on them have intimately affected the intellectual, moral, religious and even material well-being of succeeding generations, and that on the correct resolution of them depends, to a great extent, the preservation of our civilisation.

A NEW UNIVERSITY
FOR A NEW WORLD

I

IT WILL have been noted that in the controversy which
we have been recording between the Edinburgh reviewers
and the Oxford fellows, there were really two main issues
at stake. The first was the relative values as cultural instruments of literary and non-literary studies in themselves.
The second, and quite a different one, was the relative places
that these studies should hold in the curriculum of a particular university. The Oxford champions were on surer
ground with regard to the first issue, and it will probably
be granted that on the whole they had the better of their
opponents. The second issue was not very satisfactorily
thrashed out, partly because the Edinburgh reviewers based
their claim for non-literary studies on the unsure ground
of their utility, and partly because both parties concentrated
mainly on the question of how much attention was actually
being given to these studies at the older universities, and
only touched in passing on the larger question of the place
they should hold in any university.

In point of fact it was clear that in spite of the recent reforms the bias in favour of literary studies was still exceedingly strong in the older universities, and that they were making only very tentative efforts to assimilate, organise and utilise the body of scientific knowledge which was growing with such rapidity all over the world. With the growth of that knowledge had come the beginnings of the industrial revolution and the rise of the new manufacturing class, the younger members of which found themselves excluded from university studies either by class privilege or by the unsuitability for their needs of the courses provided. As early as 1764 Joseph Priestley had clearly stated the problem.

> It seems to be a defect in our present system of public education that a proper course of studies is not provided for gentlemen who are designed to fill the principal stations of *active life*, distinct from those which are adapted to the *learned professions*. We have hardly any medium between an education for the counting-house, consisting of writing, arithmetic and merchants' accounts, and a method of instruction in the abstract sciences; so that we have nothing liberal that is worth the attention of *gentlemen* whose views neither of these two opposite plans may suit.[1]

From our study of the attacks of the Edinburgh reviewers some forty years later we have seen that this dissatisfaction had by no means been allayed, and that in spite of the exaggerations which are always associated with public controversy, it was not altogether unfounded.

Furthermore there was, as we have already seen, the still

more serious bar of religious exclusiveness. Subscription to the Thirty-nine Articles was obligatory at Oxford on entrance and at Cambridge on taking a degree. In addition, by the Act of Uniformity no form of prayer or administration of sacraments in ceremonies was permitted in either university unless in accord with the book of Common Prayer of the Church of England, and by the Statutes of the University of Oxford members of that university were forbidden to be present at any religious service except in places consecrated or licensed by the Anglican bishops.

2

Owing then to new social and political conditions and to the defects and limitations of the older universities there existed in England at the opening of the nineteenth century a demand for a higher education which would be wider both in its educational scope and in the constitution of its student body. This demand was translated into action in the third decade of the century by a group of men of whom the leader was the poet, Thomas Campbell. Campbell was a native of Glasgow, had studied law at the university there, and was in later life its Rector for three terms, defeating on his third election so formidable a rival as Sir Walter Scott. He travelled much on the Continent, and in 1820 visited the University of Bonn, where he was much struck by the tolerance that existed between Catholics and Protestants, and the liberal treatment that was accorded to Jews. In conversation with the professors there he conceived the idea of founding in England a university which would be similarly open to students of all creeds, and which would provide more liberally than the older universities for scientific and professional studies.

Various contemporary events encouraged Campbell in his project. There had been during the preceding century a great revival of academic activity in his own country, Scotland, especially in philosophical and scientific fields. Dugald Stewart, Playfair, Adam Smith, Thomas Reid, David Hume, Joseph Black, Thomas Brown and William Robertson were thinkers whose influence extended widely beyond the bounds of Glasgow and Edinburgh. The best medical education was to be found in the schools of Scotland, and they formed the foundation of the great scientific departments of the modern universities. It was obvious that the example of the Scottish universities influenced very deeply the constitution of London University. The wide range of subjects, the lecture system, non-residence of students, their admittance to single courses, the absence of religious tests, the dependence of the professors on fees for their support, and the democratic character of the institution, were all features which had long been familiar in the Scottish system.

There was too at this time considerable activity in university life in Germany. The University of Berlin had been founded in 1809 and that of Bonn in 1816. We have noted Campbell's visit to Bonn in 1820 as the starting point of his London project. A visit to Berlin in 1825 encouraged him in the preference he had derived from Scotland for the professorial rather than the tutorial system of instruction, and established further contact with continental academic thought.

Another source of inspiration came from beyond the Atlantic, the foundation in 1819 by the efforts of Thomas Jefferson of the first modern university in the United States, that of Virginia. The main ideals of this institution were set out in the Report of a State Commission which met at Rockfish Gap in the Blue Ridge in 1818, known in American educational history as the Rockfish Gap Report. Jefferson was a member of the Commission, and it is generally held that the Report was mainly his work. It thus defined the purposes of the higher education envisaged:

> To form the statesmen, legislature and judges, on whom public prosperity and individual happiness are so much to depend;
>
> To expound the principles and structure of government, the laws which regulate the intercourse of nations, those formed municipally for our own government, and a sound spirit of legislation which, banishing all arbitrary and unnecessary restraint on individual action, shall leave us free to do whatever does not violate the equal rights of another;
>
> To harmonize and promote the interests of agriculture, manufactures and commerce, and by well informed views of political economy to give a free scope to the public industry;
>
> To develop the reasoning faculties of our youth, enlarge their minds, cultivate their morals, and instil into them the precepts of virtue and order;
>
> To enlighten them with mathematical and physical sciences, which advance the arts, and administer to the health, the subsistence and comforts of human life;
>
> And, generally, to form them to habits of reflection and correct action, rendering them examples of virtue to others, and of happiness within themselves.

This report has been described by one American historian of the University of Virginia as " perhaps the most pregnant and suggestive document of its kind that has been issued in the history of American Education." [2] We may grant that there is much in it which is unexceptionable, though by no means new. We shall have something to say later in this lecture and in our next lecture on the subject of the liberal ideal in education, and it is sufficient to draw your attention to its appearance in the second paragraph where individual freedom, as long as it does not violate the rights of others, is assumed to be the criterion of good legislation, and therefore of the education which is to produce it. There is also, possibly, discernible that over-emphasis of the aim of producing good rulers that characterised certain phases of Greek educational thought.

For the carrying out of these aims the Rockfish Gap Report recommended an institution which would provide a wide curriculum, imparted by the professorial method. Students of all denominations were to be admitted, but each denomination was to be free to provide whatever instruction it deemed necessary in its own particular tenets. One noteworthy provision was that students should have complete freedom in the choice of their courses. It is needless to point out that this is a provision which has constantly appeared in American education, and has given rise to much controversy. We shall see that it was adopted by the founders of London University with unfavourable consequences.

Direct communications were shortly established between Jefferson and Campbell, who had a personal interest in Virginia, since his father had had trade relations with that state, his eldest brother was living in Richmond, and another had married a daughter of Patrick Henry. Jefferson in 1824 sent over a young Virginian lawyer, Francis W. Gilmer, to look for professors in Europe, and Gilmer interviewed Campbell and encouraged him in his plans.

3

Meanwhile in England there was considerable educational activity on foot. We recall that one of the founders of the *Edinburgh Review* had been Henry Brougham. By this time he was one of the most prominent figures in political life in England, had been appointed by Queen Caroline to be her Attorney-General, and had won immense popularity by his speech in her defence against the Bill of Divorce introduced into the House of Lords in 1820. Among his many enthusiasms was education. He had forced two Select Commissions on Parliament, and in 1820 had brought in an unsuccessful bill to establish schools at public expense in every parish. He was, however, opposed to government control of education, and his aim was to secure assistance for voluntary bodies. At this time two of the best known figures in the educational world in England were Andrew Bell, an Anglican clergyman, and Joseph Lancaster, a Quaker, remembered for their advocacy of the monitorial system. In 1810 the Royal Lancasterian Society was founded to promote voluntary elementary schools, and Brougham was one of the Committee. This Society adopted the non-sectarian principle, and in 1811 the Anglican party founded in opposition the National Society (for promoting the Education of the Poor in the Principles of the Established Church). In 1814 the Lancasterian Society became the British and Foreign

School Society, and modified its non-sectarian character to the extent of permitting Bible reading in its schools. These two societies constituted the beginning of the English voluntary system of primary education, which lasted up to the Elementary Education Act of 1870 on which the English system was based until the Act of 1944.

Brougham now joined forces with Campbell, and they were further strengthened by the accession of Zachary Macaulay, the famous anti-slavery reformer, and father of Lord Macaulay. Macaulay was personally in favour of denominational education, but agreed to the non-denominational principle in order to provide for the needs of the Dissenters, who had been induced by Brougham to support the new project. On 11 February 1826 the first formal step was taken towards the founding of a university college in London by the setting up of a Council which, in addition to Brougham, Campbell and Macaulay, included James Mill, the father of John Stuart Mill, and the Duke of Norfolk to represent the Catholic interests. Though the ideas of Bentham played such a part in the conception of the university, he was now too old to take any active part in it, but he was registered as one of its proprietors and bequeathed to it part of his library. Brougham had now supplanted Campbell as leader of the project, and under his vigorous, if somewhat intolerant guidance, it took immediate shape. The novel plan was adopted of floating a public company to finance the college; building was begun in Gower Street, and professors engaged, provision being made for chairs of chemistry, biology, the various branches of medicine and oriental languages, as well as the usual literary and mathematical subjects.

4

In one most important respect Campbell allowed himself to be diverted from the model of Bonn. At that university provision was made for chairs of Catholic and Protestant theology. We may note in passing that this is one of the various expedients which have been adopted to solve the problem of religious teaching in universities, the others being to have frankly denominational institutions, as was the case on the Continent from the Reformation up to the middle of the nineteenth century, or to have a faculty in which various denominations endeavour to sink their difficulties and present a synthesis of teachings, a system which prevails today, for instance, in the Universities of Manchester and Birmingham. However, in the case of the nascent university of London the alliance of nonconformists and radicals against High Church and Tories made the total exclusion of theology the only possible course. It is interesting to note that the members of the Council defended this course purely on pragmatic grounds, and expressed their belief that religion constituted an essential part of education. They stated that they

found it impossible to unite the principles of free admission to persons of all religious denominations with any plan of theological instruction, or any form of religious discipline; and they were thus compelled by necessity to leave this great and primary object of education, which they deem far too important for compromise, to the direction and superintendence of the natural guardians of the pupils.[3]

It may be noted that trouble arose almost immediately on this issue. Many of the most zealous Dissenters, led by Edward Irving, founder of the Catholic Apostolic Church, withdrew their support at once. The Evangelicals vainly endeavoured to provide for a series of lectures which would be acceptable to all Christians, as, for instance, on Biblical Literature or on the Evidences of Christianity. The religious difficulty was one of the main reasons for insisting on non-residence, though it had also been suggested by the Scottish and German systems. However, in 1827 the Council went so far as to insist that the boarding-house keepers whom it recognised should " require their boarders to be regular in their attendance at some place of public worship," but this regulation was abandoned after a year. Then a group of professors, who were also clergymen of the Established Church, announced that with the approval of the Council they proposed to give religious instruction outside the curriculum for students of their faith, and that they had purchased an adjoining chapel for that purpose. The Dissenters protested against what they believed to be a breach of faith, and when their protests were unavailing, they announced that a series of religious lectures would be provided for their students; but neither of these projects met with much success. Even the exclusion of all theological lectures did not give that spiritual peace that had been hoped for. It was soon realised that even in the department of philosophy religious differences might be manifested, and disputes over the orthodoxy of candidates led to the two philosophical chairs being yet unfilled when the university opened.

It was not surprising that such a novel phenomenon as a

university which explicitly excluded theology from its halls should provoke an outcry in a country which was still predominantly Christian. The chaplain to the Lord Mayor of London, the Rev. T. W. Lancaster, denounced it in a pamphlet in which he expressed the view that religion is an instrument of government, and that purely secular education could not produce a generation of sound governors " No civil society," he said, " can, without the sanctions of religion, maintain the obligations of morality among its members." It is necessary to provide " a national religious education," and to exclude religion from it is to exclude " the only thing, for the sake of which education as a national measure can justly be considered needful." [4] A much greater man than the Lord Mayor's chaplain, Thomas Arnold, was also critical of the new venture, but his criticism was more reasoned. He offered himself unsuccessfully as a candidate for the Chair of History in 1827, and in 1835, when Headmaster of Rugby, became an examining fellow to the university. But his correspondence shows that he hoped thereby to mitigate the effects of what he believed to be a radically defective system. He wrote to W. Empson on 28 November 1837: "The Gower Street College I therefore hold to be Anti-Christian, inasmuch as it meddles with moral subjects—has lectures in History—and yet does not require its Professors to be Christians." [5]

It was not only on religious grounds that the new venture met with opposition. The prospectus had made no formal allusion to the granting of degrees, but it was assumed that as a natural development such power would be sought later. This was denounced as an usurpation of the long established rights of Oxford and Cambridge, and in the case of medical degrees of the existing medical schools. Ridicule was cast on the idea that a joint-stock company could constitute a university, and—a more serious objection—it was pointed out that the exclusion of theology, apart from its purely religious significance, deprived the new college of that universality of studies which was at least traditionally associated with, and according to many formed an essential feature of a university curriculum.

The democratic constitution of the student body was also a stumbling-block to conservative tradition, and there was much ridicule of it. The popular journal *John Bull* was one of the most virulent critics of what it called " The Cockney University." It depicted a gentleman asking the way to the college from a local lady. " Don't you know it? " is the reply. " Dear me, it's the second door from the Lansdowne Arms, at the corner, on the left hand as you go out of the New Road." " Can a man graduate there, Madam? " says the gentleman. " Sir? " says the lady. " I mean, do they give degrees? " " Oh, no, they don't do anything by degrees, Sir, there, they learn everything at once."

However, the college was not without its champions, of whom the most notable was Lord Macaulay, who defended it in the *Edinburgh Review*.[6]

The new institution did not aspire to participate in the privileges which had been so long monopolized by those ancient corporations (the older Universities). It asked for no foundation, no lands, no advowsons. It did not interfere with that mysterious scale of degrees on which good churchmen look with as much veneration as the Patriarch on the ladder up which he saw the angels ascending. It did not ask permission to search houses with warrants (an allusion, presumably, to the power of the Proctors), or to take books from publishers without paying for them. There was to be no melodramatic pageantry, no ancient ceremonial, no silver mace, no gowns either black or red, no hoods either of fur or satin, no public orator to make speeches, which nobody hears, no oaths sworn only to be broken.

The new university would be free from many of the defects of the old ones.

It cannot cry up one study or cry down another. It has no means of bribing one man to learn what it is of no use to him to know, or of exacting a mock attendance from another who learns nothing at all. To be prosperous, it must be useful.

We have by now learned to be on our guard against this watchword of utility, but it would appear that Macaulay uses it only to condemn indirectly some of the empty formalities and sham tests which, as we have seen, undoubtedly existed in the older universities, at least before the reforms of the early nineteenth century.

Macaulay concluded by a prophesy which, if somewhat flamboyant in its language, was on the whole to be fulfilled.

We predict that the clamour by which it has been assailed will die away—that it is destined to a long, a glorious, and a beneficent existence, that, while the spirit of its system remains unchanged, the details will vary with the varying necessities and facilities of every age—that it will be the model of many future establishments—that even those haughty establishments which now treat it with contempt, will in some degree feel its salutary influence—and that the approbation of a great people, to whose wisdom, energy and virtue its exertions will have largely contributed, will confer on it a dignity more imposing than any which it could derive from the most lucrative patronage, or the most splendid ceremonial.

5

There were 250 students on the roll when the college opened its doors in 1828, and by 1830 these had increased to 600. But difficulties soon made themselves felt. Financial troubles were among the worst. Strange to say, Sydney Smith, though he must have been in sympathy with many of the ideals of the new institution, directed the barb of his wit against it.

I understand that they have already seized on the air-pump, the exhausted (sic) receiver, and galvanic batteries; and that the bailiffs have been chasing the Professor of Modern History round the quadrangle.[7]

A much more fundamental difficulty was the lack of organization in the curriculum. In imitation of the Virginian system the students were not required to follow definite courses, and few troubled to take examinations. Cavour, who visited the university in 1835, was very unfavourably impressed.

The students are absolutely free to follow whatever courses they wish, independently of one another. Their only obligation is to be enrolled, and to pay fees in proportion to the number of courses they choose.[8]

Certificates were granted on the successful passing of an examination, but Cavour pointed out that, as one student might aim at only one certificate, another at two, another at three or more, the certificates had no absolute value. This system was abolished in 1839, when formal degrees were established, and fixed subjects prescribed for the B.A. examination. The requirements in those early days were considerable enough. The candidate had to show a competent knowledge in the four branches of examination: Mathematics and Natural Philosophy, Animal Physiology, Classics and Logic and Moral Philosophy. In addition, he might sit for honours in Mathematics and Natural Philosophy, Classics, Chemistry, Animal Physiology and Vegetable and Structural Botany. The examinations were of portentous length. Jevons, the logician and economist, complains that in 1853 the examination in mathematics lasted six hours, while that in chemistry lasted for eight.

In spite of all its initial difficulties University College met with sufficient success to prompt imitation on the part of the Anglican body. In 1828 the Duke of Wellington, who had recently become Prime Minister, presided at a public meeting at which it was decided to establish a college to be known as King's College, in which " an essential part of the system " should be " to imbue the minds of youth with a knowledge of the doctrines and duties of Christianity, as inculcated by the United Church of England and Ireland." [9] A charter of incorporation was granted to King's College in 1829, and in 1831 it was opened in the Strand, adjoining

Somerset House, the curriculum being similar to that of University College, with the addition of religious training. The staff and students had to be members of the Church of England, a requirement which persisted until 1903. The Principals were all clerics until 1913, and the classes are still arranged so that students who so desire may attend a weekly lecture in theology. Curiously enough, the College had no theological department until 1846. Since 1908 this department has been an independent body with its own Dean and Governing Body. In the same year that King's College was opened, 1831, University College received a Charter with the title of London University, but opposition on the part of Oxford, Cambridge and the medical schools succeeded in preventing it for another eight years from obtaining power to grant degrees.

It is difficult for us in these days of religious indifference to realise how fundamental was the opposition of the older universities. It may be granted that they were unconsciously biassed by the desire to maintain their long-standing mono-poly, but it cannot be denied that their main inspiration was a deeply rooted conviction of the unity of Church and State. The Privy Council met three times at the end of April and the beginning of May 1834 to hear the petition of London University for a charter, and the counter-petitions of Oxford and Cambridge and the medical bodies. A long speech was made by Sir Charles Wetherell on behalf of Oxford, arguing the case from the constitutional standpoint. The King, he held, could not legally incorporate a university in England other than such as should conform with the doctrines, discipline and worship of the Church of England, since " the regulation and government of a University is

. . . matter ecclesiastical . . . (and) by the law of England
a University is subject to the ecclesiastical visitation of the
Archbishop."[10] Furthermore, to incorporate a university
upon the principle, and for the purpose that it should not
so conform would be a breach of various statutes and laws
of the realm. In addition to such fundamental objections he
also held that it would be an injustice to allow such an
institution to confer the title of Master of Arts, which had
hitherto denoted conformity with the established doctrine
of the Church, and which therefore had been accepted as
a qualification to exercise duty in the ecclesiastical courts,
and to fulfil certain offices in schools, hospitals and other
bodies endowed in the interests of the Anglican faith.

This latter objection was also made at great length by
William Sewell, Fellow of Exeter College, a prominent
member of the earlier Tractarian Movement, and later
founder of St Columba's College, Dublin, and of Radley
College, near Oxford. His views were published in pam-
phlets entitled: *A First and Second Letter to a Dissenter on the
Opposition of the University of Oxford to the Charter of the London
College.* Newman, then a Fellow of Oriel of some ten years'
standing, expressed in a letter of 14 March 1834 to his
friend, J. W. Bowden, the same view, that a professedly
irreligious institution should not be allowed to distribute
titles which had hitherto been recognised as the badge of
a Christian education.

The Duke has begun his campaign by advising us
strenuously to resist the London University granting
degrees in arts and divinity, and there is to be a convocation next week about it. Indeed it does seem a little

too bad that the Dissenters are to *take our titles*. Why should they call themselves M.A., except to seem like us? Why not call themselves Licentiates etc.? And what is to hinder the Bishops being bullied into putting up with a London M.A.? Certainly they would soon.[11]

The opposition of the medical schools was on a lower plane. They had no objection to the setting up of a non-denominational establishment, since religious considerations did not enter into their own constitution or policy. But they did object to the singling out for the favour of conferring medical degrees a new establishment which was in no way superior to those already in existence, which was financially embarrassed, and which, by combining the offices of teaching and examining, would injure the valuable system of private teaching.

The Privy Council came to no decision, but a few years later events forced a decision. In addition to their fundamental objections the Anglican party had a more pragmatic reason for opposing the granting of degrees by London University. There was all through this period continual agitation going on to obtain the admission of Dissenters to Oxford and Cambridge and it was feared that to grant to any other body the power of conferring degrees would lessen the claims of the older universities to confine such academic recognition to members of the Establishment. However, in 1836 the Bill admitting Dissenters to Oxford and Cambridge, which had been passed by a large majority in the Commons, was rejected by the Lords. It was felt that some provision must be made for Dissenters, and in 1836 a settlement was come to. The original University College reverted from its status as a university and was chartered as University College, London, whilst a new body was established and chartered to be known as the University of London, which was empowered to give degrees in all subjects to students who had pursued approved courses in University College, King's College, and other institutions afterwards approved.

6

In spite of this reorganisation the University of London had for many years a hard struggle for existence. It provoked opposition which, though healthy in itself, tended to draw away students. The medical schools and the Law Society were stirred into activity. The University of Durham was projected in 1831 and chartered in 1837. Cambridge, as we have seen, established a natural science Tripos in 1848, and in 1854 Oxford opened its doors to Dissenters to the extent of admitting them to the primary degree.

There were, furthermore, internal difficulties. There was serious mismanagement, and the system of affiliation to teaching institutions all over the country led to an injurious lowering of standards. In 1858 the system of affiliation was abandoned, and the University of London became a purely examining body, prepared to examine all comers, and having no specific connection with its two parent colleges. This step was generally acknowledged to be retrograde, though it undoubtedly was the means of stimulating to further studies many students prevented by circumstances from attendance at formal university courses.

From that on the university experienced fluctuating fortunes.[12] Between 1858 and 1868 its ranks were augmented by the admission of women, a decade before such a step was taken in Oxford or Cambridge. In 1898 by the London University Commission Act an Internal Side was added to the University. Special examinations were instituted to be held by boards composed of external examiners and of teachers from the colleges whose students were presenting themselves. These examinations led to an " Internal Degree," giving credit for formal university education, but the system of external degrees was preserved and still prevails.

The present constitution of London University was determined in its main outlines by the University Act of 1900, whose statutes admitted a large number of affiliated Colleges as Schools of the University, which thereby became a teaching university. The general administration is controlled by a number of bodies. The court which manages finance, has, besides its academic members, representatives of the Government and the London County Council. The Senate, controlling academic matters, consists of the Chancellor, the Vice-Chancellor, the Chairman of Convocation (elected by the graduates), the Principal (a permanent official, who with a large staff organises and conducts the financial and administrative business of the University), and the Heads of the chief colleges, together with seventeen members elected from the teaching staff of the University, seventeen from Convocation, and two from the General Medical Schools. It relies for its decisions mainly on the recommendation of its many committees, of which the chief are the Academic Council, which correlates the activities of the Faculties, the Boards of Studies and the Boards of Advisors for appointments, and the Boards of Studies which are composed of the senior teachers in each subject for each institution, and conduct all business relating to individual subjects.

Among the affiliated bodies chief place is taken by the two original parent institutions, University College and King's College, with their numerous departments in every branch of the Arts and Sciences. Other teaching institutions are recognised as "schools of the University" in one or more faculties. Thus, the Women's Colleges, Bedford and Holloway, are in the faculties of Arts and Science. The medical schools, of which there are about a dozen, are in the Faculty of Medicine. In various faculties there are such institutions as the Imperial College of Science and Technology, the Royal College of Science, the Institute of Education, the Royal School of Mines, the London school of Economics, the Royal Veterinary College. In the faculty of Theology there are two Church of England colleges, two Congregational, one Wesleyan, one Baptist. Many other institutions, as, for instance, the Royal Academy of Music, the Royal College of Music and Trinity College of Music, have recognized teachers and provide training for some internal degrees, though they are not fully constituted Schools of the University.

7

Having now briefly outlined the history of London University, we are in a better position to consider the place occupied by it during its early years in the intellectual life of England. We have already indicated that its coming into being was a natural result of the scientific progress of the eighteenth century, the age of Newton, Halley, Herschel, Boyle, Lavoisier, Priestley, Hutton, Haller, Linnaeus and Buffon, and of the technological progress of the late eighteenth and early nineteenth centuries, the age of the spinning jenny and the steam engine, the age of coal, steam, macadamised roads, canals and power printing, gas and electricity. This technological progress was in large part due both to the further investigations of scientists and to the co-operation of the new race of professional engineers who held a place between the skilled mechanic and the scientist proper. It was inconceivable that the university should take no cognisance of the immense new field of human knowledge that was being opened up by these busy investigators and inventors, and should feel no urge to take a hand in their studies and training.

We have also seen how this scientific and technological progress had served in another way to create the demand for increased university education, by bringing about the industrial revolution and with it the rise of the new middle class, who naturally challenged the tradition whereby the university population was almost exclusively recruited from among the sons of the landed aristocracy. We may note further that with the industrial revolution had also come the great increase in wealth and population of the cities, and that they were the centres where the influence of the middle class was mainly exercised. There arose, therefore, a natural demand that whatever new centres of university education were provided should be situated in their midst.

When we say that the foundation of London University was a symptom of the liberal ideals which were abroad in England in the early nineteenth century, we must make a distinction. That it was inspired by English political liberalism hardly needs demonstration. It was just at this period, in the third decade of the nineteenth century, that the Whigs committed themselves to the policy of reform. The creed of the new Liberal Party was based on the Benthamite ideal of the greatest good of the greatest number. It presumed that as a rule the individual was the best judge of what was for his good, and hence the measures inspired by it aimed at the maximum of personal liberty. The party's strongest supporters were found among the wealthy middle class, who were also the strongest supporters of the university. As we have seen, their mere rise to wealth and power had created among them a demand for higher education, and their determination to abolish its former exclusive character was naturally intensified by their newly-found political creed.

Religious liberalism, whether in the form of active opposition to religion or of mere indifferentism, was something very far removed from English political liberalism. It is very doubtful that such liberalism had any considerable influence on the foundation of London University, in spite of its non-religious character. Religious liberalism had very little hold on the English people at the time, and Brougham was the only one of the founders of the university who was in any way influenced by its tenets. Moreover, the theory of state absolutism, which on the Continent was so often allied with liberalism to exclude religion from education, was quite repugnant to all of them, including Brougham.

They intended the university to be, as it still is, an independent, privately owned institution. It is clear, therefore, that they excluded religion from its curriculum as a purely practical measure, framed to avoid what they thought to be the insuperable difficulty of providing suitable religious instruction for a student body of mixed creeds.

This point is of interest, since the same difficulty was shortly to present itself on a much larger scale when in 1870 the English government embarked for the first time on a large measure of state-controlled education. As is well known to all students of education, the principle then adopted, which was embodied in the famous Cowper-Temple clause, was that education provided for public consumption must be free from any religious colour. It is well to note that English politicians have followed the lead of the founders of London University in defending this provision not on philosophical, but on pragmatic grounds. It has never been held that it would be positively immoral for a government to subsidise denominational education, but merely that in practice no way can be found to do this with fairness to all. The fact that the principle is a purely pragmatic one is confirmed by the many partial exceptions that are made to it, and by its complete abandonment in the Scottish system.

London University was not, therefore, in its beginnings an anti-religious institution. It cannot, however, be maintained that its foundation was without religious significance in the religious life of England. On the contrary it marked a most revolutionary change. It must be remembered that up to this time it had been taken for granted that education and religion went hand in hand at all stages. The Lancasterian schools were the first manifestation of the new creed of separation, and even they adopted a compromise. But the foundation of a university was an event of far greater import, and there can be no doubt that the spectacle of the non-denominational principle in action in London helped to pave the way for its adoption in state education forty years later. Believing Christians like Campbell and Zachary Macaulay can hardly have foreseen that the system which they adopted, as they said, because they deemed religion " far too important for compromise," was to prove one of the most deadly solvents of religious belief in the minds of later generations of English children. We should note also the date of the events which we are chronicling. It is commonly assumed today that the non-denominational principle is a long-standing tradition in English education, and it is instructive to remember that little over a century ago it was a complete novelty, rejected by the vast majority of Englishmen.

In several lesser ways London University influenced the course of education during the century that witnessed its foundation. It anticipated the spirit of the great University Commissions of 1850 by recognizing the claims of the physical sciences to a full place in the curriculum, and doubtless hastened the adoption of the recommendations of the Commissions in the older universities. It introduced into England the non-residential type of university with all its advantages and disadvantages, and the system of external degrees about whose value controversy has been hotly waged. It helped to restore the prestige of the professorial body, but, at least in its early days, subordinated teaching excessively to the examination system. Considerable though these influences were, however, they were slight in comparison with the part played by London University in securing public recognition for the first time of the principle of the divorce between secular and religious instruction. That was an influence that cut deep into the spiritual life of the nation, and indeed, in the opinion of the present lecturer, inflicted a well-nigh mortal wound.

3

THE SEED-GROUND
OF NEWMAN'S *IDEA*

I

IN THIS THIRD LECTURE we shall approach the more immediate background of Newman's *Idea of a University* which is provided by his own intellectual and spiritual development while at Oxford. Apart from the *Apologia* the most valuable source of information about this period of his life is the *Letters and Correspondence of John Henry Newman during his life in the English Church*, edited at his own request by his sister-in-law, Ann Mozley, and published in 1891, the year after his death. In addition to the letters and connecting notes contributed by Miss Mozley, the book contains an *Autobiographical Memoir* in four chapters, covering events up to 1832.[1]

Newman was received as an undergraduate at Trinity College on 14 December 1816, being then two months short of sixteen years of age, and he was called into residence in the following June, when the Trinity term was almost at an end. It may be remarked that he was abnormally young, even for those days. It is true that in the preceding century boys had entered the university at amazingly early ages—Jeremy Bentham for instance at twelve—but by the middle of the nineteenth century the age of entrance seems to have been only slightly lower than in our day. When I was enquiring into this subject, the present President of Trinity [2] kindly furnished me with the exact figures for Newman's year. He pointed out that before 1876 the precise date of birth was not entered, and the Latin formula was " circiter," followed by a round number. In Newman's year, nineteen freshmen were admitted, of whom nine were " circiter 18 annos," seven " circiter 17," two " circiter 19," and one (Newman himself) " circiter 16." This extreme youth of Newman must constantly be borne in mind when we are trying to form a picture of his mental and spiritual development at various stages of his university career.

It may perhaps come as a surprise to some of my hearers, especially if they have passed through schools of education, to find that under the heading of intellectual development, we shall have almost nothing to say about the teaching methods of Newman's tutors and professors or about his own methods of work, for the very good reason that he tells us very little about either. There are, however, at least two good reasons for this silence. We must first remember that the modern emphasis on method has arisen mainly from the necessity of training large numbers of persons for teaching who themselves have not any remarkable genius for it, and who are, moreover, destined to deal with young persons of very varying abilities, for whom it is important to devise the most helpful techniques possible. In the case of a student of such ability as that of Newman, though his education must proceed along certain ordered lines, such order is rather a spontaneous and instinctive process than a preconceived and deliberately applied discipline, and the influence of his teacher is more by suggestion and inspiration than by positive direction. Again, it must be recalled that in the learning and teaching of the classical languages and of history, which formed the basis of Newman's early undergraduate studies, there are certain fundamental processes of analysis and synthesis which have never varied, and from their nature never can vary, and on which we do not expect any comment either from Newman or any other student.

Here and there, indeed, in the *Autobiographical Memoir*, we get a chance reference to Newman's own methods of work, but they are on orthodox lines, and might have been recorded of any of his fellow-students. Thus, when speaking of his preparation for his B.A. examination of 1820—in which, for the consolation of us all, he did exceedingly badly, getting a very poor second class—he tells us that " he read books, made ample analyses and abstracts, and entered upon collateral questions and original essays . . . In the Long Vacation of 1818 he was taken up with Gibbon and Locke. At another time he wrote a critique of the plays of Aeschylus, on the principles of Aristotle's *Poetics*."[3] It cannot be said that there is anything particularly enlightening in such a bald record of work. In fact, it may be said that the only remarkable feature of Newman's method of work that emerges from his *Autobiographical Memoir* or correspondence is his incredible assiduity.

During the Long Vacation of 1819 I read nearly at the rate of nine hours a day. From that time to my examination in November 1820, it was almost a continuous mass of reading. I stayed in Oxford during the vacations, got up in winter and summer at 5 or 6, hardly allowed myself time for my meals, and then ate, indeed, the bread of carefulness. During 20 out of the 24 weeks immediately preceding my examination, I fagged at an average of more than twelve hours a day. If on one day I read only nine, I read the next fifteen.[4]

Newman had failed to distinguish himself in his primary degree examination, but two years later in 1824 he vindicated himself by obtaining a Fellowship in Oriel. And here he met with the first of the notable influences that were to shape his views, the company of a group of young men of enquiring minds, the self-styled Noetics, or as we might translate the title, the Intellectuals. They were not the founders of any particular school of thought, and, in fact, in later life they went various ways, but they infused into Oxford a spirit of enquiry and criticism that was on the whole beneficial. Mark Pattison in his *Memoirs* records that they were rather opinionated, they knew little of Continental thought, of Kant or Rousseau; but they maintained a " wholesome intellectual ferment." [5] Among the Noetics the most famous names were those of Thomas Arnold, the great headmaster of Rugby, Renn Dickson Hampden, whose name will recur again when we are touching on the Tractarian Movement, Copleston and Davison, who by now are well known to us, and Richard Whately, later Archbishop of Dublin from 1831-63.

As we have said, these men founded no school of thought, and we should hardly have found it necessary to speak of them, but that Newman lays so much stress on the influence they exerted on him. It was an influence both stimulating and steadying. Newman was, as we have noted, a very young man at the time. He had passed a somewhat secluded and sheltered adolescence in the bosom of a united and pious family and at a small public school. His undergraduate years had been absorbed in study, and as a result he was abnormally shy, self-conscious and sensitive. These characteristics were intensified by what he describes in his *Autobiographical Memoir* as a " real isolation of thought and spiritual loneliness which was the result of his Calvinistic beliefs." [6] We may note in passing that reference is often made to Newman's early Calvinism, but the word needs careful qualification. In the *Apologia* he makes it abundantly clear that he never accepted the terrible Calvinistic alternative of predestined salvation or predestined damnation. " Of the Calvinistic tenets," he says, " the only one which took root in my mind was the fact of heaven and hell, divine favour and divine wrath, of the justified and the unjustified." [7] With this went an Evangelical conviction of his own inward conversion and election to glory, but his mind balked at any definite conclusion as to the fate of the unpredestined.

Among the Noetics Newman singles out Whately as the man who, above all others, influenced his own mental and spiritual development. Whately, records Newman, was

a great talker, who endured very readily the silence of his company (a delightful example of that irony, which was Newman's almost sole form of humour), original in his views, lively, forcible, witty in expressing them . . . so entertaining that, logician as he was, he is sometimes said to have fixed the attention of a party of ladies to his conversation, or rather discourse, for two or three hours at a stretch [8]

—truly a remarkable feat. Newman found him stimulating and kind beneath his harshness, " a bright June sun tempered by a March north-easter." [9] He inspired Newman with confidence.

> Much as I owe to Oriel in the way of mental improvement, to none, I think, do I owe as much as to you. I know who it was that first gave me heart to look about even after my election, and taught me to think correctly, and . . . to rely on myself.[10]

Both in the *Apologia* [11] and the *Autobiographical Memoir* Newman records that he owed to Whately one fundamental theological conviction, " the idea of the Christian Church, as a divine appointment, and as a substantive visible body, independent of the State, and endowed with rights, prerogatives, and powers of its own." [12] This concept was one of the two great features of the Tractarian Movement, which in essence was a reaction against Erastianism from without and Liberalism from within. Newman makes no comment on the curious fact that he should have imbibed this teaching from one who was afterwards to be more or less a law unto himself in theological matters.

2

From 1825-6 Newman acted under Whately as Vice-Principal of Alban Hall (united with Merton in 1882). He was already in orders, having in 1824 been ordained deacon and appointed to the curacy of St Clement's. His church was the old St Clement's, which stood where the High Wycombe, Cowley and Iffley roads meet at the Plain near

Magdalen Bridge. He was in charge of it for two years and collected the money with which the present St Clement's was built, but had resigned before it was completed.

In 1826 he was appointed one of the public tutors of Oriel, and resigned his curacy to devote himself to teaching. Almost from the start, a difference of opinion manifested itself between Newman and Dr Hawkins, a St John's man, who had been Vicar of St Mary's and became Provost of Oriel in 1827.

The history of this difference of opinion might perhaps appear to be that of a mere domestic quarrel, but it merits notice here, as it records a fundamental concept of the teaching function which will re-appear when we are dealing with Newman's views on moral training. Briefly, what happened was this. Newman at the beginning of the Easter term, 1826, found himself the junior of four tutors, the others being Richard Hurrell Froude, Robert Isaac Wilberforce and Joseph Dornford. In Newman's opinion, the influence of the tutors over the undergraduates had hitherto been too purely academic, and any other influence they exerted was purely disciplinarian. The spirit of the undergraduates was bad. Excessive privileges were claimed by and conceded to wealthy gentlemen commoners, and religious training was confined to an automatic insistence on periodical reception of the Holy Communion. Newman believed that the function of the tutor should be a paternal one, that he should map out the course of studies of his pupils and be constantly aware of their progress, and that he should endeavour to cultivate their friendship and thus exert a moral and spiritual influence over them. His appointment as Vicar of St Mary's in 1828 increased for himself personally the spiritual ascendancy he aimed at, but he believed that, quite apart from his rights and duties as a clergyman, he had " in his Tutorial work the aim of gaining souls to God." [13]

He held almost fiercely that secular education could be so conducted as to become a pastoral cure . . . He recollected that in the Laudian statutes for Oxford, a Tutor was not to be a mere academical Policeman or Constable, but a moral and religious guardian of the youths committed to his care.[14]

Dr Hawkins, however, held other views. He supported the tutors, indeed, in their efforts to restore discipline, and, as Newman drily puts it, " it began to be the fashion at Oriel to be regular in academical conduct." [15] But on the question of pastoral supervision there was a sharp difference from the first. When the final break came in 1830, it was over an academic issue, the right of the tutors to arrange their own time-table of lectures, but the fundamental cause of the difference was undoubtedly the pastoral conception advocated by Newman and taken up by the other tutors. Hawkins avoided an open rupture, but effectively dislodged his recalcitrant subordinates by ceasing to allot them pupils.

It has been very well pointed out by Miss Maisie Ward in her *Young Mr Newman* that there was probably another consideration at work in Hawkin's mind which forced him to a decision. He might have compromised on the main issue of the abstract relation between tutor and pupil, but he saw that in the concrete a close pastoral relationship would tend to increase Newman's influence enormously, and at this moment Newman was showing clear signs of becoming a

leader of the inchoate Tractarian Movement. As Miss Ward
admirably puts it:

> Whately had seen in Newman a tendency to become a
> leader of a party. One feels rather sorry for him and
> Hawkins, as they watched the promising young Liberal
> whom they had rescued from the jaws of Evangelicalism
> turning into a red-hot zealot of an equally dangerous kind.
> Anything red-hot would have annoyed them; a High but
> not Dry Churchman, a furious Church-and-King bigot,
> was gathering a formidable influence through the rising
> talent of the College. It must be stopped.[16]

In my *Newman's University: Idea and Reality*,[17] I have referred
to certain passages dealing with this passage-of-arms with
Hawkins which Newman cut out of his *Autobiographical
Memoir* before publication. In one of these Newman expresses his regret in later years for his over-insistence on
his views, and accuses himself of " provoking insubordination
and petulance." The incident, however, is worthy of record,
since it shows that at the outset of his teaching career
Newman was brought up against a problem that was to
recur thirty years later in the government of the Catholic
University of Ireland, the problem of the moral and religious
guidance of undergraduates.

3

The next landmark which we come to in Newman's
Oxford career is the famous election of 1829. I may note
here that I have deliberately abstained so far from anything
more than passing references to the development of New-

man's religious convictions. I have done so because I think it is better that we should survey that development rapidly at the close of this lecture. And note that we cannot do more than make such a rapid survey. In another series of lectures in the second session of this school the subject will be dealt with at length. Our purpose here, as we have seen, is merely to pick out those events and influences which are necessary for the understanding of Newman's later expressed views on university education. A detailed knowledge of his own religious development would, doubtless, be required for the fullest understanding of all his later views, but we can find time only to point out its main lines, especially in so far as they bear on our proper subject.

Hence, at this date, 1829, we will content ourselves with recording that Newman was firmly fixed in the concept which he owed to Whately of the church as a visible society, but that he had outgrown the scepticism of the Noetics, and had come to the concept of an abiding body of doctrine preserved in the church through the action of the Holy Spirit, and independent of the passing theories even of the most brilliant contemporary minds. That body of doctrine, preserved, developed and lived in the church of the Fathers, he believed to be still possessed, though enfeebled and obscured, in the Anglican Church. The immediate need of the times was to form a party to defend that church against the assaults of brilliant intellectualism. Indifferentism was the great peril of the day, and Newman believed that the passing of Catholic Emancipation was a public manifestation of the growth of Indifferentism. Peel, who was then Home Secretary and Leader of the House, felt obliged to resign his seat for the university and offer himself for re-election.

He was opposed by Sir Robert Inglis, a champion of the Low Church, and Newman threw himself with ardour into the election campaign which ended in Peel's defeat.

It is not easy to form a perfectly clear picture of Newman's convictions on the immediate issue at stake. Apparently he did not think it necessary to come to any definite conclusion on the Emancipation issue itself. In a letter to his mother [18] announcing the victory, he speaks of himself as having no definite opinions in favour of the Catholics. On the other hand, he tells us in the *Apologia* [19] that, two years before the election, he had been opposed to a petition brought into Convocation of the University calling on Parliament to reject the Catholic claims, and this on two grounds, firstly because he had been reading a work entitled *Letters of an Episcopalian* attributed to Whately, and secondly, because he shrank from the bigoted " two-bottle orthodox " who were the chief opponents of Catholic belief. Yet in a letter to his sister Harriet he says: " I am clearly in *principle* an anti-Catholic; and if I do not oppose the Emancipation, it is only because I do not think it expedient, perhaps impossible so to do." [20] Thirty-five years later, in the *Apologia*, he stressed the rights of the University as the mainspring of his opposition to Peel. " I took part against Mr. Peel," he says, " on a simply academical, not at all an ecclesiastical or political ground . . . a great University ought not to be bullied even by a great Duke of Wellington." [21] Perhaps the clearest revelation of his mind is found in the opening words of the letter to his mother already quoted: "We have achieved a glorious victory . . . We have proved the independence of the Church and of Oxford." The two issues were, therefore, closely linked in his mind, the freedom of the Church and the freedom of the university. The linking was not entirely logical, since the university was itself by no means free from Liberalism, but Newman had high hopes for its future, and looked to it as the breeding-ground of that school of intellectual defenders of the Church's deposit of faith which was imperilled by the spirit of Indifferentism.

Miss Ward points out that youth may have played an important role in the rather perfervid opposition to Peel. Newman was only twenty-eight, his closest friends, Hurrell Froude and Wilberforce, twenty-six.

> Have we not all seen in a young group some practical issue handled in this excited over-wrought fashion? The other side have brought in outsiders, have failed to consult their friends, are electioneering, are getting at people, the skies will fall if they are not defeated.[22]

4

However, even if Newman's first encounter with Peel was not on the Liberal or Indifferentist issue alone, that issue was to be knit between the same antagonists some twelve years later. Much had happened in the interval. The Tractarian Movement had been born, had grown swiftly and had just come to a climax in February 1841 with the publication of Tract 90. Newman's opposition to Liberalism had been intensified tenfold, and he was quick to detect a new expression of it in a speech made by Peel, now Prime Minister. The occasion was the opening of a Public Library and Reading Room at Tamworth in Staffordshire, the borough for which Peel had been Member since 1830. Newman, with characteristic courage, took the Prime Minister to task in a series of letters to the *Times*, signed " Catholicus." They were later published as a pamphlet, and in 1872 appeared with other writings in the volume entitled *Discussions and Arguments*.[23]

The gist of Peel's speech is thus stated by Newman in his first letter.

Human nature, he seems to say, if left to itself, becomes sensual and degraded. Uneducated men live in the indulgence of their passions; or, if they are merely taught to read, they dissipate and debase their minds by trifling or vicious publications. Education is the cultivation of the intellect and heart, and Useful Knowledge is the great instrument of education. It is the parent of virtue, the nurse of religion; it exalts man to his highest perfection, and is the sufficient scope of his most earnest exertions.

Physical and moral science rouses, transports, exalts, enlarges, tranquillizes and satisfies the mind. Its attractiveness obtains a hold over us; the excitement attending it supersedes grosser excitements; it makes us know our duty, and thereby enables us to do it; by taking the mind off itself, it destroys anxiety; and by providing objects of admiration, it soothes and subdues us.

And, in addition, it is a kind of neutral ground, on which men of every shade of politics and religion may meet together, disabuse each other of their prejudices, form intimacies, and secure co-operation.

In his criticism of these theories, Newman points out in his second Letter that Brougham, in his Inaugural Address to Glasgow University in 1827 and in other writings, had also pointed to knowledge as the source of virtue, and that his sentiments and those of Peel appeared to echo the teachings of Bentham. There was, however, an essential difference in Bentham's concept. For Bentham "the knowledge which carries virtue along with it, is the knowledge how to take care of number one—a clear appreciation of what is pleasurable, what painful, and what promotes the one and prevents the other." Brougham had a higher ideal than this. He protests that knowledge "must invigorate the mind as well as entertain it, and refine and elevate the character, while it gives listlessness and weariness their most agreeable excitement and relaxation." But, as Newman points out, this ideal when carefully examined, is not much higher than Bentham's.

> His notions of vigour and elevation, when analyzed, will be found to resolve themselves into a mere preternatural excitement under the influence of some stimulating object, or the peace which is obtained by there being nothing to quarrel with.

This was very much the concept proposed by Peel, though in a more naïve and popular way. The philosophy which he propounded for the elevation of mankind was

> not a victory of the mind over itself—not the supremacy of law . . . not the unity of our complex nature . . . but the mere lulling of the passions to rest by turning the course of thought; not a change of character, but a mere removal of temptation.

And then there comes one of those bitingly ironical passages of which Newman was such a master.

> When a husband is gloomy, or an old woman peevish and fretful, those who are about them do all they can to keep dangerous topics and causes of offence out of the way, and think themselves lucky if, by such skilful management, they get through the day without an outbreak. When a child cries, the nursery maid dances it about, or points to the pretty black horses out of window (sic) or shows how ashamed poll-parrot or poor puss must be of its tantarums. Such is the sort of prescription which Sir Robert Peel offers to the good people of Tamworth. He makes no pretence of subduing the giant nature, in which we are born, of smiting the loins of the domestic enemies of our peace, of overthrowing passion and fortifying reason; he does but offer to bribe the foe for the nonce with gifts which will avail for that purpose just so long as they *will* avail, and no longer.

In the third Letter Newman goes on to emphasise the fact that secular knowledge can never be a positive means of moral improvement. " Science, Knowledge, and whatever fine names we use," he says, " never healed a wounded heart, nor changed a sinful one," and he contrasts the power of Divine Knowledge, which has been from the first " a quickening, renovating, organizing, principle." This is not to deny that secular knowledge has its proper place in the cultivation of the mind, but it must keep to that place. And here I would draw your attention to a short passage which is of particular significance in view of what we shall have to say later about Newman's concept of the relative places of secular and sacred knowledge in education.

Christianity and nothing short of it, must be made the element and principle of all education. Where it has been laid as the first stone, and acknowledged as the governing spirit, it will take up into itself, assimilate, and give a character to literature and science. Where Revealed Truth has given the aim and direction to Knowledge, Knowledge of all kinds will minister to Revealed Truth. The Evidences of Religion, natural theology and meta-physics,—or, again, poetry, history and the classics,— or physics and mathematics, may all be grafted into the mind of a Christian, and give and take by the grafting. But if in education we begin with nature before grace, with evidences before faith, with science before con-science, with poetry before practice, we shall be doing much the same as if we were to indulge the appetites and passions, and turn a deaf ear to the reason.

We may pass rapidly over the fourth Letter in which Newman deals with Peel's plea that secular knowledge, especially that of the physical sciences, leads naturally to knowledge of God. Newman indeed himself in his *Eighth Discourse* was to develop this theme in a masterly way, but he puts his finger shrewdly on the weak spot in Peel's reasoning. For the ordinary human mind this sequence from the knowledge of things created to the uncreated will in practice not take place unless there is at the same time a direct effort to acquire the knowledge of God from revealed sources.

Newman then passes in his fifth Letter to Peel's second

argument in favour of secular studies, that they are a principle
of social unity. Here was a novel plea for Indifferentism,
but one that was to become painfully familiar in the later
history of education. In the new Reading Room at Tamworth
Peel announced that " in the selection of subjects for public
lectures everything calculated to excite religious or political
animosity shall be excluded." Newman has some dry remarks
to make on the equiparation of religion and party politics,
but he passes rapidly in his sixth Letter to the fundamental
error of Peel that unity among men is to be got by discarding
the old bond of Faith and substituting the new bond of
Knowledge. Newman points out that in itself the acquisition
of a heterogenous body of knowledge has no unifying power.
It can only unify when the mind goes on to infer some
extra-sensible order which is proper to society, and this
inference is not science, but the beginnings of theology.
Indeed, secular knowledge, without the guiding light of
theology, in practice tends to produce unbelief. The purpose
of science is to enquire what things are, the purpose of
theology to enquire why they are. In the seventh Letter
Newman notes:

> There are two ways, then, of reading Nature—as a
> machine, and as a work. If we come to it with the
> assumption that it is a creation, we shall study it with
> awe; if assuming it to be a system, with mere curiosity.
> The essence of Religion is the idea of a moral Governor,
> and a particular Providence; now let me ask, is the
> doctrine of moral government and a particular providence
> conveyed to us through the physical sciences at all?
> Would they be physical sciences if they treated of morals?

Can physics teach moral matters without ceasing to be physics?

At the close of this Letter Newman thus briefly sums up his whole argument.

I consider, then, that, intrinsically excellent and noble as are scientific pursuits, and worthy of a place in a liberal education, and fruitful in temporal benefits to the community, still they are not, and cannot be, *the instrument* of an ethical training; that physics do not supply a basis, but only materials for religious sentiment; that knowledge does but occupy, does not form the mind; that apprehension of the unseen is the only known principle capable of subduing moral evil, educating the multitude, and organizing society; and that, whereas man is born for action, action flows not from inferences but from impressions—not from reasonings, but from Faith.

In the foregoing passage I would draw your attention to Newman's explicit admission that the study of the physical sciences is " worthy of a place in a liberal education." It will be of use to us later in determining what exactly Newman meant by liberal education, and in disposing of a common misunderstanding of his doctrine.

The episode of the letters on the Tamworth Reading Room was a comparatively slight one in the crowded life that Newman was leading at this period; but we shall find that it bears considerably on our special topic, and we shall find recurring again and again in his *Discourses on the Idea of a University* and in his correspondence concerning the Catholic University the main themes of his letters to the *Times*, the proper relations between secular and religious knowledge, and the contribution made by both to the total work of education.

5

Almost from Newman's appointment as tutor of Oriel, certainly from his appointment as Vicar of St Mary's in 1828, he exercised an extraordinary ascendency over his students and colleagues by his preaching. We are concerned here only with a few passages in one of his sermons, but we can hardly feel that we have formed an adequate picture of Newman's mental and spiritual development at Oxford without at least a passing reference to the manifestation of that development in his pulpit utterances. His sermons were almost all preached in St Mary's, and fall into three categories. There were the University sermons preached mainly during the Oxford Movement, the parochial sermons preached in his capacity as Vicar from 1828 to 1843, and the theological lectures given in Advent and after Easter in the chapel of Adam de Brome to select audiences, the matter of which afterwards formed part of *The Prophetical Office of the Church*, the *Lectures on Justification*, and some of the *Tracts for the Times*.

There have been many striking tributes paid to the genius of Newman as a preacher. We will content ourselves with that of Dean Church. The passage is found in that beautiful and admirably charitable book, Church's *Oxford Movement*.[24] The reading of it will help us, when we visit St Mary's, to live again the impressive scenes and to hear again the momentous words of just over a century ago.

None but those who remember them can adequately estimate the effect of Mr Newman's four o'clock sermons at St Mary's. The world knows them, has heard a great deal about them, has passed its various judgments on them. But it hardly realises that without these sermons the movement might never have gone on, certainly would never have been what it was. Even people who heard them continually, and felt them to be different from other sermons, hardly estimated their real power, or knew at the time the influence which the sermons were having upon them. Plain, direct, unornamented, clothed in English that was only pure and lucid, free from any faults of taste, strong in their flexibility and perfect command both of language and thought, they were the expression of a piercing and large insight into character and conscience and motives, of a sympathy at once most tender and most stern with the tempted and wavering, of an absolute and burning faith in God and His counsels, in His love, in His judgments, in the awful glory of His generosity and His magnificence. They made men think of the things which the preacher spoke of, and not of the sermon or the preacher. Since 1828 this preaching had been going on at St. Mary's growing in purpose and directness as the years went on, though it could hardly be more intense than in some of its earliest examples. While men were reading and talking about the Tracts, they were hearing the sermons; and in the sermons they heard the living meaning, and reason and bearing of the Tracts, their ethical affinities, their moral standard. The sermons created a moral standard, in which men judged the questions in debate. It was no dry theological correctness and completeness which was sought for. No love of privilege, no formal hierarchical claims, urged on the writers. What they thought in danger, what they aspired to revive and save, was the very life of religion, the truth and substance of all that makes it the hope of human society.

The *Oxford University Sermons*, which were published as a volume in 1843, had as their general theme the philosophy of faith, the demonstration of the fact that the Gospel teachings in all their simplicity were based on profound intellectual truths, and that true wisdom led to complete concurrence with divine revelation. Newman in a letter to James Hope Scott described this collection of sermons as " the best, not the most perfect book I have done. I mean there is more to develop in it though it is imperfect." [25] These words are of particular interest to us, as we shall find that one of the ideas propounded in these sermons was in fact very fully developed later by Newman in his *Idea of a University*. It occurs in the sermon entitled " Wisdom as compared with Faith and Bigotry," preached on Whit Tuesday, 1841. The relevant passages are these.

> The words philosophy, a philosophical spirit, enlargement or expansion of mind, enlightened ideas, a wise and comprehensive view of things, and the like, are, I need hardly say, of frequent occurrence in the literature of this day, and are taken to mean very much the same thing . . . Yet their meaning certainly requires drawing out and illustrating.[26]

Newman then gives examples of the contemplation of certain large bodies of knowledge which produce this enlargement of mind; the sight of the varied and complicated phenomena of Nature: the study of physical science, the wide panorama of history, the existence and effects of sin in man, the universal religious convictions of the human race. What is it, Newman asks, in the contemplation of these bodies of knowledge that produces this enlargement of mind?

A very little consideration will make it plain that knowledge itself, though a condition of the mind's enlargement, yet, whatever be its range, is not that very thing that enlarges it. Rather the foregoing instances show that this enlargement consists in the comparison of the subjects of knowledge one with another . . . And therefore a philosophical cast of thought, or a comprehensive mind, or wisdom in conduct and policy, implies a connected view of the old with the new; an insight into the bearing and influence of each part upon every other; without which there is no whole, and could be no centre. It is the knowledge, not only of things, but of their mutual relations. It is organized, and therefore living knowledge.[27]

Having established the nature of this philosophical or comprehensive knowledge, Newman goes on to demonstrate that the principle of it is the action of the reasoning faculties on the data given by the intellect. And here I would draw your attention briefly to the fact that Newman uses the term "philosophy" or a "philosophical knowledge," not in the traditional but in an analogous sense. I will recur to this point in our next lecture.

Philosophy, then, is Reason exercised upon Knowledge; or the Knowledge not merely of things in general, but of things in their relations to one another. It is the power of referring every thing to its true place in the universal system,—of understanding the various aspects of each of its parts,—of comprehending the exact value of each,—of tracing each backwards to its beginning and forward to its end,—of anticipating the separate tendencies of each, and their respective checks or counter-actions; and thus of accounting for anomalies, answering objections, supplying deficiencies, making allowance for errors, and meeting emergencies.[28]

(Those who are familiar with current educational writing, especially in the United States, will be interested to note here Newman's picking out of one intellectual activity that has been now elevated to the position of a fetish, the power " to deal with situations." The modern stress on this power is, I need hardly say, attributable to the pragmatic philosophy which pervades American educational thought, and has been so largely adopted—I believe often unconsciously—in this country.) But to return to Newman's description of the process of philosophical thought.

It never views any part of the extended subject-matter of knowledge, without recollecting that it is but a part, or without the associations which spring from this recollection. It makes everything lead to everything else; it communicates the image of the whole body to every separate member, till the whole becomes, in imagination, like a spirit, everywhere pervading and penetrating its component parts, and giving them their one definite meaning.[29]

Here, then, we have Newman's concept in 1841 of philosophic or comprehensive knowledge, and we shall find that in his *Idea of a University* he claims that it is precisely this type of knowledge that has always been considered liberal. In his *Sixth Discourse* (sections 4, 5, 6) he expressly notes that he is embodying the idea and even much of the phraseology of this sermon, but we may go further and say that in it we find the germ of thought of the whole series of *Discourses*.

Before leaving this subject I would draw your attention to the fact that among the subjects that Newman enumerates as capable of producing enlargement of mind is the study of physical science. My warnings in connection with this study may seem wearisome, but, as you will see, they are less wearisome than the perpetual misunderstanding and misrepresentation of Newman's attitude towards it which are found even in contemporary writings.

6

We have now completed our task of picking out the main influences, events, or developments of thought whose effects will be detected later in Newman's educational writings and achievement. I have warned you that I have deliberately abstained from all but a passing mention of Newman's spiritual development during this time. The division has obviously been a most artificial one, but I can offer many good excuses for adopting it. The story of the Tractarian Movement is a most complicated one; the story of Newman's influence on it and its influence on him is even more complicated; and if any simplification is possible, it can be done only by isolating the events of the Movement from the general chronicle of Newman's life at Oxford. Furthermore, as I have already said, we are not called on to study it in detail—that will be done at a later date in this course of lectures. Our main task will be to detach a certain great underlying principle of the Movement which was also the inspiration of Newman's concept of the University. But we may also say that in any event it would be a very maimed account of Newman's Oxford days that would not take at least a rapid glance at the personages and main events of the great spiritual revival which brought about two momentous events, the birth of the Anglo-Catholic movement and the reception of Newman and a host of his contemporaries into the Catholic Church.[30]

The primary, though not the most effective cause of the Tractarian Movement, was the conviction among earnest Anglicans at the beginning of the century that the Anglican Church was losing her place in the life of the nation. Neither of the two great parties within the church possessed those qualities of other-worldliness that can alone secure support for any body purporting to be religious. The Church Party claimed to base their theology on the teaching of the great Anglican divines of the seventeenth and eighteenth centuries, but according to Dean Church their main characteristic was plain commonsense rather than erudition.

> Its worst members were jobbers and hunters after preferment, pluralists who built fortunes . . . or country gentlemen in orders who rode to hounds and shot and danced and farmed, and often did worse things.[31]

Their sobriety of doctrine earned them the nickname of the High and Dry party; the convivial habits of some of them inspired the alternative title of " the two-bottle Orthodox." The Evangelicals on the other hand had been influenced by the Methodist revival. Their sincere piety displayed itself in philanthropic activities. Yet they lacked driving force. They had not the definiteness of Lutherans, Calvinists or Puritans. They had come to terms with a society whose ideal was " to be reasonable." Their fundamental idea of religion was the " assurance of salvation," and they shrank from definite theological teachings, so that their utterances became repetitious and empty. The Noetics, of whom we have spoken, could hardly be described as a party. They were confined to Oxford, and their influence was more critical than constructive. They were the type of men who later blossomed out as liberal theologians.

The general uneasiness about the state of the church was brought to a head in the early years of the century by the growth of religious liberalism, which was the second and most potent cause of the Tractarian Movement. We have already sufficiently examined the nature of English political liberalism,[32] and we may now remark that, being in itself an ethical teaching, it inevitably invaded the sphere of morals, and from that to the realm of faith was only a step. It was, therefore, when liberalism was directly or indirectly concerned with religion that it was opposed by the Tractarians. The issue was often confused by the fact that they opposed also its political or economic effects, but their key motive was the religious one. The true issue was succinctly stated by Newman in his old age in his speech at Rome on the reception of the cardinalate.

Liberalism in religion is the doctrine that there is no positive truth in religion, but that one creed is as good as another . . . Since then, religion is so . . . private a possession, we must of necessity ignore it in the intercourse of man with man. Religion is in no sense the bond of society . . . It must be borne in mind that there is much in the Liberalistic theory which is good and true . . . it is not till we find that this array of principles is intended to supersede . . . religion that we pronounce it to be evil.[33]

The whole trend of Newman's religious development brought him, from his earliest days in Oxford, into sharp conflict with the liberal concept of religion. We have already seen that even as a boy he had imbibed the Calvinist teaching, though not in its entirety, of the division of mankind into those who had a complete personal experience of salvation and those who had not. From this, as he tells us in the *Apologia*,[34] derived his early conviction of (1) the church as a visible society, (2) the absolute nature of dogma, and (3) the uncompromising acceptance of religious belief as a living force in daily life. These convictions were not shaken by his contact with the Noetics. Indeed, as we have seen, the first of them, the existence of a visible church, was strengthened for him by Whately. The general scepticism of the Noetics was the first influence that led Newman to reject his early Evangelical beliefs. For a time, indeed, it swayed him slightly towards those liberal views of which he was normally the sworn enemy; but he soon discarded the shallow intellectualism of liberalism, largely through the influence of Hurrell Froude, the elder brother of the historian, and one of Newman's fellow tutors at Oriel. Froude was one of the most brilliant and attractive figures of the Movement. His intense and ascetical sense of religious values he communicated to Newman, thereby helping him to realise the lack of supernatural content in the Evangelical faith, and the insufficiency of liberalism when faced with the realities of human temptation and suffering. From Froude too he learned the love of antiquity, and this led him in the years 1831-2 to the study of the early Fathers, where he found that complete conviction of the reality of the unseen world of grace, which he had found lacking in contemporary Anglicanism.

Though in a certain sense the Tractarian Movement may be said to have begun with the publication in 1827 of Keble's *Christian Year*, which embodied the spirit of fervent piety so characteristic of the Movement, Newman in the *Apologia* [35] dates its definite emergence from 1833. In that year occurred the suppression of two redundant Irish bishoprics, an act which seemed to the High Anglicans to be a definite challenge to the old order in which England, as a Christian nation, was part of Christ's church, and therefore bound in legislation and policy by the laws of the church. On the 14th of July Keble preached the Assize sermon in the pulpit of St Mary's. It was a call to Christians to take steps to secure the independence of the church from the state in its new concept, and was afterwards published under the title of " National Apostacy."

His call was answered by a meeting at Hadleigh in Suffolk of a small group, Hurrell Froude, Arthur Perceval, Fellow of All Souls, and William Palmer, Fellow of Worcester, formerly of Trinity College, Dublin. They decided on the publication of the memorable *Tracts for the Times*, in the first two of which were emphasised the main points of attack, the Erastianism of the supporters of the church and the Liberalism of its opponents. In 1833 the Movement was strengthened by the accession to its ranks of Edward Bouverie Pusey, Regius Professor of Hebrew and Canon of Christ Church, whose theological learning added weight, though at times dullness to the Tracts. In 1836 feelings both for and against the Tractarians were deeply intensified by the appointment of Renn Dickson Hampden, a former Fellow of Oriel and one of the Noetic group, now Principal of St Mary Hall (united with Oriel in 1902), to the Chair of Divinity in the University. Hampden's views were avowedly liberal. In the preceding year a motion to abolish subscription to the Thirty-Nine Articles on Matriculation had been proposed in Convocation. It was decisively rejected, but Hampden had openly declared on that occasion that the church formularies had no binding force. In his Bampton lectures of the same year he had expressed the view that nothing was of importance in religion but scriptural fact. His appointment to the Chair of Divinity roused the Tractarians to righteous indignation. Pusey addressed a protest to Melbourne, the Prime Minister, but the only action taken was that Hampden by way of censure was deprived by Convocation of certain rights attached to the Chair.

To form some idea of the feeling that prevailed at this period in Oxford among both the protagonists and antagonists of the Movement, we must recall that England was then still a deeply religious country, where life to a considerable degree centred on the parish church or the local chapel, as the case might be. In our age of indifference it is difficult to conceive the excitement caused by the opposition of a group of devout parsons and laymen to the appointment of a freethinking divine to the Chair of Divinity; but we must recall that the spiritual ferment which this contest signified was at work in innumerable centres all through the country, and the Oxford Tractarians were conscious that the battle they were fighting was but one incident in a larger, indeed nation-wide struggle. We must remember too that Oxford was then a small country town, not more than an appendage to the University, and that in those days of slow communication the life of the University was extremely self-contained. Even today we know that it is almost impossible to cross a quadrangle without meeting an acquaintance, and we can picture how in those more leisurely days any university interest was busily canvassed all day from mouth to mouth. And this was an interest which most Oxford men believed to concern not merely the University, but the whole destiny of mankind. It is startling to think how much the world has changed since those days, only a hundred years ago, when the College gardens and quadrangles, and the quiet roads and country lanes about Oxford saw groups of earnest young men arguing incessantly about the nature of God's Kingdom on Earth and its relation to the human soul.

Very briefly now we must review the spiritual reaction of Newman to these momentous happenings. He has made it all fairly clear for us in the *Apologia*.[36] At the beginning of the Movement, about 1832, he had already satisfied himself about certain fundamental beliefs. There was firstly the Principle of Dogma. " My battle," he says, " was with Liberalism; by liberalism I meant the anti-dogmatic principle." Secondly, as we have seen, there was the existence of a visible church with sacraments and rites which are the channels of invisible grace. Thirdly, there was that strange identification of Rome with anti-Christ, though this prejudice had been modified by the influence of Froude and by Newman's Mediterranean journey in 1832-3.

Taking the first two of these fundamental beliefs as a starting point, he had evolved the theory of the *Via Media*, enunciated in his *Prophetical Office of the Church*, which was composed in 1834-6 and published in 1837. The original deposit of faith had been given to the early church. Rome had added to it. Protestantism had taken away from it. In the Anglican Church there was preserved the most perfect presentation of it, though she had compromised her position by the tolerance of Protestant errors. But this system was no sooner elaborated than doubts arose in his mind about it. The great weakness of the *Via Media* was that it was, as he says, " a church on paper," and most of the bishops of the day were unanimous in rejecting it. These doubts were intensified by his study during the Long Vacation of 1839 of the history of the Monophysite heresy. In the pages of the Fathers he found all the characteristics of the early church to be identical with those of the Roman church of today. If the Monophysites were heretics because they broke with such a system, then were not the Anglicans heretics also? And in August of that year the same conclusion was urged on him by the reading of an article by Wiseman in the *Dublin Review* on the history of the Donatists.

The issue of whether or not the *Via Media* was a reality was knit by the publication in 1841 of Newman's Tract 90.[37] Newman's aim was to show that the Thirty-Nine Articles do not oppose Catholic teaching, that is the teaching of the early church. They but partially oppose Roman dogma, and for the most part oppose the dominant errors of Rome. To the majority of the Anglican bishops it appeared that the true gist of the Tract was that there was little in the Articles that could not be reconciled with Roman belief. Many of them denounced it, and a strong condemnation was published in March 1841 by the Heads of Houses of the University. That was the end of the *Via Media* as a possible reality, and the episode in October of that year of the appointment of a German Lutheran Bishop of Jerusalem with jurisdiction over English Protestants was but a nail in its coffin.

For our purposes it is not necessary to dwell on the remaining incidents of Newman's journey into the Catholic church, though they are so moving in view of our nearness to the scene of them. I have little doubt that all my hearers will make, during the course of this school, a pilgrimage to the old almshouses at Littlemore which are a symbol of the greatness of Newman's renunciation. There they will see the room where he composed, at white heat, his *Essay on Development*, which demonstrates how what he had once regarded as Roman corruptions of and additions to the primitive creed were legitimate developments of the original deposit of faith. There too it was that he finally convinced himself that the Roman church, no less than the Anglican church as he knew and loved it, possessed the mark of holiness. That mark he found most startlingly evident in the person of the obscure Italian Passionist, Dominic Barberi, who by a strange train of circumstances was sent by God to receive him into the Catholic church.

At the risk of appearing to " protest too much," I would again remind you that this account of the Tractarian Movement has been a very compressed one, and has not aimed at tracing all the very complex events and influences that determined its course. The same remark applies to the outline given of the part played by Newman in it and the part it played in his spiritual development. But I trust that it has sufficiently traced one underlying principle of the Movement, the belief in a fixed, objective body of religious truth, the recognition of which was not a matter of choice, but of intellectual necessity, and which therefore must determine the ethical principles, both private and social, which guide man's destiny. The recognition of such a body of truth was to be, as we shall see, the starting point of Newman's concept of university education, and it was a natural transition to recognise all truth as an objective reality. The problem of the proper approach of the mind to that reality was to lead Newman on to the elucidation of the nature of liberal knowledge and the fundamental part it plays in university education, or for that matter in all education.

THE SCIENCE OF SCIENCES

I

WE NOW APPROACH our consideration of Newman's *Discourses*. I shall first deal very briefly with their immediate historical setting. It is an interesting subject both for students of the history of education and for students of Irish history, but for one thing exigencies of time do not permit that we should delay on it, and for another it had comparatively little bearing on the philosophical content of the essays. I shall point out whatever bearing it had.

The following are the main facts. Up to the middle of the nineteenth century there had been but one university in Ireland, the University of Dublin, founded in 1592, containing but one college, the College of the Holy and Undivided Trinity. This University was from the outset Protestant in character and aims, but in the early years had no legal limitation of the students to any one denomination. It was not until the time of the Statutes of Charles I (1637) that Catholics were, in practice, excluded by the obligation laid on all students of attending divine service and receiving the Holy Communion according to the Anglican rite, and by the oath against Popery (*Pontificia Religio*) to be taken by the Fellows. Probably about the same time there was added an oath, on taking a degree, against transubstantiation, "invocation and adoration" of the Blessed Virgin, and the sacrifice of the Mass.

In 1794 a Royal Letter made it possible, by a partial abolition of religious tests, for Catholics to proceed to degrees in Trinity College, though they were still debarred from Fellowships and scholarships. Several efforts were made during the ensuing half century to secure equal treatment for Catholics, but they met with no success. Finally in 1845, moved by the increasing political power of the Catholic body, Sir Robert Peel, the Prime Minister, introduced into Parliament a Bill for the establishment of three Colleges at Belfast, Cork and Galway, to be known as the Queen's Colleges, and later to be united as the Queen's University. These colleges were to be completely non-denominational in character. No religious tests were to be imposed either at entrance or on admission to degrees, no religious instruction was to be given, except what might be provided by the various religious bodies at their own expense, no religious topics were to be introduced into the classrooms, and no religious considerations were to weigh in the appointment or dismissal of officials.

The Queen's Colleges were rejected by the majority of the Catholic laity under the leadership of O'Connell and by the majority of the Irish bishops. The matter was referred to Rome, and in two Rescripts the Congregation of Propaganda condemned the Colleges, and urged on the Irish bishops the establishment of a Catholic University on the model of the recently revived University of Louvain. In August 1850 a General Synod of the Irish bishops was held at Thurles in Co. Tipperary, where the condemnation of the

Colleges by Rome was endorsed, and a Committee set up to forward the establishment of the Catholic University of Ireland.

This Committee was under the chairmanship of Dr Paul Cullen, Archbishop of Armagh, later Archbishop of Dublin, who had been appointed Apostolic Delegate to convoke the Synod of Thurles and forward the University project. Largely on his initiative Newman in the summer of 1851 was invited to be the first Rector of the University, and to come to Dublin to deliver a series of lectures on mixed or undenominational education as a send-off. Newman accepted both invitations, and came to Ireland in October of that year, to draw up a preliminary report, to which we shall have occasion to refer later, and to inform himself on the state of affairs with a view to the preparation of his lectures. These lectures were eventually delivered in Dublin in May 1852. Actually only the first five were given, on Monday May 10th and the four successive Mondays. Newman finished the second five, which were never spoken, in the autumn of 1852 in Birmingham, and added a preface and appendix. The first complete published edition bears the date "In Fest. Praesent. B.V.M. Nov. 21st, 1852"; but a pencilled note in one of Newman's copies in the Oratory at Birmingham gives the actual date of appearance as "Feb. 2nd (Feast of the Purification of the B.V.M.) 1853."

It is clear from his correspondence that Newman accepted with alacrity the invitation to deliver these lectures. The original purpose of the lectures was to expose the nature of undenominational education, and we have seen that this was a subject that had occupied Newman's thoughts during the preceding thirty years. We recall that he looked upon the struggle against Liberalism as his life-work, and he considered undenominational education to be a striking manifestation of the liberal frame of mind. He had witnessed in 1828, when he was a young don at Oriel, the foundation of London University, the first embodiment of the undenominational principle in higher education to appear on British soil. The following year, as we have seen, he had been one of Peel's most vigorous opponents in the Oxford election on the issue of Catholic emancipation, which he then conceived to be a manifestation of the Liberal spirit. In 1834-5 he had read Sir William Hamilton's plea for fair treatment of Dissenters in education, and in 1841 in the Tamworth Letters he had crossed foils with Peel on the whole issue of religion in education. Now there had come this new application of the undenominational principle in the Queen's Colleges, and Newman was asked to discuss it in the country where it was being put into force. No issue could have been more topical, more dear to his heart, or of greater importance to religion.

But, from another aspect also the delivery of these lectures had a strong appeal for him. Actually we may note in advance, though it will become clearer as we proceed, that Newman's *Discourses* are a skilful blending of two themes, the necessity of including religious teaching in any scheme of studies, and the fact that the cultivation of the mind rather than immediate preparation for professional occupations is the primary end of a university. These two themes flow from one common consideration, namely the nature of human knowledge. Accepting the moderate realist position that knowledge is a valid mental grasp of reality, and that real things are not isolated in the universe, but stand in various relations to one another, it follows that the truest knowledge is that which grasps not only the various objects, material or spiritual, which make up the universe, but also—in as full a degree as possible—their mutual relations. The development from this simple yet fundamental consideration of Newman's two themes will be demonstrated from the analysis of his *Discourses*. All we have to do here is to note that the second theme, the nature of liberal knowledge and its essential place in the University curriculum, was also peculiarly topical. It had been thrashed out, as we have seen, in the early years of the century in the *Edinburgh Review* controversy. It has been the theme of Sir William Hamilton's criticisms of Oxford. It had become a living issue in the foundation of London University, with its stress on scientific and professional studies, and it was one of the main pre-occupations of the two University Commissions set up in 1850 for the reform of the studies and government of Oxford and Cambridge. Everything combined then to make Newman eager to develop publicly these two closely related themes, and thus to give a wide and complete view of the whole scope and aim of university education. We may note in passing that it is the second of these two themes that receives almost exclusive attention from writers on educational topics today. There is in fact at least one well-known edition of Newman's *Idea of a University*, which omits altogether the *Discourses* that deal with the place of theology in the curriculum. It will, however, be obvious that such a mutilation destroys the entire great sweep of the *Discourses*, and robs them of half their force.

It will, I believe, help to clarity, to reverse to some extent in our consideration of the *Discourses* Newman's order of treatment, and to deal first with his concept of liberal knowledge. However, it will be essential, in order to preserve the order and unity of his thought, to give in outline the arguments of the earlier *Discourses* which deal with the place of theology in the curriculum, reserving for a later lecture the detailed analysis of them.

2

Already in his preface, which we recall to have been added after the completion of the *Discourses*, Newman gives us a glimpse of his concept of that cultivation of the mind which he equiparates with a liberal education.[1] He thus enumerates the mental advantages to be gained by the students of the proposed university: " the force, the steadiness, the comprehensiveness and the versatility of intellect, the command over our own powers, the instinctive just estimate of things as they pass before us." The characteristics to which I would draw your attention are " comprehensiveness " and " the just estimate of things." A few lines further on Newman tells us that liberal education " brings the mind into form." Again, he gives a few vivid pen-pictures of uncultivated or illiberal minds.

. . . Such persons have no difficulty in contradicting themselves in successive sentences, without being conscious of it . . . Others, whose defect in intellectual training is more latent, have their most unfortunate crotchets, as they are called, or hobbies, which deprive them of the influence which their estimable qualities would otherwise secure . . . Others can never look

straight before them, never see the point, and have no
difficulties in the most difficult subjects. Others are
hopelessly obstinate and prejudiced, and after they have
been driven from their opinions, return to them the next
moment without even an attempt to explain why. Others
are so intemperate and intractable that there is no greater
calamity for a good cause than that they should get hold
of it.

On the other hand Newman enumerates the characteristics
of the intellect which has been " properly trained," and I
would draw your attention to the definition he gives of this
proper training, that it has been " formed to have a connected
view or grasp of things."

In the case of most men it makes itself felt in the
good sense, sobriety of thought, reasonableness, candour,
self-command, and steadiness of view, which characterize
it. In some it will have developed habits of business,
power of influencing others, and sagacity. In others it
will elicit the talent of philosophical speculation, and
lead the mind forward to eminence in this or that
intellectual department. In all it will be a faculty of
entering with comparative ease into any subject of thought,
and of taking up with aptitude any science or profession.

We may omit from our consideration the *First Discourse*.
It merely dwells on the considerations which urged Newman
to base his arguments mainly on his actual experience of
university life in Oxford. One point alone is worth attention,
namely that in view of the mixed nature of his audience
Newman elected to omit all arguments based on the authority
of the Catholic church, and to confine himself to philosoph-

ical reasoning, or at least to such theological considerations as would be accepted by all believers in the existence of God. We shall see that in the event Newman did not keep absolutely to this purpose, though in the edition as now printed he adheres to it, in the main, for the course of the first seven *Discourses*.

In his *Second Discourse* Newman plunges at once into the discussion of the new type of university that had appeared on the intellectual horizon, exemplified by the University of London and the Queen's Colleges in Ireland, one namely in which the study of theology was excluded on principle. There had been, even in medieval times, universities in which there was no faculty of theology, but this had been regarded as an accidental state of affairs, dictated by reasons of expediency. Here, however, was a new concept of a university, one which claimed that a complete view of knowledge need not include the knowledge of God and man's relation to him.

We will deal here very briefly with Newman's argument to the contrary, and we may best do so by quoting the syllogism which he propounds at the opening of his *Discourse*.

A University, I should lay down, by its very name professes to teach universal knowledge, Theology is surely a branch of knowledge: how then is it possible for it to profess all branches of knowledge, and yet to exclude from the subjects of its teaching one which, to say the least of it, is as important and as large as any of them.[2]

We will revert later to Newman's statement that a university by its very name professes to teach universal knowledge. We shall see that this does not mean that a

university must teach every conceivable subject, but that
its idea involves a certain breadth of curriculum, and that
if it excludes any subject of major value, it must show cause
for this exclusion. We shall also see that in claiming breadth
of curriculum for a university Newman is not merely
depending on the etymology of the name *Universitas*. It is
enough to note here that all that Newman intends is to
make the very modest claim, as he does at the close of this
Discourse, that to exclude on principle theology from a
university course is " simply unphilosophical." " Theology,"
he says, " has at least as good a right to claim a place there
as astronomy." [3] This simple yet telling reasoning of Newman
has been strongly endorsed by that Scarlet Pimpernel of the
academic world, Mr Bruce Truscot, whose two books,
Redbrick University and *Redbrick and these Vital Days*, have
done more, perhaps, than any other modern works to
stimulate interest in university problems in the English-
speaking world. Mr Truscot says: " The arguments of
Newman's well-known lecture, ' Theology a Branch of
Knowledge ' have never been answered, probably because
they are unanswerable." [4]

In the *Third Discourse* Newman pushes the argument a
stage further, and urges that the omission of theology will
falsify the content of all the other subjects in the curriculum.
Here again let us be careful to get the exact gist of his
argument. There is, of course, no question of demanding
that every student must necessarily pursue a formal course in
theology, or that every professor must have done so. The
argument is that if in the study of other subjects theological
considerations are systematically excluded, those other
subjects will be mutilated, and to that extent falsified.

In support of this contention Newman brings forward what is the key argument, the fundamental theme of the whole series of *Discourses*, and the link between the two great propositions contained in it. Taking for granted the moderate realism propounded in Aristotelian and Scholastic philosophy, he bases his argument on the very nature of knowledge.

Truth is the object of Knowledge of whatever kind; and when we inquire what is meant by Truth, I suppose it is right to answer that Truth means facts and their relations, which stand towards each other pretty much as subjects and predicates in logic. All that exists, as contemplated by the human mind, forms one large system or complex fact, and this of course resolves itself into an indefinite number of particular facts, which, as being portions of a whole, have countless relations of every kind one towards another. Knowledge is the apprehension of these facts, whether in themselves, or in their mutual positions and bearings. And, as all taken together form one integral subject for contemplation, so there are no natural or real limits between fact and fact; one is ever running into another; all, as viewed by the mind, are combined together, and possess a correlative character one with another.[5]

Newman then points out that the human mind is incapable of taking in all these facts at once, but does so by partial views, which we call the various sciences.

Now these views or sciences as being abstractions, have far more to do with the relations of things than with things themselves. They tell us what things are, only or principally by telling us their relations, or assigning predicates to subjects; and therefore they never tell us all that can be said about a thing, even when they tell something, nor do they bring it before us, as the senses do. They arrange and classify facts; they reduce separate phenomena under a common law; they trace effects to a cause.

They are, however, all imperfect.

They proceed on the principle of a division of labour, even though that division is an abstraction, not a literal separation into parts; and, as the maker of a bridle or epaulet has not, on that account, any idea of the science of tactics or strategy, so in a parallel way, it is not every science which equally, nor any one which fully, enlightens the mind in the knowledge of things as they are, or brings home to it the external object on which it wishes to gaze. Thus they differ in importance; and according to their importance will be their influence, not only on the means of knowledge to which they all converge and contribute, but on each other.

Since then sciences are the results of mental processes about one and the same subject-matter, viewed under its various aspects, and are true results, as far as they go, yet at the same time separate and partial, it follows that on the one hand they need external assistance, one by one, by reason of their incompleteness, and on the other that they are able to afford it to each other, by reason, first, of their independence in themselves, and then of their connexion in their subject-matter. Viewed all together, they approximate to a representation or subjective reflection of the objective truth, as nearly as is possible to the human mind, which advances towards the accurate apprehension of that object, in proportion to the number of sciences which it has mastered; and which, when certain sciences are away, in such a case has but a defective apprehension, in proportion to the value of the sciences which are thus wanting, and the importance of the field on which they are employed.[6]

You will observe the masterly way in which Newman has set out his premises, so that the rest of the argument hardly needs to be put formally. The late Charles Frederick Harrold, Professor of English in Ohio State University, in his Preface to the 1947 edition of the *Discourses*, points out how Newman's method of argument resembles that of Cicero. Indeed the analysis of Cicero's style given by Newman in his *Historical Sketches* might well be an analysis of Newman's own style in controversy. It is the technique of multiple advance on one front. Both great writers, the rhetorician and the apologist, have perfected the art of approaching a subject from all sides, examining and re-examining it, until to use Newman's words of Cicero "the hearer feels ashamed of doubting a position which seems built on a foundation so strictly argumentative."[7]

In this instance Newman drives home his conclusion with skilful iteration through twenty more pages, but sums it up in one concluding paragraph.

I say, then, if the various branches of knowledge which are the matter of teaching in a University, so hang together, that none can be neglected without prejudice to the perfection of the rest, and if theology be a branch of knowledge, of wide reception, of philosophical structure, of unutterable importance, and of supreme influence, to what conclusion are we brought from these two premises but this: that to withdraw Theology from the public schools is to impair the completeness and to invalidate the trustworthiness of all that is actually taught in them? [8]

But not only will there be untrustworthiness in the various subjects of the curriculum, if theological consideration be excluded; there will be an untrustworthiness, a deformity in the curriculum as a whole. This is the theme of the *Fourth Discourse*. You will recall how Newman had emphasised the fact that each science reveals to us a part of truth, which it is its special function to reveal. To take the instance of man. History is the name given to the collection of facts concerning what man has done in the past. Biology, chemistry, physics, each contribute their quota of facts about the constitution of his body. Economics deals with his efforts to produce the real wealth necessary for his life and well-being. Psychology records and theorises about the nature and functions of his mind and will. Newman points out that if, in some fantastic and absurd way, the study of any of these sciences were prohibited, the human mind would not be satisfied merely to leave a gap where that science had been, simply to disregard the mass of facts which that science had formerly presented to it. Its inevitable tendency would be to explain these facts by the findings of the other sciences. One example given by Newman is that of history. If we can imagine such an absurdity as the total exclusion of its study from a curriculum, the mind would inevitably seek to find some way of discovering how man behaved himself in the past, and would endeavour to substitute a conjecture as to how he must have behaved, basing it on metaphysics, or as we should say on psychology and ethics.

I observe then that, if you drop any science out of the circle of knowledge, you cannot keep its place vacant for it; that science is forgotten; the other sciences close up, or, in other words, they exceed their proper bounds, and intrude where they have no right . . . The case is the same with the subject-matter of Theology; it would be the prey of a dozen various sciences, if Theology were put out of possession; and not only so, but those sciences would be plainly exceeding their rights and their capacities in seizing upon it. They would be sure to teach wrongly, where they had no mission to teach at all. [9]

We have seen that it is difficult even to imagine the suppression of any other subject. Let it be once again recalled that we are not speaking merely of the absence of such a subject from the curriculum, but its total exclusion, on principle. We do not mean the case, which might well occur, in which a university would have, let us say, no faculty of law. But we mean such an absurd state of affairs as that in which all consideration of the subject of law would be banned, and history, for instance, would have to be expounded without the slightest reference to the development of legal systems or their effect on the progress of mankind.

Newman's argument is that the omission of theology is just as fantastic, and here again it must be clear that he does not mean the absence of a theological faculty, but the banning of all religious considerations. On the face of it, his contention is unanswerable, but he sustains it by numerous examples, of which one will suffice to cite, the case in which Political Economy (now generally termed Economics) goes beyond its proper sphere of investigating the laws governing the production and distribution of wealth, and presumes (Benthamite utilitarianism and Marxian materialism occur as obvious instances) to propose the proper distribution of it as the total end of man's existence. It is the function of theology to convey to man all that he can know about his final end in life. Put theology aside, refuse to it the right to expose to man that particular facet of truth, and at once you observe the efforts of some other science, in Newman's words, " to close up," to usurp to itself a task it was never made for and is incapable of fulfilling, thus falsifying the whole content of truth which the curriculum under consideration is supposed to convey.

3

In his *Fifth Discourse* Newman passes by an easy transition to the second part of his theme, that with which we are mainly concerned today. A university, he points out, may be regarded with reference either to its studies or its students. He has so far applied the fundamental principle of the unity of knowledge to the curriculum, in order to vindicate the inclusion of theology in it. Now he proposes to apply it to the students, in order to decide what type of learning the university should give them. Should it be useful in the common acceptance of the term, or should it

have some other character? And at this point I would
remind you of the distinction made in our first lecture
between the ultimately useful and the immediately useful.
It is of the latter that Newman speaks here.

Newman now repeats his fundamental principle that " all
branches of knowledge are connected together, because the
subject-matter of knowledge is intimately united in itself,
as being the acts and work of the Creator." [10] I will here
draw your attention to a title which he had given in his
Third Discourse to knowledge, which particularly emphasises this connection, a title which will constantly recur,
and which, if not explained, might cause confusion. This
knowledge, says Newman, " is my own conception of what
is meant by Philosophy, in the true sense of the word, and
of a philosophical habit of mind, and which in these Discourses I shall call by this name." [11] You will recall that we
saw in our last lecture how Newman, eleven years previously
in one of his Oxford sermons, had used the term " philosophy " in the same applied sense. It may possibly be
objected that Newman's usage is somewhat arbitrary.
Universal tradition applies this term, philosophy, to the
study of things under their most universal aspects, comprising the recognized branches of ontology, cosmology,
psychology, ethics and natural theology, with which is
commonly included the science of knowledge, epistemology
or criteriology. In Newman's defence it may be acknowledged that there is a certain fitness in the analogy by which
he applies the term to the knowledge of things under ever
widening, though not necessarily ultimate aspects. However,
whether his use of the term be approved or not, he makes
his meaning clear, and adheres to it consistently. He now

points out that it is philosophical knowledge in his sense which he holds to be the result of liberal education, and to be "the main purpose of a university in its treatment of its students."[12] Note that he says "the main purpose," implying therefore that it may have professional training as a secondary purpose, a fact which he explicitly emphasises later on. The fruits of such an education are thus briefly described by him.

> A habit of mind is formed which lasts through life, of which the attributes are, freedom, equitableness, calmness, moderation, and wisdom; or what in a former Discourse I have ventured to call a philosophical habit.[13]

He now pushes further his enquiry into the nature of this knowledge by asking the commonly heard question, "What is the use of it?", and points out that the answer to this question will constitute the main subject of the *Discourses* which are to follow.

His first answer is the enunciation of the famous dictum which gives its name to the *Discourse*: "Knowledge is capable of being its own end."[14] It is certainly strange that this dictum should have been a stumbling-block to so many, and the fact that it has been such seems to suggest that the number of those who have read, or at any rate digested Newman's *Discourses* is very few. There is no question whatever of the mind wrapping itself up in a cocoon of knowledge and going into a fruitless sleep. Newman's meaning simply is that the human intellect is a perfectible faculty. It is something that grows, accidentally if you will, but really, and what makes it grow is knowledge. Any knowledge, says Newman, "if it be really such," adds thus

to the perfection of the mind, but more particularly that
" comprehensive view of truth in all its branches, of the
relations of science to science, of their mutual bearings and
their respective values " which he calls " philosophy." [15]
In practice this perfection of the mind can and must be
directed to further ends, for the accomplishment of the
whole end of man, his own good and that of his fellow men.
Newman indeed, as we shall see shortly, was to devote one
entire *Discourse* to the manner in which this " philosophic
knowledge " could subserve professional, utilitarian aims,
and another to the manner in which it could subserve
religion. But even before it serves these ultimate aims, it
achieves an aim of its own. This doctrine is succinctly stated
by Newman in a passage so clear that one can only charitably
assume that it has been overlooked by his critics.

> That further advantages accrue to us and redound to
> others by its possession, over and above what it is in
> itself, I am very far from denying; but, independent of
> these, we are satisfying a direct need of our nature in
> its very acquisition. [16]

Newman goes on to confirm his statement that knowledge
is, or can be, its own end, from the title which such
knowledge has commonly borne, " Liberal Knowledge."
He points out that in its original sense it was opposed to
servile knowledge, knowledge namely of mechanical or
bodily employments in which the mind has little part.
Liberal knowledge, therefore, is primarily " exercises of
mind, of reason, of reflection." [17] There is, however, a
further distinction to be made, since there are some mental
pursuits which are not commonly termed liberal. Commer-

cial and professional pursuits, though involving great mental activity are not commonly thus termed. Hence we arrive at the full idea of liberal knowledge, that, namely,

> which stands on its own pretensions, which is independent of sequel, expects no complement, refuses to be *informed* (as it is called) by any end, or absorbed into any art, in order to present itself to our contemplation.[18]

This concept Newman confirms by quotations from Cicero and Aristotle, warning us, however, that he is not merely relying on the extrinsic authority of these ancient writers, but confirming from their words

> a specific idea, which ever has been, and ever will be, while the nature of man is the same, just as the idea of the Beautiful is specific, or of the Sublime, or of the Ridiculous, or of the Sordid.[19]

It is not possible here to go into any detailed history of the growth of the idea of liberal education. It is enough to record the fact that both Greeks and Romans commonly spoke of *mathemata eleuthera, studia liberalia, artes liberales*; and that the term received universal acceptance from the Middle Ages on. The studies understood by this term varied according to the different ideals of different ages, but the general meaning was always the same, namely the studies which would produce the best type of man. The sense, too, in which the word liberal was used, varied also, sometimes, emphasising the difference between slave and freeman, sometimes merely emphasising the qualities of the citizen of a free state, and in mediaeval times emphasising rather the freedom of the studies, namely that they were not directed to professional purposes. But the underlying idea, as Newman states, always remained the same, that of a type of education complete in itself and forming the complete man in himself.

4

Newman now proceeds to a closer analysis of the nature of liberal or philosophical knowledge, with a view to vindicating his claim that it is " the main purpose " [20] of a university education. He introduces this study by a paragraph which, for reasons to which I will draw your attention, needs close examination.

> I consider, then, that I am chargeable with no paradox, when I speak of a Knowledge which is its own end, when I call it liberal knowledge, or a gentleman's knowledge, when I educate for it, and make it the scope of a University. And still less am I incurring such a charge, when I make this acquisition consist, not in Knowledge in a vague and ordinary sense, but in that Knowledge which I have especially called Philosophy, or, in an extended sense of the word, Science; for whatever claims Knowledge has to be considered as a good, these it has in a higher degree when it is viewed not vaguely, not popularly, but precisely and transcendently as Philosophy. Knowledge, I say, is then especially liberal, or sufficient for itself, apart from every external and ulterior object, when and so far as it is philosophical, and this I proceed to show. [21]

It would appear to me that this paragraph provides two instances of a defect that is fairly often found in the *Dis-*

courses, and which I would attribute to the pressure under which they were composed. It is the throwing in casually of some new idea or distinction, which creates confusion in the mind of the reader either because it passes unobserved, or because it is insufficiently explained or developed. Thus, in this paragraph Newman gives us casually two new names for liberal knowledge. The first is " a gentleman's knowledge," a dangerous phrase which might easily be interpreted as " the knowledge proper to the wealthy or leisured " or " the knowledge of an amateur," and which in modern times is used humorously to denote a very sketchy knowledge. But from all that goes before it is clear enough that Newman is using it simply in the sense of the knowledge of an educated man. We may note in passing that the phrase " a gentleman's knowledge " was in much more common use in Newman's day and was less susceptible of misunderstanding than in our more democratic age. The dictionaries still give it as the first meaning of " liberal," though the *Oxford Concise* warns us that it is " now rare, except in education." The second new name for liberal knowledge is " science "; and Newman adds, " in an extended sense of the word," leaving us to guess how it is extended. The word " science " is generally applied to a systematical study of one branch of knowledge, but Newman apparently uses it here to describe systematical study of knowledge in general. There is, indeed, a partial excuse for his rather casual and compressed introduction of this new title. In the original *Fifth Discourse*, which came before the one now under consideration, and which, as we shall see, was omitted in the second edition, there was a more explicit explanation of his use of the title and of the sense in which it may be called "extended." Newman there declares that liberal knowledge views all the sciences as one. "Imagine," he says, "a science of sciences, and you have attained the true notion of the scope of a University." With this explanation the use of the title "science" in the present *Fifth Discourse* is clear enough, but it may fairly be said that, having omitted the *Discourse* in which it is found, Newman should have given some compensating explanation in the context in which the title now occurs.[22]

Besides these two new titles for liberal knowledge, Newman introduces casually into this paragraph an explanation that would seem worthy of greater emphasis.

> Whatever claims Knowledge has, to be considered as a good, these it has in a higher degree when it is viewed . . . as Philosophy . . . Knowledge . . . is then especially liberal . . . when and so far as it is philosophical.[23]

Newman here implies that there is not an essential difference between liberal knowledge and any other kind of knowledge, but only one of degree. This, I think, must be acknowledged, and the impression that Newman makes an essential difference between the two has led to a mistaken criticism of his praise of liberal knowledge. After all, what is mental culture in its simplest definition, but the perfecting, the enlarging, the enriching of the intellect? And this can only be done by the formation of concepts and the action of the judgment on them. These two fundamental processes enter into the acquisition of all knowledge, even of the most mechanical type. The difference between it and scientific or philosophical knowledge can be due, therefore, only to the greater influence of the reason, and, in point of fact, this is the difference which Newman finds between the two, as he goes on to elaborate in Section 6 of this *Discourse*.

Knowledge is called by the name of Science or Philosophy, when it is acted upon, informed, or if I may use a strong figure, impregnated by Reason. You see, then, here are two methods of Education; the end of the one is to be philosophical, of the other to be mechanical; the one rises towards general ideas, the other is exhausted upon what is particular and external.[24] Let me not be thought to deny the necessity, or to decry the benefit, of such attention to what is particular and practical, as belongs to the useful or mechanical arts; life could not go on without them; we owe our daily welfare to them; their exercise is the duty of the many, and we owe to the many a debt of gratitude for fulfilling that duty. I only say that Knowledge, in proportion as it tends more and more to be particular, ceases to be Knowledge . . . When I speak of Knowledge, I mean something intellectual, something which grasps what it perceives through the senses; something which takes a view of things; which sees more than the senses convey; which reasons upon what it sees, and while it sees, which invests it with an idea . . . [25]

The last three sections of this *Discourse* are devoted to answering the objection that intellectual culture has failed to produce virtue. One passage gives the gist of the whole argument.

To open the mind, to correct it, to refine it, to enable it to know, and to digest, master, rule, and use its knowledge, to give it power over its own faculties, application, flexibility, method, critical exactness, sagacity, resource, address, eloquent expression, is an object as intelligible (for here we are inquiring, not what the object of a Liberal Education is worth, nor what use the Church makes of it, but what it is in itself), I say, an object as intelligible as the cultivation of virtue, while, at the same time, it is absolutely distinct from it. [26]

Having established the thesis that knowledge can be an end in itself, and that the kind of knowledge best fitted to be such an end is philosophic or comprehensive, Newman goes on to enquire more particularly into the nature of this knowledge, as shown by its effects on the mind. With this purpose he compares it, first with mere knowledge of isolated facts (*Sixth Discourse*), second with professional knowledge (*Seventh Discourse*) and third with religious knowledge (*Eighth* and *Ninth Discourse*).

We may pass fairly rapidly over the *Sixth Discourse*, as it consists chiefly of illustrations by examples of the nature of liberal knowledge, as already defined in the *Fifth Discourse*. It is noted by Newman that much of this *Discourse* is taken almost *verbatim* from his Oxford University Sermon of 1841, which we considered in our last lecture. The examples chosen are: the impressions made by foreign travel, the study of astronomy, zoology, the physical sciences, history, the religious beliefs of mankind. All these produce what even the common man will call enlargement of mind, which is thus analysed by Newman.

The enlargement consists, not merely in the passive reception into the mind of a number of ideas hitherto

unknown to it, but in the mind's energetic and simul-
taneous action upon and towards and among these new
ideas, which are rushing in upon it. It is the action of a
formative power, reducing to order and meaning the
matter of our acquirements; it is a making the objects
of our knowledge subjectively our own, or, to use a
familiar word, it is a digestion of what we receive into
the substance of our previous state of thought . . . And
therefore a truly great intellect . . . possesses the
knowledge, not only of things, but also of their mutual
and true relations; knowledge, not merely considered as
acquirement, but as philosophy.[27]

The rest of this *Discourse* we may omit. It deals with the
defects of universities at that date, which Newman points out
to be precisely due to lack of a liberal or philosophical
approach. It may be observed that the two defects he picks
out, the imparting of a mass of undigested facts, or the
attempt to cover too many subjects, are still the main
defects that a university, or indeed any teaching institution,
has to guard against.

I may remark that in section nine there is an obvious attack
by Newman on London University, the fairness of which
all may not admit. Newman contrasts a resident university
with tutorial superintendence with one which relies mainly
on examinations, greatly to the disadvantage of the latter.
As we shall see, he believed strongly in the value of both
residence and the tutorial system, and while granting that
these two provisions are probably necessary for the ideal
university, we must allow that without them, but with
lesser provisions for superintendence of studies, at least a

very good second best can be attained. Newman backs up
his advocacy of residence by an argument which is open
to criticism. He claims great educative value for the mere
companionship of students. "The conversation of all," he
says, "is a series of lectures to each." [28] The cynic will
smile at this, and even the serious critic may doubt whether
the interchange of ideas between immature minds, though
not without value, can be put in comparison at all with the
direction of mature and skilled teachers. However, the
point is quite a secondary one, and is not essential to
Newman's claim for the benefits of residence, much less to
his main theme of the liberalising effect of university life.

The *Seventh Discourse* is devoted by Newman to discussion of
the relation between liberal and professional knowledge.
He commences by recalling the memorable controversy with
which we are now familiar, between the *Edinburgh Review*
and the Oriel Fellows. He points out that the Fellows were
replying, not only to the *Edinburgh Review*, but also to Locke,
who in his treatise on Education, had extolled utility as the
main purpose of education, limiting utility to the value of
education for the future profession or trade of the pupil,
what we have called in a previous lecture " immediate
utility."

Newman's first reply, based on that of Copleston, is
perhaps a little subtle, yet nevertheless is cogent. He
returns to the idea that liberal knowledge is an end in itself,
since it constitutes a perfecting of the intellect, and argues
that, even if we accept the useful as the criterion of education, such a perfection, or health of the mind is surely a
useful thing, as much as is bodily health. [29]

Much more telling is his second argument, hinted at by

Copleston, but more fully elaborated by Davison, and succinctly stated by Newman himself :

Again, as health ought to precede labour of the body, and as a man in health can do what an unhealthy man cannot do, and as of this health the properties are strength, energy, agility, graceful carriage and action, manual dexterity, and endurance of fatigue, so in like manner general culture of mind is the best aid to professional and scientific study, and educated men can do what illiterate cannot; and the man who has learned to think and to reason and to compare and to discriminate and to analyse, who has refined his taste, and formed his judgment, and sharpened his mental vision, will not indeed at once be a lawyer, or a pleader, or an orator, or a statesman, or a physician, or a good landlord, or a man of business, or a soldier, or an engineer, or a chemist, or a geologist, or an antiquarian, but he will be placed in that state of intellect in which he can take up any one of the sciences or callings I have referred to, or any other for which he has a taste or special talent, with an ease, a grace, a versatility, and a success, to which another is a stranger. In this sense, then, . . . mental culture is emphatically *useful*." [30]

Newman fittingly closes this *Discourse* by an exposition of the value to society of a liberally trained mind. " If then," he says, " a practical end must be assigned to a University course, I say it is that of training good members of society." [31] Then follows a passage which illustrates remarkably Newman's power of enlarging on an idea without ever being diffuse, of displaying its many facets without needless repetition, of creating, by a masterly synthesis of detail, an inspiring view of the whole.

A University training is the great ordinary means to a great but ordinary end; it aims at raising the intellectual tone of society, at cultivating the public mind, at purifying the national taste, at supplying true principles to popular enthusiasm and fixed aims to popular aspiration, at giving enlargement and sobriety to the ideas of the age, at facilitating the exercise of popular power, and refining the intercourse of private life. It is the education which gives a man a clear conscious view of his own opinions and judgments, a truth in developing them, an eloquence in expressing them, and a force in urging them. It teaches him to see things as they are, to go right to the point, to disentangle a skein of thought, to detect what is sophistical, and to discard what is irrelevant. It prepares him to fill any post with credit, and to master any subject with facility. It shows him how to accommodate himself to others, how to throw himself into their frame of mind, how to bring before them his own, how to influence them, how to come to an understanding with them, how to bear with them. He is at home in any society, he has common ground with every class; he knows when to speak and when to be silent; he is able to converse, he is able to listen; he can ask a question pertinently, and gain a lesson seasonably, when he has nothing to impart himself; he is ever ready, yet never in the way; he is a pleasant companion, and a comrade you can depend upon; he knows when to be serious and when to trifle, and he has a sure tact which enables him to trifle with gracefulness and to be serious with effect. He has the repose of a mind which lives in itself, while it lives in the world, and which has resources for its happiness at home when it cannot go abroad. (We think here of all that is said today about "education for leisure"). He has a gift which serves him in public, and supports him in retirement, without which good fortune is but vulgar, and with which failure and disappointment have a charm. The art which tends to make a man all this, is in the object which it pursues as useful as the art of wealth or the art of health, though it is less susceptible of method, and less tangible, less certain, less complete in its result.[32]

5

THE STUDY OF MAN

I

WE HAVE NOW ESTABLISHED Newman's fundamental concept of liberal knowledge, and we may proceed to deal with some secondary considerations which will help to clarify that concept and answer possible difficulties.

There is first the question whether Newman considered that, for the obtaining of this wide grasp of knowledge which he calls " philosophy," it was necessary that a wide curriculum of subjects should be studied. It may be stated at once that he held that such a wide curriculum was not an absolute necessity, and indeed that even one subject may, and should be, thus philosophically, comprehensively, liberally studied.

We may consider, first of all, a passage in the original *Fifth Discourse*, which was afterwards omitted by Newman, but from the doctrine of which he did not depart.

A science is not mere knowledge, it is knowledge which has undergone a process of intellectual digestion. It is the grasp of many things brought together in one, and hence is its power; for properly speaking, it is

Science that is power, not Knowledge. Well then, this is how I would act towards the Sciences taken all together; we view them as one and give them an idea; what is this but an extension and perfection . . . of that very process by which science exists at all. Imagine a science of sciences, and you have the true notion of the scope of a university. We consider . . . that there is an order and precedence and harmony in the branches of knowledge one with another, as well as one by one.[1]

But, indeed, even without this explicit statement, it is obvious from all that Newman says about the nature of liberal knowledge that the approach of the mind even to a single fact, a single concept, is always of the same comprehensive nature. Its natural tendency is to seek relations between this fact and other facts, to view it as part of some set of correlated facts which correspond to related beings in the real order. Still more is this so when the mind approaches a single science, that is a systematic collection of facts dealing with one particular aspect of a certain being or beings.

Nevertheless it is equally clear that for the perfection of this liberal knowledge Newman does demand a certain breadth of curriculum. This is obvious from the passage just quoted, in which he speaks of the " science of sciences " as being the true scope of a university. This demand for breadth of curriculum is indicated even more clearly in a passage from the present *Fifth Discourse*. It may be noted that this passage did not occur in the *Discourses* as originally delivered, but was added in the second edition in 1859, possibly to make up for the omission of the passage in the original *Fifth Discourse*.

It is a great point then to enlarge the range of studies which a University professes, even for the sake of the students; and though they cannot pursue every subject which is open to them, they will be the gainers by living among those and under those who represent the whole circle. This I conceive to be the advantage of a seat of universal learning, considered as a place of education. An assemblage of learned men, zealous for their own sciences and rivals of each other, are brought, by familiar intercourse and for the sake of intellectual peace, to adjust together the claims and relations of their respective subjects of investigation. They learn to respect, to consult, to aid each other. Thus is created a pure and clear atmosphere of thought, which the student also breathes, though in his own case he only pursues a few sciences out of the multitude . . . He apprehends the great outlines of knowledge, the principles on which it rests, the scale of its parts, its lights and shades, its great points and its little, as he otherwise cannot apprehend them. Hence it is that his education is called Liberal. A habit of mind is formed which lasts through life, of which the attributes are freedom, equitableness, calmness, moderation, and wisdom; or what in a former Discourse I have ventured to call a philosophical habit.[2]

It must be granted that this noble idea of Newman is not always realised in modern universities. The sheer number of the faculties and of their members acts as a barrier to intercourse between them, intense specialisation tends to exclude interest in other subjects, and personal antagonisms sometimes exert a regrettably centrifugal force.

Nevertheless, it cannot be denied that in a university, if anywhere, there exists the opportunity for that sane and generous adjustment of views of which Newman speaks, and that breadth and tolerance are found to a high degree in those academic minds which are great enough to profit by it.

We may note here that Newman has given us in the passage quoted a fundamental principle for the drawing up of any curriculum. At each stage of development it is all-important to keep in view the primary aim of comprehensive or philosophical or liberal knowledge. We have thus to ask ourselves not only whether the student is capable of commencing the study of some additional subject, but also whether he can do so in the same comprehensive way in which he has mastered others, and without doing damage to his further comprehensive grasp of those which he already possesses.

There will, of course, be other considerations. There will be the question whether a new subject is best fitted for the general culture of the student in the particular age and circumstances in which he finds himself, apart from the question of its usefulness to him vocationally. But it is at least satisfactory to feel that we have got down to bedrock on one point. Whether it is a question of a syllabus for elementary, secondary or university students, we must satisfy ourselves about the ability of the student at each stage, not only to grasp, but to grasp with some degree of comprehensiveness, the new subject. He must be able, as we commonly say, to digest it and assimilate it to the already digested knowledge which he possesses. This is, in some ways, a principle of elementary simplicity, but it is well to realise that it is also one of fundamental importance.

2

In connection with this question of the wide curriculum, we may deal briefly with the question whether any argument in its favour may be drawn from the name " University." Does this name, as is sometimes assumed, indicate some degree of universality in studies, and can it therefore be held that, in the common view of men, a university is an institute which essentially covers a broad field of knowledge?[3]

It may be granted at once that the title originally had no such meaning. It is found in the Latin form *Universitas* in documents before the end of the twelfth century, meaning simply a corporation or association. It is only at the end of the twelfth and beginning of the thirteenth centuries that we find it applied to a corporation or association of masters or students or of both combined. From then on the use of it gradually became restricted to describe some such academic body.

The common mediaeval term for what we now call a university was not *Universitas*, but *Studium Generale*. There is considerable vagueness as to what exactly the various writers meant by *generale*, or in other words, what were the essential features of an institution to which the name *Studium Generale* was given. However, there is fairly unanimous consent that these features were: (1) the admission of students from all parts—and this was probably the primary meaning of *generale*; (2) the promotion of higher education by at least one of the higher faculties of Theology, Law or Medicine, in addition to Arts; and (3) a plurality of Masters. The three great institutions to which the title of *Studium Generale* was pre-eminently applied were the Universities of Paris, founded 1210-16, noted for Theology and Arts; Bologna, founded about 1158, noted for Law; and Salerno, founded about 1231, noted for Medicine.

In course of time it became the prerogative of either the Pope or Emperor to grant the Bull by which such *Studia Generalia* were officially recognised, and by virtue of which their Masters held the *ius ubique docendi*, that is the right to teach in any similarly constituted *Studium Generale*. Thus the idea spread that the *ius ubique docendi* was the essential mark of a university.

The *Universitas*, as has been said, was originally not the whole teaching institution, but merely a guild, either of students or masters, or, as in Bologna, of both combined. Those guilds gradually grew in power, but owing to the wider membership of the faculty of Arts, the guilds of this faculty came to assume the government of the whole institution. They at first had separate Rectors or Presidents, but in time a common Rector of the Faculty of Arts was appointed, who became the real head of the University. The Chancellor was an extra-academic official, who usually represented the local Bishop. And so it came about that the term *Universitas*, originally applied to a mere guild, became closely associated with the *Studium Generale*, and in the fifteenth century had become synonymous with it.

Towards the end of this century we find what is probably the first suggestion that a new meaning was being attributed to the word *Universitas*, and that it was being taken to emphasise the breadth of studies common to universities. In the original Bull of the foundation of the university of Tübingen, founded in 1477 by Count Eberhard of Würtemberg, we find the words *Publicas scolas atque universale divi-*

narum humanarumque scientiarum studium . . . fundare cura-vimus.[4] This meaning has certainly persevered, not merely in the popular mind, but among writers of weight, to the present day.

Newman is perfectly aware of this gradual change in the significance of the word " university." In his *Second Discourse* he refers to the original meaning of " a corporation," and also mentions the fact we have already alluded to, that the early *Studium Generale* was so called on account of its being open to students from all parts.[5] He is, as usual, most carefully accurate in his approach to the question. He contents himself with pointing out that many writers on the subject have accepted the later meaning, thus showing that they considered a breadth of studies to be an essential of the university, even if that were not the original connotation of the term.

Students who are particularly interested in this point may note that in the original first edition of the *Discourses* it is treated at great length in the Appendix, but the passages quoted at the opening of the *Second Discourse* give the gist of what is there stated.

Newman further points out that if we go back to the original term *Studium Generale* and accept the common view that this indicated a place of resort for students from all parts, this necessarily involves a certain degree of breadth of course to suit these various students. But finally he declares that he does not base his claim for breadth of course merely on the etymology of the word " university " but on the nature of the institution itself as a source of liberal knowledge.

It is interesting to note that some forty years later a very different thinker, T. H. Huxley, in his Rectorial Address to Aberdeen University, 1874, gives a definition of a university which combines both the original idea of the *Studium Generale* and the later meaning which Newman declares to be of general acceptation.

> I shall contrive my endeavours to . . . do what in me lies to bring this University to the ideal . . . of all Universities; which, as I conceive, should be places in which thought is free from all fetters; and in which all sources of learning and all aids to learning should be accessible to all comers. [6]

Before leaving this topic, we may remark once more how often Newman has been misrepresented by those who have read him hastily, and have not realised that, to get his true meaning, every word must be pondered. In Mr Bruce Truscot's *Redbrick University*, first published in 1943, the author takes Newman to task, firstly for holding that " every kind of subject must be studied at a university." [7] We have seen how utterly contrary to the truth is this accusation. Newman first of all excludes all non-liberal subjects, and secondly he makes it clear that not every subject need be included in the curriculum, or should be attempted by the students, but only that none should be excluded on principle. Mr Truscot goes on to express astonishment

> that Newman should not only have been so vague about the history of the word, but should have been so easily content to adopt the popular sense in which it is used and say that a University should teach universal knowledge.

All of which goes to show that Mr Truscot has not only misread the text of the *Discourses*, but is utterly ignorant of the existence of Newman's Appendix to the first edition. But this is not the worst. Mr Truscot, to substantiate his charge against Newman, quotes him as asking, " What ought the term University to mean, but a place where every science is taught which is liberal, and at the same time useful to mankind? " [8] When we turn to the passage cited,[9] we find that this is part of a lengthy quotation from the Edinburgh Reviewers whose views Newman was refuting.

We have already seen this passage in our first lecture, and it was certainly enough to make Newman turn in his grave to have the words of Sydney Smith quoted as his. Moreover, Mr Truscot has not even understood Smith. The whole tenor of the passage, as you may recall, is to extol utility as the criterion of excellence in university studies. The question of a wide curriculum is not being discussed at all, and the adjective " every " is merely used to confine such studies to those which are useful as well as liberal. Such wild misquotations should surely make us very cautious in accepting modern criticism of Newman, even from apparently learned sources.

3

It was laid down by Newman in his *Third Discourse* that, although all sciences worthy of the name are capable of a liberal or philosophic treatment, and therefore can form part of the curriculum of a university, yet

it is not every science which equally, nor any one which fully, enlightens the mind in the knowledge of things as they are, or brings home to it the external object on which it wishes to gaze. Thus they differ in importance; and according to their importance will be their influence, not only on the mass of knowledge to which they all converge and contribute, but on each other.[10]

There is, in fact, one particular group of studies in which Newman observes a peculiar quality which renders them specially suitable to be the instrument of liberal education. In his *Seventh Discourse* he quotes with approbation the teaching of Davison, who points out that in the acquisition of liberal knowledge there is a certain quality of the intellect which is commonly called judgment, and which enables the student, as he phrases it, " to seize the strong point "[11] in any subject.

Newman continues with the passage from Davison's review in the *Quarterly*, which we have already considered, in which the subjects which Davison holds to be peculiarly the province of the judgment are enumerated: religion, ethics, history, eloquence, poetry, theories of general speculation, the fine arts and works of wit. We recall that Davison found in this group of studies two common characteristics: firstly that they all have as their subject man's intellectual and volitional nature, and secondly that they demand wider and more elastic and more subtle use of the reasoning power than other studies.

It may be observed that here is another instance of that imperfection in the composition of Newman's *Discourses* to which allusion has already been made. This peculiar character of certain types of study, the group, theology, philosophy, literature, history, is a subject worthy of great emphasis, yet Newman indicates it here by a passing allusion in a quoted source. One would expect some further comment, some emphasis on Newman's own part. We do, indeed, find that emphasis later in the *Discourses*, but we have to search for it, and we find it in the *Ninth Discourse*. But even there that peculiar quality of those philosophic-literary-historical studies is not mentioned for its own sake, but to emphasise the control which the Church must exercise over such studies. The reference is to literature only, but if we refer to the end of the second paragraph of this *Discourse*, we find that literature is used in a wide sense to denote all those studies that do not fall under the heading of the physical sciences.

> Literature stands related to Man as Science stands to Nature; it is his history. Man is composed of body and soul; he thinks and he acts; he has appetites, passions, affections, motives, designs; he has within him the lifelong struggle of duty with inclination; he has an intellect fertile and capacious; he is formed for society, and society multiplies and diversifies in endless combinations his personal characteristics, moral and intellectual. All this constitutes his life; of all this Literature is the expression; so that Literature is to man in some sort what autobiography is to the individual; it is his Life and Remains.[12]

It may be noted here that this peculiar value of the philosophic-literary-historical group of subjects has not been universally recognised by writers and thinkers on education. Nevertheless, it has been recognised by many educationists of the first rank, and in more recent times has tended to be

more generally accepted, doubtless owing to the philosophical bankruptcy that is discernible in those whose
education has been almost completely limited to the
physical sciences. The question receives admirable treatment,
for instance in *A Defence of Classical Education*, published in
1917 by Sir Richard Livingstone.[13] One brief passage may
here be quoted, which echoes the argument of Davison and
Newman, and clothes it in somewhat more modern
phraseology.

> As science reveals to us the physical constitution of
> ourselves and the world round us, so the humanities
> reveal to us man. There is no science of man: anatomy
> and biology, while they have much to say about his body,
> throw little light upon his behaviour, nor explain why he
> makes a French Revolution or a European war, why he
> is a miser or a spendthrift, a Machiavelli or a Frederick
> the Great. Yet the " science " which everyone needs,
> and statesmen above all, is such a knowledge of man.
> Now there is, if not a science, yet a recorded account
> of man; we call it, according to its various aspects, by
> the various names of literature, history, philosophy. And
> this is the justification of the literary-philosophic-
> historical education which prevails in our schools and
> universities.

In the following pages the three main fruits of these
studies are expounded: the knowledge of man, the mental
elasticity acquired by the effort to enter into the mind of
man in all its varying types, and the elevation of the mind
acquired from contact with the imaginative beauty of great
literature. Sir Richard Livingstone does not formally

include theology among these specially cultural subjects but doubtless philosophy is intended to include it. Davison, we recall, heads the list of such subjects with "religion (in its evidences and interpretations)."

It may be noted that the claims of these subjects have perhaps been damaged by the mistaken notion that their supporters look on them as the only ones capable of giving a truly liberal culture to the mind. It may even be granted that some of these supporters have been led into making such a claim as a reaction to the exaggerated importance attributed to scientific training. As we shall see shortly, Newman himself clearly admitted the liberal character of the physical sciences when treated properly. Many persons, indeed, when they talk of "general education," are thinking of a literary education only. We may lay it down briefly here that the correct meaning of "general education" is an education which fits the student to be a better man, both in himself and with reference to society, prescinding from, though not excluding, his ability to perform specific tasks in life. It is clear that such "general education" cannot be restricted to literary education, but it is also clear, from all that has been said, that literary education plays a very special part in such "general" training, and that its omission will be a fatal defect.

4

You will recall that in our third lecture I drew your attention to a passage in the Seventh Letter on Peel's speech at Tamworth, in which Newman expressly acknowledges that scientific pursuits are "worthy of a place in a liberal education," and also to the passage in his Oxford University Sermon on Wisdom as compared with Faith and Bigotry, in which he included physical sciences among the subjects capable of producing that "enlargement of mind" or "philosophical knowledge" which we have seen to be identical with liberal knowledge. These two passages would be enough to put us on our guard against any hasty, off-hand judgment that Newman restricted the term liberal studies to mean literary studies only. But indeed any such judgment would indicate a most superficial knowledge of his *Discourses*. It is true that in them he constantly contrasts liberal with professional education, and it happens that most of what are commonly called professions, namely callings which adapt intellectual knowledge to the immediate welfare of mankind, are scientific ones, medicine, engineering, architecture and the innumerable practical applications of chemistry, physics, biology and their sub-divisions. It is clear, however, that Newman makes a distinction between the study of these sciences in themselves and their study with a view to immediate utility, and that to the former he does not hesitate to attribute the characteristic of liberality. Thus, in his *Third Discourse*, when elaborating the concept of liberal knowledge as a grasp of objective facts and their relation to one another, he makes mention of the various sciences which divide up these facts and relations so as to make them comprehensible to the human mind, and shows how all of them—he mentions, as examples, Optics, Astronomy, Geology, Comparative Anatomy, Chemistry, Dynamics—"arrange and classify facts" . . . "reduce separate phenomena under a common law" . . . "trace effects to a cause," and thus " transfer our knowledge from the custody of memory to the surer and more abiding protection of philosophy " [14]—the term " philosophy " here bearing that special sense given to it by Newman which we have already explained.

Again, we find repeated almost *verbatim* in the *Sixth Discourse* that passage from the Oxford University sermon describing the nature of enlargement of mind. We have already mentioned that Newman includes the physical sciences as being among the subjects capable of producing it. We may cite here one short passage which surely leaves Newman's critics with very little excuse for misunderstanding him. Having spoken of Astronomy and Zoology, he proceeds thus:

> Hence Physical Science generally, in all its departments, as bringing before us the exuberant riches and resources, yet the orderly course of the Universe, elevates and excites the student, and at first, I may say, almost takes away his breath, while in time it exercises a tranquilizing influence upon him.[15]

And in the *Ninth Discourse* you will recall that Newman's aim is to establish the proper relations that should exist between theology and secular knowledge. He makes of secular knowledge two great divisions: knowledge of the physical and social worlds. These, says Newman, " when respectively subjected to Human Reason, form two books: the book of Nature is called Science, the book of man is called Literature." It is clear from the whole tenor of the *Discourse* that Newman is envisaging Science not merely as applied, but as purely intellectual knowledge. However, he also explicitly classes Science and Literature together. " Literature and Science," he says " thus considered (namely as ' the book of nature ' and ' the book of man ') nearly constitute the subject-matter of Liberal Education,"[16] " nearly," because both of them need the saving guidance of theology.

It is only when the pursuit of scientific knowledge is narrowed down to subserve immediate utilitarian ends that Newman would deny to it the character of liberality. In the *Fifth Discourse*, in the well-known passage where he is explaining in what sense knowledge should be its own end, he points out that the Baconian philosophy " by using its physical sciences in the service of man, does thereby transfer them from the order of Liberal Pursuits to, I do not say the inferior, but the distinct class of the Useful."[17] And again, in the *Seventh Discourse* he explicitly admits that scientific pursuits—he instances Medicine and Geology —may take their place with other subjects in the university curriculum, but adds this warning:

I do but say that there will be this distinction as regards a Professor of Law, or of Medicine, or of Geology, or of Political Economy, in a University and out of it, that out of a University he is in danger of being absorbed and narrowed by his pursuit, and of giving Lectures which are the Lectures of nothing more than a lawyer, physician, geologist, or political economist; whereas in a University he will just know where he and his science stand, he has come to it, as it were, from a height, he has taken a survey of all knowledge, he is kept from extravagance by the very rivalry of other studies, he has gained from them a special illumination and largeness of mind and freedom and self-possession, and he treats his own in consequence with a philosophy and a resource, which belongs not to the study itself, but to his liberal education.[18]

Indeed, it is very strange that any careful reader of the *Discourses* should go away with the impression that Newman, in defending liberal education, was advocating a purely literary education. As we have seen, there are only two passages, one of them a quotation from another writer, in which he emphasises the special value of literary studies, whilst the passages in which he deals with scientific pursuits and their proper place in a university, are far more numerous. Yet misunderstanding of Newman on this issue still persists. The late Charles Frederick Harrold, Professor of English in Ohio State University, was a great admirer of Newman, and his *John Henry Newman*, published in 1945, is a careful and scholarly work. Yet in the Introduction to the latest edition of the *Idea of a University* [19] Professor Harrold writes as follows:

In many ways the *Idea of a University* bears the marks of that clerical and humanistic Oxford which, more or less, came to an end with the publication of the Royal Commission's Report (1852), a report which proposed the liberalising and secularizing of Oxford and Cambridge. Newman's book appeared at an opportune time for him to vindicate, not only for his Irish audience but also for the world at large, the theological and humanistic culture which the Oxford of Newman and Pusey and Copleston had symbolized for so many years.

It is true that Copleston and Davison, as we have seen, were largely concerned with vindicating the worth of the Greek and Latin classics, and in this, though their defence was sound enough, they unduly narrowed the field of liberal knowledge. The Edinburgh Reviewers, on the other hand, wished the field of liberal education to be enlarged so as to include the physical sciences. But they wrongly narrowed the field of these sciences to their merely practical applications. Newman preserves that very balance and comprehensiveness which he claims to be characteristic of liberal knowledge. He goes beyond Copleston and Davison in extending the field of liberal knowledge to all sciences; but, on the other hand, he points out that the aspect of utility, which for the Edinburgh school was the great advantage of the physical sciences, is precisely that which, if emphasised, excludes them from the field of liberal knowledge.

5

At this stage a point may be cleared up which perhaps may have occurred to some of my hearers. The distinction drawn by Newman between liberal and professional, or, utilitarian study of a subject, is, of course, not absolutely water-tight in practice. A course, for instance, in pure chemistry, will aim at laying down general principles and introducing the student to broad classifications. But, obviously, much of its teaching may be of practical use to him in his after career in a brewery or a soap manufactory. On the other hand, the most narrowly utilitarian course, destined to fit him for some specific job in a commercial chemical works, will necessarily include many applications of broad principles and general classifications, and will often draw attention to connections of his subject with others. This point is even clearer when we consider a literary subject such as history. A young teacher may follow a history course in a Training College with an almost purely professional purpose. He may confine himself to a course which will be suitable for teaching to children of a certain age. But it is obvious that even such a course will have a certain liberalising effect on his mind. It will be impossible for him not to detect certain broad currents, certain connections of this section of history with others. And, on the contrary, though a university course on the same period will be broader, deeper and more philosophical, it cannot fail to be useful to him in the classroom. In practice, then, we may say that the liberal, or the utilitarian purpose will predominate in one or other course, but that neither will be absolutely excluded.

And, while we are on this subject, we may also point out that even the distinction between manual and intellectual pursuits is not absolutely water-tight in practice. It is obvious that even the most mechanical trades, those of carpenter, mason, bricklayer, involve a considerable amount of intellectual activity—all the deliberate actions of man do —and the same applies in a higher degree to the more skilled trades, such as those of electrician, fitter or weaver. And, on the other hand, there are certain scientific pursuits whose character is highly intellectual, but which depend for their success on a certain degree of manual dexterity. No man can be a successful chemist or physicist who is unskilled in the handling of his apparatus. The surgeon's application of his science is done by actions which are very similar to those of a highly skilled carpenter or tailor, but they presume a wide knowledge of anatomy, physiology, chemistry and biology. Newman went so far as to say that " mercantile occupations are not liberal at all," [20] and this perhaps may be granted of the fundamental processes of handing goods out and taking the money in. But in the complexity of modern commerce, especially on a large scale, there is much knowledge required of economics and sociology which, if it does not elevate commerce to the level of a liberal subject, at least gives it a liberal tinge. Commerce is one of those subjects concerning whose admission to the university curriculum controversy is possible, and you can see that the whole point at issue is whether the broader subjects which generally form part of the course for a degree in commerce, economics, sociology, politics, geography, predominate over the more mechanical studies such as book-keeping. The case against a commercial degree is stronger in those universities, as in the United States, which conduct separate business schools, where shorthand, typing, filing systems, etc., constitute a large portion of the course.

The main point to be remembered is that, whether it is a case of distinguishing between the liberal and professional or utilitarian study of an intellectual subject, or between an intellectual and non-intellectual, or manual subject, we can rarely, if ever, draw a hard and fast line, but must endeavour to decide what, in practice, is the predominant characteristic of the study or subject under discussion.

6

One last topic may now be dealt with, namely the teaching of Newman regarding the place of the classics in liberal education, " classics " being here understood in the strict sense of the study of the Greek and Latin languages. It may be noted that this topic is barely touched on in the *Discourses*. In the *Seventh Discourse* Newman refers to the Edinburgh attack on the classics, but observes that he is not at present " concerned with the specific question of classical education," [21] and passes on to the more fundamental consideration of whether liberal education can be truly considered useful.

For a fuller treatment of the subject we must turn to Newman's Lecture on *Christianity and Letters*, delivered in the School of Philosophy and Letters in the Catholic University of Ireland on 9 November 1854. This is the lecture which Quiller-Couch in his Seventh Lecture On the Art of Reading commends so enthusiastically to his students. It may be remarked, however, that it should not be regarded as a complete defence of classical studies. It confines itself to one great consideration, namely the unique part played by these languages in forming the common culture of Europe. It traces, in broad and sweeping lines, how the great thoughts and modes of thought of the ancient Greeks were perfected by them and handed on to the Romans, who adopted them, not in slavish imitation, but because of their intrinsic excellence. Into this stream of classical culture there flowed from Palestine a new and higher stream of knowledge, the Christian revelation. In time the civilisation of Greece, Rome and Palestine passed away, but Christian Europe emerged, preserving the precious heritage of sacred and profane knowledge inherited from all three. In the Christian era the study of classical literature emerged in the form of the traditional Seven Liberal Arts: Grammar, Rhetoric, Logic, and the fourfold division of Mathematics, Geometry, Arithmetic, Astronomy and Music. Newman points out how these liberal studies, based on classical reading, long held the field as the foundation of all culture. The rich flowering of Scholastic theology and philosophy in the Middle Ages, and the growth of the great faculties of Law and Medicine in the mediaeval universities did not deprive the Liberal Arts of their fundamental position, and Newman argues with much cogency that the great modern/output of scientific knowledge will not " detrude classical literature and the studies connected with it from the place they have held in all ages in education." [22]

It must be granted that this argument of Newman needs some qualification in our day. It will be noted that what he is specifically defending is the study of the Liberal Arts, that philosophic-literary-historical group of subjects to which we have so often alluded. He assumes, however, and rightly, that originally this group of studies was given to mankind with great depth and ability by the Greek and Latin writers, and has been most fruitfully studied in the works of those writers by educated Europeans throughout the history of the Christian world. He does not enter into any discussion of the question how far that study should continue to be drawn from these ancient languages, and to what extent it can be supplied by the modern languages and literatures to which they have given birth. In his day such discussion was of less import than today, since the study of the classics was still taken for granted as an essential of the curriculum of all secondary schools. We today find that discussion much more urgent, since our schools are thronged with young people who are either incapable of gaining sufficient mastery over the classics to derive true cultural fruit from them, or for whom the exigencies of utility demand so many other subjects as to render a study of the classics a physical impossibility. It may be granted, too, that the teaching of the vernacular and of foreign languages and of history is now more systematic and thorough than in Newman's day, and hence provides a better alternative to the classics. But Newman's main contention remains as true today as it was a century ago. The study of the classics gives a unique understanding of the formation of European culture, and provides the competent student, as no other studies can, with a store of those beliefs and ideals which, ennobled and supernaturalised by Christianity, went to make up that culture.

In his *Understanding Europe*, Mr Christopher Dawson, who of all English Catholic writers deserves to be listened to on this subject, issues a very pertinent warning. He points out that up to modern times European culture was based on the study of the two classical languages, but that this did not mean that that culture consisted merely in the knowledge of these two languages. They were, however, the common vehicles of that culture, but it was the culture, not the vehicle that was the essential thing.[23]

In the past the traditional system of classical education provided a common intellectual background and a common scale of values which transcended national

and political frontiers and formed the European or
Western republic of letters of which every scholar was
a citizen . . . But we must be careful to distinguish
between this particular form of higher education and
higher education in general, and not to reduce the central
inescapable problem to the old controversy between
conservative classicism and radical modernism. It is quite
possible that the traditional form of classical education has
become completely antiquated and can no longer provide
the unifying element which our civilisation requires.[24]

In the later chapters of his book Mr Dawson, with great
force, develops the main theme of his work, which is that
this unifying element consists in a return to a broad and
complete view of European civilisation as a common
Christian civilisation. I am certain, however, that he would
agree with the proposition we have enunciated, that we
must still preserve the actual study of the classics as instruments for the obtaining of that broad and complete view,
even though we must face the fact that only an élite can be
trained to use them. But Mr Dawson is perfectly correct in
his assumption that they are only instruments, and that the
exigencies of modern conditions demand that all other
possible instruments must be used to attain the end which
he shows to be of such urgent necessity,

> to study Western Christian culture from the Christian
> point of view—to see it as a new way of life which was
> brought into Europe nearly nineteen hundred years ago,
> when St. Paul set sail from Troy to Macedonia, and
> gradually expanded until it became accepted as the
> universal standard of the European way of life.[25]

6

SACRED AND SECULAR KNOWLEDGE

I

IT WILL BE RECALLED that in our fourth lecture, we noted that Newman's *Discourses* were a skilful blend of two themes: the necessity for the inclusion of theology in the university curriculum and the claim that liberal knowledge is the primary end of university education. We noted, further, that these two themes were based on one common consideration, the nature of human knowledge. We stated that we would take the second theme first, but found that it was necessary, for its understanding, to give a preliminary outline of the first. Our purpose in this lecture is to give a more complete account of Newman's views as to the place held by religion in education. He is, of course, dealing specifically with university education, but the principles he lays down are applicable, *mutatis mutandis*, to education at every stage.

For the sake of clarity I will point out to you that these views are found mainly in the *Second*, *Third* and *Fourth* *Discourses* and in the *Eighth* and *Ninth*. The *Second*, *Third*, and *Fourth*, which we have considered in outline, deal with the necessity for including theology in the curriculum. Then follow the *Fifth*, *Sixth* and *Seventh*, which deal with the nature of liberal knowledge and its claim to be the primary end of university education. The *Eighth* and *Ninth*, which as yet we have not considered, deal with the relations between Knowledge and Religious Duty and between the Church and Knowledge respectively. They presume all that we have learned in the preceding *Discourses*, both about religious knowledge and about liberal knowledge. They do not add to our information about either in themselves, but expound the relations that exist, or should exist between them.

Now, reverting to the *Second*, *Third*, and *Fourth Discourses*, we may first briefly recall what they tell us about theology. It must be included in a university curriculum, firstly because it is a true science, secondly because its omission means that our knowledge of truth is mutilated, and thirdly because if it is omitted, some other science will inevitably intrude itself, to explain the range of facts with which theology or religious knowledge properly deals.

As thus enunciated, Newman's claim is a very modest one, and could be made for any other science. As he says at the conclusion of the *Second Discourse*:

> Religious doctrine is knowledge, in as full a sense as Newton's doctrine is knowledge. University Teaching without Theology is simply unphilosophical. Theology has at least as good a right to claim a place there as Astronomy.[1]

But Newman goes much further than this. In the *Second* and *Third Discourses* he has many magnificent passages expounding the nature of theology, and showing that it is not only a true science, but the greatest of all sciences, both in itself and in its bearings on all other sciences. The knowledge of God, he points out in the *Second Discourse*, comes to us through every channel of human knowledge.

> Is not the being of God reported to us by testimony, handed down by history, inferred by an inductive process, brought home to us by metaphysical necessity, urged on us by the suggestions of our conscience? [2]

And, if we deny the validity of any of these sources, we find ourselves forced to exclude other sciences of common reception.

> For instance are we to limit our idea of University Knowledge by the evidence of our senses? Then we exclude ethics; by intuition? we exclude history; by testimony? we exclude metaphysics; by abstract reasoning? We exclude physics. [3]

Furthermore, when we have come to the knowledge of God, we find that we possess already a science of unique comprehensiveness.

> The word " God " is a Theology in itself, indivisibly one, inexhaustibly various, from the vastness and simplicity of its meaning. Admit a God, and you introduce among the subjects of your knowledge a fact encompassing, closing in upon, absorbing, every other fact conceivable. How can we investigate any part of any order of Knowledge, and stop short of that which enters into every order? All true principles run over with it, all phenomena converge to it; it is truly the First and Last. In word, indeed, and in idea, it is easy enough to

divide Knowledge into human and divine, secular and religious, and to lay down that we will address ourselves to the one without interfering with the other; but it is impossible in fact.[4]

Then there follows a passage to which I would particularly draw your attention, as it supplies a complete refutation of the insinuation so often made, and even still heard, that Newman betrayed sympathy with the non-intellectual concept of faith propounded by the Modernist school. He addresses himself to the problem of how it could be possible that men who recognise the existence of God could deny to the knowledge of him the title of true science, and he points out that in the original Lutheran doctrine and in certain schools of Protestant thought commonly called Evangelical, there is found the assumption " that Religion consists, not in knowledge, but in feeling or sentiment."

The old Catholic notion which still lingers in the Established Church, was that Faith is an intellectual act, its object truth, and its result knowledge. Thus if you look into the Anglican Prayer Book, you will find definite *credenda*, as well as definite *agenda*; but in proportion as the Lutheran leaven spread, it became fashionable to say that Faith was, not an acceptance of revealed doctrines, not an act of the intellect, but a feeling, an emotion, an affection, an appetency; and, as this view of Faith obtained, so was the connexion of Faith with Truth and Knowledge more and more either forgotten or denied. Men learned to believe and to take it for granted that Religion was nothing beyond a *supply* of the wants of human nature, not an external fact and a work of

God . . . Thus Religion was useful, venerable, beautiful, the sanction of order, the stay of government, the curb of self-will and indulgence, which the laws cannot reach.

It was " based on custom, on prejudice, on law, on education on habit, on loyalty, on feudalism, on enlightened experience, on many, many things, but not on reason." [5] Such a concept of religion, Newman points out, has led in modern times to a conclusion which its originators never dreamed of, and would heartily denounce.

It has been taken up by that large and influential body which goes by the name of Liberal or Latitudinarian; and . . . where it prevails, it is as unreasonable, of course, to demand for Religion a chair in the University, as to demand one for fine feeling, sense of honour, patriotism, gratitude, maternal affection or good companionship, proposals which would be simply unmeaning. [6]

As against this sentimental concept of theology, Newman sets the concept of God revealed to us even by purely natural reason, and again emphasises the fact that this concept is not only a science, but the greatest of all sciences, and one which is inextricably connected with all other sciences. God, says Newman,

is One who is sovereign over, operative amidst, independent of the appointments He has made; One in whose hands are all things, who has a purpose in every event, and a standard for every deed, and thus has relations of His own towards the subject-matter of each particular science which the book of knowledge unfolds; who has, with an adorable, never-ceasing energy, implicated Himself in all the history of creation, the constitution of nature, the course of the world, the origin of society, the fortunes of nations, the action of the human mind; and who thereby necessarily becomes the subject-matter of a science, far wider and more noble than any of those which are included in the circle of secular Education.[7]

This permeation, as it were, of every other subject by theology naturally receives ever greater stress in the *Third Discourse*, the theme of which, as you recall, is that truth is one great system, and that if any section of it is removed, the whole becomes falsified. Newman applies this principle to the study of theology, and points out that the argument, which would be valid for any subject, is peculiarly cogent for it. I can only refer you to that magnificent passage in which he enlarges, far more fully than in the *Second Discourse*, on the nature of theology.[8] The passage is too long for quotation, but it is one with which every student of Newman should be familiar. It is a remarkable instance of that power which he possessed, similar to that of a great musician who builds up a symphony on a single theme, of enlarging, illustrating, developing a central idea, returning to it again and again from every angle, yet always avoiding mere iteration, always revealing some new facet, always making some distinction that is required for clarity, or drawing some conclusion that better illustrates the nature of its premise.

One brief passage must serve to give an idea of the whole. Newman has dwelt on the nature of God, designer and creator of the universe, both inanimate and animate. He then passes to God's intellectual creation.

Man with his motives and works, his languages, his propagation, his diffusion, is from Him. Agriculture, medicine and the arts of life, are His gifts. Society, laws, government, He is their sanction. The pageant of earthly royalty has the semblance and the benediction of the Eternal King. Peace and civilization, commerce and adventure, wars when just, conquest when humane and necessary, have His co-operation and His blessing upon them. The course of events, the revolution of empires, the rise and fall of states, the periods and eras, the progresses and retrogressions of the world's history, not indeed the incidental sin, over-abundant as it is, but the great outlines and the results of human affairs, are from His disposition . . . His are the dictates of the moral sense, and the retributive reproaches of conscience. To Him must be ascribed the rich endowments of the intellect, the irradiation of genius, the imagination of the poet, the sagacity of the politician, the wisdom (as Scripture calls it) which now rears and decorates the Temple, now manifests itself in proverb or in parable. The old saws of nations, the majestic precepts of philosophy, the luminous maxims of law, the oracles of individual wisdom, the traditionary rules of truth, justice, and religion, even though imbedded in the corruption, or alloyed with the pride, of the world, betoken His original agency, and His long-suffering presence.[9]

2

Having thus established by many examples, of which the passage just cited contains only a portion, the fact that theology has innumerable bearings on every form of creation, it is an easy matter for Newman to draw the conclusion which is the theme of this whole *Discourse*, that theology cannot be omitted from the circle of human sciences without mutilating that circle and each of its component parts. We are, however, here interested not so much in this conclusion, which we have already considered, as in the fact, not necessary for the bare conclusion, but strengthening it immeasurably, that the relations of theology to other sciences are universal and are on the highest intellectual plane.

If this be a sketch, accurate in substance and as far as it goes, of the doctrines proper to Theology, and especially of the doctrine of a particular Providence, which is the portion of it most on a level with human sciences, I cannot understand at all how, supposing it to be true, it can fail, considered as knowledge, to exert a powerful influence on philosophy, literature, and every intellectual creation or discovery whatever. I cannot understand how it is possible, as the phrase goes, to blink the question of its truth or falsehood.

(I would draw your attention here in parenthesis to a feature of Newman's style exemplified in the last sentence, the skilful use of common, popular, almost slang phrases, to drive home a point.)

It meets us with a profession and a proffer of the highest truths of which the human mind is capable; it embraces a range of subjects the most diversified and distant from each other. What science will not find one part or other of its province traversed by its path? What results of philosophic speculation are unquestionable, if they have been gained without inquiry as to what Theology had to say to them? Does it cast no light on history? has it no influence upon the principles of ethics? is it without any sort of bearing on physics, metaphysics and political science? Can we drop it out of the circle of knowledge, without allowing, either that that circle is thereby mutilated, or on the other hand that Theology is really no science? [10]

Newman then adds two considerations, on which we need not delay, but which further strengthen the conclusion he has drawn. The first is that theology is not only a science, but a science " precise and consistent in its intellectual structure." [11] The second is that it has been accepted as a science from time immemorial and by the greatest intellects, whether pagan or Christian. [12] He then sums up the whole gist of his *Discourse*, and in this summing up we will again note the point with which we are here concerned, that theology holds not only a place, but the supreme place, among the sciences.

I say then if the various branches of knowledge, which are the matter of teaching in a University, so hang together, that none can be neglected without prejudice to the perfection of the rest, and if Theology be a branch of knowledge, of wide reception, of philosophical structure, of unutterable importance, and of supreme influence, to what conclusion are we brought from these two premises but this? that to withdraw Theology from the public schools is to impair the completeness and to invalidate the trustworthiness of all that is actually taught in them. [13]

We recall that Newman in these *Discourses* professedly confined himself to arguments from natural reason. At the close of this *Discourse*, he reminds his hearers of this fact, and remarks in passing that the argument he has propounded should be of greater influence with Catholics, whose knowledge of God from revelation goes far beyond even the vast array of truths that reason alone can deduce from the idea of God.

I would ask you to note that we have now almost completed the main outline of Newman's teaching in his *Discourses*, as now printed, on the place of theology in the curriculum. It is found almost entirely in the *Second* and *Third Discourses*. However, at the beginning of the *Fourth Discourse* there is an important addendum. One often hears the argument against an all-Catholic school, whether at the University level or below it, put in some such words: " I am all in favour of Catholics learning their religion, and of course the only satisfactory teacher of the Catholic religion must be a Catholic. But I cannot for the life of me see how you can have Catholic mathematics, or Catholic chemistry and physics, much less Catholic engineering, and hence the religious convictions of the teachers of these subjects are a matter of indifference. " It will be noted that this is an obvious instance of the well-known technique of attacking the most vulnerable part of an argument, and implying that the rest of the argument is equally vulnerable. Newman points out the obvious fact that the relations of theology to secular subjects vary in extent and closeness.

I do not say that every science will be equally affected by the omission (of theology); pure mathematics will not suffer at all; chemistry will suffer less than politics, politics than history, ethics or metaphysics.[14]

We may remark in passing that Newman would hardly make such a complete concession concerning mathematics today when the boundaries between that subject and philosophy are so disputed. But his main contention is sound, and gives us the answer to the objection made. There is a further point, but we will postpone consideration of it until later, since Newman dealt with it more fully elsewhere, namely that the internal principles of the various branches of knowledge are not in themselves theological, and may be studied fully without reference to theology. It is only when these subjects are regarded as set in their place in the universe that theological relations arise. In that sense there is most surely a Catholic history, Catholic economics, Catholic physics and chemistry. And it may be remarked that the extreme complication and interdependence of modern social life has obtruded theological considerations into subjects that once were regarded as purely secular, so that we find engineers, architects and lecturers in commerce being forced, if not into the field of theology, at least into those of sociology and ethics where they are next door to it.

The main body of the *Fourth Discourse* may be passed over rapidly. It contains, as we have seen, a very illuminating consideration, but one that can be put very briefly, and that, moreover, applies to every subject, not to theology alone. If any subject in the whole circle of knowledge is neglected, there is a tendency for some other subject to intrude, owing to the natural tendency of the human mind to find an explanation for all observed phenomena. You have there

the gist of the whole *Discourse*, and the rest of it consists
in the skilful working out of examples, the demonstration
of how the fine arts may tend to guide religion rather than
to subserve it, and how political economists may come to
think that their science can conduce to virtue.

The *Fifth*, *Sixth* and *Seventh Discourses*, as we have seen,
deal almost exclusively with the nature of liberal knowledge.
There is, however, one passage in the *Fifth Discourse* which
touches on the subject of theology, and which is of importance, since it has a bearing on a topic which will
concern us later. Newman's concept of the relation between
College and University. We recall that Newman had defined
liberal knowledge as that whose aim is the cultivation of the
mind, and which, in that sense, is its own end. He points
out that such liberal knowledge may be, and in fact always
is diverted to other ends; but in proportion as it is thus
directed, it becomes less liberal. Among other examples
he takes theology.

If, for instance Theology, instead of being cultivated
as a contemplation, be limited to the purposes of the
pulpit or be represented by the catechism, it loses
—not its usefulness, not its divine character, not its
meritoriousness (rather it gains a claim upon these titles
by such charitable condescension)—but it does lose the
particular attribute which I am illustrating; just as a face
worn by tears and fasting loses its beauty, or a labourer's
hand loses its delicateness;—for Theology thus exercised
is not simple knowledge, but rather is an art or a business
making use of Theology.[15]

Now, I would ask you to observe most closely Newman's exact contention in these words, for they led later to criticism. Newman does not for a moment belittle that practical application of theology to our lives that constitutes the good life, the Christian life. He does not for a moment state that the cultivation of the whole, perfect man can take place without this practical application of theology. He does not state that such practical application of theology is not an essential part of the life of a university student. He merely states that, if it be granted that the cultivation of the mind or liberal knowledge be the primary object of a university, then the theology that must find a place in its curriculum must be a speculative science. Such a science will, of course, include a study of the principles of ethics and Christian morality, but, as such, it will not go further, it will not aim at securing the application of such principles. There we can leave the matter for the moment.

As for the *Eighth* and *Ninth Discourses*, although they professedly treat of the relations between secular knowledge and religion, their themes are secondary. They presume that the nature and place of the two great divisions of knowledge have already been defined. Before dealing briefly with them, I would draw your attention to the fact that they are, in another respect also, a form of addendum to the main work. They do not conform to Newman's original intention that his *Discourses* should be based on natural reason alone, but discuss the relations between liberal knowledge and the Catholic Faith and Church. The reasons for this change we shall see shortly, when we are considering the original *Fifth Discourse*, which was omitted by Newman from the second and succeeding editions of his work.

Briefly here is the gist of these two *Discourses*. The *Eighth* points out that liberal education, though not in itself religious, may subserve religion by preparing the human mind for it, firstly by disentangling it from the thraldom of sense, and secondly by producing in it a refinement and fastidiousness that is inimical to certain forms of vice. Liberal education can even produce a certain religion of philosophy, which, however, unless elevated by Christianity, is only a subtle form of pride. It is, perhaps, hardly necessary to point out to the present audience, that Newman's famous description of a gentleman, which occurs towards the end of this *Discourse*, is given only as an example of this religion of philosophy. It is the description of a pagan gentleman, but is frequently taken to be more. I remember having seen it quoted without comment in a Catholic school magazine as an ideal for youth, but it must be remembered that Newman pointed out that such an ideal may serve the course of religion or do it infinite harm. It may produce a Basil the Great or a Julian the Apostate, a St Francis de Sales or a Gibbon.

The central theme of Newman's *Ninth* and last *Discourse* is that it is not sufficient for the constitution of a Catholic university that theology should be taught in it. The Church must also exercise some direct and active jurisdiction over it, so that the proper position of theology may be safeguarded.

It is no sufficient security for the Catholicity of a University even that the whole of Catholic Theology should be professed in it, unless the Church breathes her own unearthly spirit into it, and fashions and moulds its organization, and watches over its teaching; and knits together its pupils, and superintends its action.[16]

I would draw your attention in passing to the fact that this does not by any means require that the government of a Catholic University should be purely or even predominantly clerical. Newman correctly expresses the function of the Church in wide terms, without defining, how in practice her jurisdiction is to be exercised, since this will vary in varying circumstances. The Canon Law, for instance, prescribes that a Catholic University or Faculty in the strict sense must be established only by the authority of the Holy See (Can. 1376), but it also recognises (Can. 1379 Sec. 2) that there may be universities not thus canonically erected, but which are sufficiently imbued with the Catholic spirit to receive the approbation of the Church. Canon 1381 gives to the local ordinary, the bishop of the diocese, the right to see that the teaching in all schools in his diocese conforms to Catholic principles, but leaves to him the determination of how this right shall be exercised.

To prove the necessity for this authority of the Church, Newman considers how the two great divisions of secular knowledge, science and literature, if left to themselves, have a tendency to develop hostility to religion, science by excluding it, literature by corrupting it. There can be, Newman maintains, no real collision between science and theology, since both come from the same divine Author, whose works cannot contradict one another, but historically there has been a constant jealousy between them, for which Newman gives three main causes. Firstly, the absorption of scientists in the laws of nature has led to a reluctance to admit higher laws, a reluctance which has been intensified by the occasional interference of religious criticism in purely scientific matters. Again, the methods of the two forms of knowledge differ. Science depends mainly on induction from phenomena, theology on deduction from first principles. Finally, revealed religion, which constitutes the major part of the Catholic faith, has reference to circumstances that arose after the creation of the universe, and therefore deals with a different order of religious truth from that conveyed to man by the mere contemplation of created things. The interposition of the Church is therefore constantly needed in the schools, not to watch over and protect science, but to protect theology from the undue pretensions of science.[17]

With regard to literature the function of the Church is somewhat different. The danger here is not that of intrusion on theology. It arises from the fact that literature, as Newman briefly puts it, " stands related to man as science stands to nature, it is his history." Or in other words, it " is to man in some sort what autobiography is to the individual; it is his Life and Remains."[18] And though it may at times have a deeply religious tinge, yet it is in the main the history of natural man, often of sinful man. In the seventh and eighth sections of this *Discourse* Newman gives a rich and thoughtful development of this idea which is one of the most memorable passages in the whole book. What is to be the attitude of the Church towards this chronicle of man and his failings? If she merely proscribes its study, what preparation has the student received for meeting in contemporary writings and in real life the same problems, the same temptations, the same evils that are found in its pages? Her function, rather, though Newman admits that in practice it is often a difficult and delicate one, is to guide and expound.

> The Church's true policy is not to aim at the exclusion of Literature from Secular Schools, but at her own admission into them. Let her do for Literature in one way what she does for Science in another; each has its imperfections, and she has her remedy for each. She fears no knowledge, but she purifies all; she represses no element of our nature, but cultivates the whole . . . Her principle is one and the same throughout: not to prohibit truth of any kind, but to see that no doctrines pass under the name of Truth but those which claim it rightfully.[19]

3

We have now completed our survey of Newman's views as to the place of theology in the university curriculum. I would, however, draw your attention to one feature of his treatment which is more clearly grasped at the close of this survey than during its progress. You will recall that Newman's primary purpose was to vindicate the inclusion of theology in the curriculum, or at least to show that its exclusion on principle was unphilosophical. There is, however, another conclusion which follows from his argument, which is of equal importance, namely that whether or not theology is formally included in the curriculum, it must be always informally included by the fact that every other subject must take cognisance of its own relations to theology. I do not think it necessary to labour this point further. It follows at once from the argument on which Newman relies in the *Second* and *Third Discourses* for his vindication of the place of theology. If theology cannot be omitted because it has innumerable bearings on every other subject, then no other subject can be completely and correctly studied unless due cognisance is taken of its relation to theology.

It may, however, be well to add a word in defence of Newman for the fact that he treats the relations of other subjects to theology as a secondary theme, and the relations of theology to other subjects as his primary theme. I remember on one occasion hearing a distinguished Catholic professor say that in vindicating the position of theology in the curriculum, Newman was merely pushing an open door, since his *Discourses* were addressed mainly to Catholics, to whom such a theme must be a truism. In answer to such a criticism it must be pointed out, firstly that Newman addressed his arguments as much to his non-Catholic hearers as to Catholics; secondly, that in his day the idea of the exclusion of theology, even as a formal subject, was something quite novel, and it was necessary to demonstrate clearly the philosophical error it contained even to those who by tradition were totally opposed to it; and thirdly that, in fact, he does deal most adequately with the other side of the relation, namely that of other sciences to theology. It is, perhaps, a little confusing for the student, coming first to these lectures, to find the *Fourth Discourse* entitled " Bearing of Other Branches of Knowledge on Theology," and to find discussed therein, as we have seen, not the fundamental issue of the relation of these other branches to theology but rather a secondary consideration,

namely the tendency of other subjects to usurp the function
of theology if it is excluded. For the more fundamental
issue, he must go back to the *Third Discourse* and re-read it,
this time not attending so much to the relation it establishes
between theology and secular sciences, as to the other
branch of the relation which inevitably follows, and which
is vindicated equally by the argument which establishes the
primary relation.

It may, however, be granted that, as the *Discourses*
stand today, they do not, perhaps, emphasise sufficiently for
our present-day needs the necessity of what we may call
the implicit inclusion of theology in the teaching of every
other subject. If this criticism be admitted, it may be met
by pointing out that in the original scheme of the *Discourses*,
there was a much fuller treatment of this subject. The
Discourse containing it is known as the original *Fifth Discourse*. It was the last of those actually delivered in Dublin
in May 1852, and it appears in full in the first edition. It
was omitted from all succeeding editions, but is found with
minor corrections in a volume to which we shall have
occasion to refer to again, *My Campaign in Ireland*.[20] This
latter text is reprinted in Professor Harrold's 1947 edition
of the *Discourses*.[21]

In the opening passages of this *Discourse* Newman deals
with the very issue we have just alluded to, namely the
relation of secular subjects to theology. He quotes from
the *Edinburgh Review* of February 1826 an article voicing
the usual argument of the protagonists of non-denominational education, namely that, whilst they have no objection
to religious teaching in its proper place, they cannot see
how secular teaching need take any account of religion.

Take the case of a young man, a student, we will suppose, of surgery, resident in London. He wishes to becomes a master of his profession, without neglecting other useful branches of knowledge. In the morning he attends Mr. McCulloch's Lecture on Political Economy. He then repairs to the Hospital, and hears Sir Astley Cooper explain the mode of reducing fractures. In the afternoon he joins one of the classes which Mr. Hamilton instructs in French or German. With regard to religious observances, he acts as he himself, or those under whose care he is, think most advisable. Is there anything objectionable in this? Is it not the most common case in the world? And in what does it differ from that of a young man at the London University? . . . Have none of those who censure the London University on this account, daughters who are educated at home, and who are attended by different teachers? The music master, a good Protestant, comes at twelve; the dancing master, a French philosopher, at two; the Italian master, a believer in the blood of St. Januarius, at three. The parents take upon themselves the office of instructing their child in religion. She hears the preachers whom they prefer, and reads the theological works which they put into her hands . . . Who can point out any material difference between the situation in which this girl is placed, and that of a pupil at the new University.[22]

Newman points out first of all the confusion in this argument of intellectual with non-intellectual pursuits; but he goes on to show that there is in it a deeper fault, namely,

a lack of comprehension of the fact he has so often emphasised, that knowledge is one comprehensive whole, made
up of ordered parts of varying values.

The majestic vision of the Middle Age which grew
steadily to perfection in the course of centuries, the
University of Paris, or Bologna, or Oxford, has almost
gone out in night. A philosophical comprehensiveness,
an orderly expansiveness, an elastic constructiveness,
men have lost them, and cannot make out why.[23]

The new notion of a university is " a sort of bazaar or
pantechnicon, in which wares of all kinds are heaped together
for sale in stalls independent of each other." [24]

And now, to illustrate more clearly this doctrine of the
philosophical comprehensiveness of knowledge, Newman
introduces a metaphor drawn from a fundamental teaching
of Scholastic Philosophy.

We form and fix the Sciences in a circle and system,
and give them a centre and an aim, instead of letting
them wander up and down in a sort of hopeless confusion. In other words, to use scholastic language,
we give the various pursuits and objects, on which the
intellect is employed, a *form*; for it is the peculiarity
of a form, that it gathers up in one, and draws off from
everything else, the materials on which it is impressed.[25]

It is obviously impossible here to give a detailed exposition
of the doctrine of matter and form adopted by St Thomas
from Aristotle. It is probably quite familiar to many of my

hearers. For the understanding of Newman's figurative use of the term "form," it is enough to say that the theory is invoked primarily to explain the nature of substantial change. It postulates two elements in material beings, the element of indetermination which is matter, and the element determining matter to a specific substantial nature which is the form. We may note that this explanation of the nature of material beings, though it is commonly held by scholastic philosophers, carries with it no obligation of faith. Only with regard to the human soul is it defined in Catholic theology that it is the form of the body, since it fulfils the definition of a form, being an incomplete substance, whose nature it is to be united with another incomplete substance, thereby determining it to be a substantial whole. Newman, indeed, proceeds to give this very example of a form, the human soul which, as he says, " gives unity to the various parts which make up the human frame." [26] He then, by a very striking and just analogy, compares the philosophic comprehensiveness, the principle of unity in Liberal Knowledge to the form of material things or to the human soul viewed as a form. Without that form knowledge is an agglomeration of dead members. Each can come to life only when the form is complete.

It will be recalled that the whole aim of this *Discourse*, as of the preceding ones, especially the *Third*, is to demonstrate that theology is an essential component—indeed the highest component of this " form " of Liberal Knowledge. And Newman goes on to drive home his point that the absence of this essential element in the form, and the consequent absence of the form itself, must alter every subject of knowledge.

This then is the obvious answer to the objection with' which I opened this *Discourse*. I supposed it to be asked me, how it could matter to the pupil, who it was that taught him such indifferent subjects as logic, antiquities, or poetry, so that they be taught him. I answer that no subject of teaching is really indifferent in fact, though it may be in itself; because it takes a colour from the whole system to which it belongs, and has one character when viewed in that system, and another viewed out of it. Accordingly then, as a teacher is under the influence, or in the service of this system or that, so does the drift or at least the practical effect of his teaching vary.[27]

4

At this point Newman somewhat abruptly interjects a warning, the full purport of which we shall consider a little later. He asks his hearers to note that, though he claims that no subject can be completely known without some reference to theology, he is not claiming thereby for theology anything " singular or special, or which is not partaken by other sciences in their measure."

Far indeed am I from having intended to convey the notion . . . that Theology stands to other knowledge as the soul to the body; or that other sciences are but its instruments and appendages . . . On the contrary, Theology is one branch of knowledge, and Secular Sciences are other branches. Theology is the highest, indeed, and widest, but it does not interfere with the real freedom of any secular science in its own

particular department . . . Not Science only, not
Literature only, not Theology only . . . but all knowledge
whatever, is taken into account in a University, as being
the special seat of that large Philosophy, which embraces
and locates truth of every kind, and every method of
attaining it.[28]

We will just note, for the moment, that Newman objects
to the description of theology as being the soul of Liberal
Knowledge, and that his objection is based on the view that
such terminology would imply that theology could affect
other knowledge in the latter's intrinsic principles. The
further history of this objection we will pursue shortly.

The last few pages of this *Discourse* are devoted to a
consideration of a special type of non-religious education,
or rather a system of compromise between religious and
non-religious education which is familiar to us today under
the title of the " Agreed Syllabus." [29] Here is Newman's
straightforward description of the system, and it is interesting
to note that his words, written a century ago, need absolutely
no change to be applicable to the system as propounded
today.

As there are many persons . . . who maintain that
Religion should not be introduced at all into a course
of Education, so there are many too, who think a compromise may be effected between such as would and such
as would not introduce it, viz., by introducing a certain
portion, and nothing beyond it; and by a certain portion
they mean just as much as they suppose Catholics and
Protestants to hold in common. In this way they hope,
on the one hand, to avoid the odium of not teaching

religion at all, while on the other they equally avoid any show of contrariety between contrary systems of religion . . .[30]

Newman points out that an initial difficulty in this system is to find out exactly what are the tenets held by the various denominations outside the Catholic Church. There is, however, a much more fundamental difficulty, which is that in reality the various denominations hold nothing in common in religion, however they may seem to do so. This difference is most striking of all when the belief of Catholics is opposed to that of any other Christian denomination. As Newman puts it, " to teach half of any whole is really to teach no part of it."[31] The Catholic faith is one, complete, interdependent system. Non-Catholic beliefs embrace only parts of that system. Hence a tenet which a non-Catholic appears to hold in common with a Catholic is not really held in common, because the Catholic holds it as being inextricably connected with other tenets which the non-Catholic rejects. Thus, for a Catholic, belief in the Incarnation necessarily involves belief in the Mass. If, then, a Catholic and a Protestant simultaneously avow their belief in the Incarnation, they are, though using the same words, avowing their belief in different things.

Newman acknowledges that this may seem a hard doctrine, especially to those of charitable feelings, who do not like to think unfavourably of any one.

And when they find a man of another denomination differ from them in religious matters, they cannot bear the thought that he differs from them in principle, or that he moves on a line, on which did he progress for centuries he would but be carried further from them, instead of catching them up. Their delight is to think that he holds what they hold, only not enough; and that he is right as far as he goes. Such persons are very slow to believe that a scheme of general education, which puts Religion more or less aside, does *ipso facto* part company with Religion; but they try to think, as far as they can, that its only fault is the accident that it is not so religious as it might be. In short they are of that school of thought (and here we find an instance of Newman's power of expressing a very deep truth in very simple language) which will not admit that half a truth is an error, and nine-tenths of a truth no better; that the most frightful discord is close upon harmony; and that intellectual principles combine, not by a process of physical accumulation, but in unity of idea.[32]

5

We have already mentioned that this original *Fifth Discourse*, delivered in Dublin on 7 June 1852, the last to be spoken, was omitted by Newman from all editions after the first. We will now consider briefly the reasons for this omission, not that the matter is one of first-class importance, but because the discussion of these reasons will help to clarify still further Newman's teaching on the place of theology in liberal education.

We noted earlier in this lecture that in this *Discourse* Newman expressed his dissent from the view that theology could be regarded as the "form" of Liberal Knowledge, taking the word "form" in an analogical sense, as something

that gives to liberal knowledge its peculiar unity, in some
such manner as the form of material things was held by the
scholastics to determine matter to their specific substantial
nature, or as the soul determines the body to form one
substantial whole. We may presume, therefore, that already
in 1852, he had heard such a view propounded by either
English or Irish theologians or educationists. On 20 March
1854 a Brief was published by Pius IX urging the Irish
Bishops to carry into effect the project of the Catholic
University decided on at the Synod of Thurles in 1850,
and suggesting the main lines on which the University
should be conducted, so that it might be worthy of the
title of Catholic which it was to bear. The Latin text of this
Brief is given in *My Campaign in Ireland*.[33]

Three points are especially emphasised:

1. Our holy religion is to be, as it were, the soul of the
whole educational system.

2. All the various branches of knowledge are to advance
in the closest union with religion, so that the different
studies may be illumined with the light of Catholic teaching.

3. The professors are not only to give good example in
their teaching and the uprightness and propriety of their
lives, but are to make it their earnest endeavour to mould
the characters of their pupils to piety, good conduct, and
all the virtues, and to instruct them in science and letters
according to the traditions of the Catholic Church.

In Newman's manuscript memorandum, *My Connection
with the Catholic University*, which was written between 1870
and 1873, there are certain comments on this Brief, from
which one paragraph concerns us here.

The Pope exhorts the Bishops to make ' divina nostra religio *tamquam anima* totius litterariæ institutionis ' in the University; that is the *form*. ' Omnes disciplinae ' are to go forward in the most *strict league* with religion, that is, with the assumption of Catholic doctrine in their intrinsic treatment; and the professors are directly to mould ' totis viribus ' the youth to piety and virtue, and to ground them in literature and science in conformity with the Church's teaching. I wrote on a different idea my ' Discourses on University Education ' in 1852; vid. especially the original 5th Discourse.[34]

Newman's disatisfaction with these words of the Brief, though only hinted at, is unmistakable. Was there then a fundamental difference between his concept of the place of theology in liberal education and that of the Pope? My view is that there was not, and that Newman, for once, did not display his usual accuracy of thought in his consideration of the Pope's words.

To clear the issue, let us say briefly that there was no quarrel whatever about the necessity for the inclusion of theology in the curriculum, or about the nature of liberal knowledge. The only issue is whether the different meanings given by the Pope and Newman to the term " the soul " or " form " of education imply a real difference in doctrine. Now, let us remember that both are using the term merely metaphorically. This is obvious from the very nature of the case, and it is confirmed by the fact that the Pope deliberately uses the adverb " tamquam," " as it were." A metaphor depends for its meaning on the intention of the user, and both the Pope and Newman have made their meanings clear.

Newman was approaching the question from the purely philosophic stand-point, and his purpose was to illustrate the nature of that liberal knowledge whose value he was so resolutely defending. He quite rightly pointed out that its very liberal nature, its comprehensiveness, " that large Philosophy," as he put it, " which embraces and locates truth of every kind, and every method of attaining it,"[35] could be suitably spoken of as its form or soul.

When we examine the wording of the Brief, we find clear evidence that the Pope was speaking of religion as being the " soul " of education in a very different sense. In the very same sentence in which he introduces the metaphor, he goes on to specify the characteristics of education which he means to illustrate by its use. Reverence for, and worship of God are to be fostered. The faith is to be guarded, secular studies are to be in harmony with Catholic principles, sound doctrines are to be proposed, the declarations of the Holy See are to be accepted, false teachings to be avoided, the professors are to give good example by their teaching and conduct, and to be zealous for the moral and intellectual training of the youth under their care.

It will be seen at once that this passage merely enunciates the traditional Catholic teaching that religious and secular teaching form one whole. Confirmation of every statement in it can be found in Newman's own writings.[36] The fact was that the Pope was really dealing with the issue raised by Newman in his earlier *Discourses*, the denial that there was any relation at all between the other sciences and religion. He was concerned not to emphasise the inter-relation of all sciences, but to emphasise the one relation which was rejected by liberal thought. He used, therefore, the metaphor of the "soul" or "form" to denote the paramount importance of that relation, a theme which Newman himself had exhaustively treated in the first five and last three of his *Discourses*.

But, all along, let us remember that the question is one of an analogy. If then we are asked, "What is the soul or form of education?" we rightly reply that literally it has none. It has, however, two characteristics, either of which may fittingly be compared to a soul or form. It has a philosophical comprehensiveness which gives to it its complete nature, and without which it is mutilated. But it also is dominated by theology in the sense that theology is the highest of all branches of knowledge, and has deeper and more significant relations with all knowledge than any other branch of it.

I have said that in his consideration of the Pope's words Newman did not exhibit his usual clarity of thought, and I believe that this is manifested by a curious comment which he makes on one passage in the Brief. "Omnes disciplinae" he says, "are to go forward in the most *strict league* with religion." And he adds, "that is, with the assumption of Catholic doctrine in their *intrinsic* treatment."[37] We have already remarked that it was possible that Newman had heard certain theologians propounding the view that theology could affect the intrinsic principles of other sciences, and giving it the title of the "soul or form" of education in that sense. But let us observe that there is not a trace of such a doctrine in the Pope's Brief. The word "intrinsic" does not appear anywhere, and Newman certainly appears to have gone too far in translating the words "arctissimo foedere conjunctae" by "with the assumption of Catholic doctrines in their *intrinsic* treatment." As far as I know, no such doctrine has ever appeared in any authoritative papal pronouncement, and we may remark that the very opposite is stated in the decrees of the Vatican Council (Sess. 3 Cap 4).[38] Speaking of " human arts and sciences," the Council declares:

> Nor does the Church forbid these sciences to use their own principles and methods in their respective spheres. This liberty is their right and she acknowledges it. But she does take every means to prevent them from opposing God's teaching and so falling into error, and from over-stepping their own borders, trespassing upon the field of faith, and so causing confusion therein.

Before leaving this topic I would draw your attention to a well-known passage in Newman's address on *Christianity and Scientific Investigation*, which he composed in 1855 for the School of Science in the Catholic University. It was one of those reprinted in a volume entitled *Lectures and Essays on University Subjects addressed to members of the Catholic University*, and now known as *The Idea of a University Part II*.[39] In this essay Newman gives a balanced statement of the relations between religion and secular knowledge. He once more asserts the view which, whether he realised it or not, has always been that of the Church, that a scientist must be " at liberty to investigate on the basis, and according to the peculiarities, of his science." [40] Yet on the other hand Newman shows how that liberty is perfectly compatible with the demands of faith. The Catholic scientist, says Newman,

> is sure, and nothing shall make him doubt, that, if anything seems to be proved by astronomer, or geologist, or

chronologist, or antiquarian or ethnologist, in contradiction to the dogmas of faith, that point will eventually turn out, first *not* to be proved, or secondly, not
contradictory, or thirdly, not contradictory to anything
really revealed, but to something that has been confused
with revelation. And if, at the moment, it appears to
be contradictory, then he is content to wait, knowing
that error is like other delinquents; give it rope enough,
and it will be found to have a strong suicidal propensity.[41]

I have said that the question why Newman omitted the
original *Fifth Discourse* from the later editions is not one
of major importance. However, we have now touched on
one possible reason for this omission, namely the opposition
which he—in my opinion wrongly—thought he detected
between the teaching of Pius IX and his own on the subject
of the "soul" or "form" of education. Newman did not
retract his own view. He states it, though with less emphasis,
in some of the *Discourses* which remained (*Sixth Discourse*,
p. 121; *Eighth Discourse*, p. 159) but he may have thought it
wiser to omit the express rejection of theology as the soul
of education which the original *Fifth Discourse* contains.
There were, however, other reasons for the omission of
this *Discourse*. They are of interest only to Newman specialists, and you will find them discussed on pp. 287-91 of
my *Newman's University: Idea and Reality*. Briefly, the main
reason there suggested is that the *Discourse* merely reiterated
the themes of the *Third*, *Fifth* (of present edition) and *Sixth*
Discourses, namely that theology must influence all subjects,
and that the "form" of liberal knowledge is its own comprehensiveness. A contributory reason may have been that

Newman in this *Discourse* abandoned his plan of dealing with his topic from the philosophical standpoint only, and treated of certain matters that involved acceptance of the Catholic religion. By omitting the *Discourse*, he got back to his original standpoint, and maintained it until the last two *Discourses*, which deal professedly with the Church and liberal knowledge.

6

One last topic will bring to a close our consideration of Newman's views on the relations between religious and secular knowledge. You will recall a distinction made by Newman in the *Fifth* (as now printed, originally *Sixth*) *Discourse*, between theology as a speculative science and that application of theology to the life of man which tends towards his sanctification. Only the former would Newman admit as a strictly liberal science and hence as an essential part of the curriculum of a university. It is clear from letters and documents contained in the archives of the Oratorian Fathers at Birmingham that he submitted this *Fifth Discourse* to some of his fellow-religious, who objected to the distinction he had made. To clarify the position, Newman composed an Introduction which was printed separately, and omitted when the *Discourses* were published in their entirety, the reason for the omission being that Newman considered that by the time he had got to his last *Discourse* his views were sufficiently clear without the Introduction. He went to great pains in the composition of this Introduction, composing at least three drafts and submitting them to various friends for criticism.

It would be wearisome to follow in detail Newman's reasoning on this point.[42] The gist of it is this. Looked on in its bare idea, a university as such is not an institution for the sanctification of men, but for their instruction. However, when a Catholic, or for that matter any man believing in God, considers what a university should be in the concrete, he cannot look upon the sanctification, that is the religious and moral welfare of the students, with indifference, but must provide for it. But the necessity for this provision does not arise out of the nature of the university, but out of the nature of the students as creatures of God and Christians. Newman believed that this distinction had been historically observed by the Church in the foundation of Colleges or Halls, and he later elaborated this notion in the papers which he contributed to the University Gazette in 1854, which were described as "Illustrations of the Idea of a University," and which were reprinted in his *Historical Sketches*, Volume III, the first part. In one of these papers he concisely defines a College as

> a place of residence for the University student, who would then find himself under the guidance and instruction of Superiors and tutors, bound to attend to his personal interests, moral and intellectual.[43]

Such institutions Newman considered to be necessary, not indeed for the strict idea of a university, but for its "integrity," using the word in the recognised scholastic sense, as he explains, of "a gift superadded to its nature, without which that nature is indeed complete, and can act and fulfil its end, but does not find itself . . . in easy circumstances." [44]

It is, of course, obvious that it is a matter of opinion whether actual residence on the part of the students is required, as Newman thought, for the "integrity" of a university. It was largely the custom in the mediaeval universities, but usage has varied greatly since then at different times and in different places. If however such actual residence is not postulated, it is clear that it is the duty of a university to provide in other ways for the religious and moral welfare of its students. But if Newman's contention is correct, such provision is made by the university authorities, not in virtue of their being university authorities, but on the general ground of their responsibility as guardians of their students.

Let us remember in any case that whatever is thought of Newman's distinction in this matter, it was only a mental distinction. It is perfectly plain that in a Catholic university in existence he envisaged the most ample means for the religious and moral welfare of the students; and this contention is borne out by his practice in the Catholic University of Ireland, where he prescribed residence for as many of the students as possible, and for all students the usual provision of public religious services, religious societies, encouragement in the frequentation of the sacraments, and whatever disciplinary regulations were needed as safeguards against moral evils.

7

THE *IDEA* IN PRACTICE

I

WE HAVE ALREADY ALLUDED to the fact that New-
man's *Discourses on the Idea of a University* should not be
regarded as a complete compendium of his views on the
constitution of a university. They were planned with one
great aim in view, namely to emphasise the fact that a
university, whatever its constitution and whatever its total
aims, has one primary aim, the production of educated men.
They describe fully, perhaps even with a certain amount of
iteration that is confusing, what is the nature of this education
which is the primary end of a university, namely the formation of a cast of mind which disposes its possessor to view
knowledge, not as a agglomeration of truths, but as a con-
catenation of related truths, each having its particular
ontological or ethical value.

We have also conceded that owing to the strained
circumstances in which the lectures were composed, and the
unchartered nature of their subject, there is in them at
times a lack of proportion, an excess of repetition, sometimes excessive or defective emphasis, all of which may
mislead the casual reader.

We have, however, pointed out that careful analysis of

the lectures reveals their complete soundness, their consistency, their breadth of view, their permanent value.
But it will be of very great assistance to us in clarifying the
main and subsidiary themes of the lectures to turn to their
practical application by Newman himself in the constitution
and day by day working of the Catholic University of
Ireland, of which these lectures were intended as an
adumbration, and whose foundation followed so closely
after their publication. It is surely only fair to Newman to
form our idea of his total concept of the University not
merely on his educational treatises, but also on his educational
practice. A military leader is judged even more by his
tactics on the field of battle than by his writings or declarations on general strategy.

I have said that time does not permit of any detailed
history of the events which led up to the establishment of
the Catholic University, and similarly we cannot give any
detailed account of the gradual evolution of its constitution.
I propose, therefore, that we confine ourselves to certain
key documents, mainly or totally composed by Newman,
which are extant and easily accessible. This procedure has
at least two great advantages. It avoids confusion by side-
stepping all the complicated events and conflicting interests
that accompanied the foundation of the university, and it
enables us to base our study on that most satisfying source
of all historical research, authentic first-hand documents.

The first of these documents is known as the Report of
October 1851, the full title of which is *Report on the Organisation of the Catholic University of Ireland*. It was drawn up at
the request of the University Committee by a small sub-
committee consisting of Newman, Dr Patrick Leahy,

Vicar-General of Cashel and President of Thurles Diocesan College, later Vice-Rector of the university from 1854 to 1857, when he became Archbishop of Cashel, and Myles O'Reilly, a prominent Catholic layman of the day, a wealthy Co. Louth landowner, B.A. of London University and LL.D. of Rome, who later commanded a battalion of Papal Volunteers against Garibaldi, was a member of Parliament and an Assistant Commissioner of the Board of Intermediate Education in Ireland. They met at Thurles, in Co. Tipperary, and after some days of consultation issued this first key document.[1]

Its very first lines dispose completely of the assumption that Newman had any hankering after the excessive literary education which had characterised Oxford in the days of its decline.

The university was to consist of four Faculties, 1. Arts, which was divided into two sections, Letters and Science. 2. Medicine. 3. Law. 4. Theology.

As, however, only the Faculty of Arts could be founded as a beginning, the Committee gave in detail only its branches and extent. For either Letters or Science the time to be devoted to the course up to the primary degree of B.A. (as yet the distinctive title of B.Sc. was not used for a Science degree) was to be four years. It was to be settled later what further study should be required for the M.A.

The branches of study embraced by the Faculty of Arts were to be:

In the division of Letters: Latin, Greek; the Semitic and Modern Languages; History, Ancient and Modern, both National and Ecclesiastical; Archaeology, Christian and Profane; English Literature and Criticism.

In the division of Science: Logic, Metaphysics, Ethics, including Economy and Politics; Philosophy of Religion; Mathematics; Natural Philosophy (i.e. Physics); Chemistry; Natural History (the usual title then used for Botany); Mineralogy and Geology, etc. etc.

Subsidiary to the Faculty of Arts should be organised a School of Engineering.

The remarkably wide nature of this curriculum will be at once noticed. It may be said that it embraced the entire field of liberal learning, as far as it was then known. I will draw your attention especially to two points in it. One is the addition of the abbreviations " etc. etc." after the enumerated subjects of physical science. Newman was a man who never misused a word, never used it superfluously, never above all used it as padding or to conceal unclear thought. Hence I do not think it far-fetched to see in the addition of the abbreviations " etc. etc." a far-seeing pre-vision on Newman's part of the establishment of new branches of science or of the subdivision of the existing branches. The other point worthy of special note is the provision for an engineering school. We have seen how it was only in the early decades of the nineteenth century that the profession of engineering came into being as the result of the development of technology. Newman, therefore, showed great elasticity of mind in being prepared to admit engineering studies into the curriculum of the university.

In later years there was to be much controversy as to what subjects were or were not admissible into that curriculum, and there is much controversy still. Forestry, agriculture, commerce, dramatics, even art and architecture and pedagogy are examples of subjects which are admitted by some and excluded by others. Let us remember that there can be no mathematical line drawn in the matter. The original idea of the *Studium*, as the university was first, called, was that it should be a centre of knowledge or learning. Inevitably that also meant that it should be a place of professional training, since a profession is nothing more than a calling which utilises certain branches of human knowledge for the welfare of mankind. Training for merely mechanical pursuits, however, was excluded, not because they were despised, but because they required a far lesser share of knowledge and hence did not naturally find a place in the *Studium*. But it is clear that it must always be merely a matter of human judgment whether any calling involves enough intellectual activity to be called a profession and to be worthy of inclusion in the university curriculum. Up to the eighteenth century the traditional three great faculties of Theology, Law and Medicine, with the introductory faculty of Arts, covered clearly enough all the pursuits that could be fairly called professional or intellectual. But since the end of the eighteenth century, especially in the domain of applied science, it has become increasingly difficult to decide the point at which certain pursuits lose their mechanical nature and become predominantly intellectual. All that can be said is that the university must endeavour to keep its old aim of being a *Studium*, a centre of learning, and must apply that criterion to the admission or rejection of any form of vocational training. In Newman's day the profession of engineering had established itself as a calling which, though demanding a certain degree of manual dexterity, also demanded such a knowledge of mathematics, physics and chemistry as fully to warrant its inclusion among the learned professions. That he readily acknowledged this, is a proof not only of his awareness of the changing nature of human knowledge, but also of his entire consistency with his own principles.

We may pass rapidly over the other provisions of this first Report of October 1851. They deal mostly with the government of the university, and are not connected with our main theme, its studies. The government of the university was to be a blend of the monarchical and democratic. The supreme government was to be entrusted to a Rector appointed by the bishops, and for the first ten years, the professors were to be appointed in the same way, on the recommendation of the Rector. The professors, however, were to elect their own Deans in each faculty, and these Deans, with the Vice-Rector, formed the Rectorial Council. The Academic Senate was to consist of all the officers and professors, and, after ten years, of such a number of graduates, annually elected by the graduates of their respective faculties as should not exceed one-fourth of the total. All ordinary business was to be transacted by the Rectorial Council, but graver matters, such as the framing of statutes, were to be referred to the Senate.

2

The next document which we will consider is known as the Statement of 14 August 1852.[2] It was addressed by Newman to Dr Paul Cullen, Archbishop of Dublin and Chairman of the University Committee. The main theme of it is Newman's conviction that the best way to secure a good spirit among a large number of university students is to divide them into small self-contained communities, living in Inns or Halls, as in the mediaeval universities. Newman proposed that each of them should lodge about twenty students (though he also envisaged other students living with their families or in licensed lodgings, affiliated with the Halls). A Dean should preside over each Hall, and some of the tutors of the university should reside in each. There would be a private chapel in each Hall and a chaplain who could act as confessor to the students.

There are just two points which require emphasising in this plan. Firstly, we see the predilection of Newman for a residential university. It may be remarked that there is nothing in the concept of a university which essentially demands residence. As long as the ideal of a centre of knowledge is maintained, it is immaterial whether the students live under the same roof as their rulers and teachers, or only come to meet them at stated times. In the mediaeval universities of the Continent the practice varied, and it was only in the two great English universities that residence gradually became the rule, and that the Halls developed into formal colleges, whose Heads assumed complete government of the university. It is, however, undeniable that a strong case can be made for residence as being a great help to that unity of aim and community of ideas that must prevail if the university is to attain its end of liberal culture.

The second point to be stressed is the brief, but important indication that there should be a certain degree of supervision of the students by the Dean, and that hand-in-hand with this should go some provision for their religious life. We recall that Newman, in pursuance of his theory that the primary end of the university was mental culture, had claimed that the proper place of theology in the curriculum was as a theoretic study. It did not, however, follow, as some of his critics have held, that he would thereby absolve the university authorities from all responsibility with regard to the religious and moral life of the students, or that he would exclude religious training from among the total ends of education. We have already seen that this can be gathered even from his writings, but here we find clear proof of it in his first sketch of the practical organisation of the university.

The first steps in the setting up of the Catholic University of Ireland took place during the summer of 1854. On 18 May the bishops met in synod at the Presbytery, Marlborough Street, Dublin, and after some days of deliberation published thirteen decrees, which embodied the main provisions of the Report of October 1851.[3] The university was to have five faculties, Newman's faculty of Arts being divided into two, the faculty of Philosophy and Letters and the Faculty of Science. The bishops reserved to themselves the *supremum ius* over the university, which in practice meant the appointment of Rector, Vice-Rector, and for the time being of the professors designated by the Rector. All ordinary administration was vested in the Rector. On 4 June, Whit Sunday, Newman was solemnly installed as Rector after High Mass celebrated in the Pro-Cathedral, Marlborough Street.

3

Before the synod Newman had submitted to the bishops a memorandum dealing in much greater detail than the Report of October 1851 with the aims and organisation of the university. The memorandum was considered by the bishops at the synod, but no comment on it was issued. It is evident, however, that it found favour, since most of its provisions were afterwards put into effect. It calls for detailed consideration here, as giving the views which had crystallised in Newman's mind during the three years of waiting that had elapsed, and which he now considered definitive on the eve of the opening of the university.[4]

The memorandum begins by setting out a number of the main aims of the university. We may pick out half a dozen of the more important.

2. To provide a professional education for students of law and medicine, and a liberal education for youths destined to mercantile and similar pursuits, as far as their time will admit it.

4. To form a school of theology and canon law suited to the needs of a class of students who may be required to carry on their sciences beyond the point of attainment ordinarily sufficient for parochial duty.

5. To provide a series of sound and philosophical defences of Catholicity and Revelation, in answer to the infidel tracts and arguments which threaten to be our most serious opponents in the era now commencing.

6. To create a national Catholic literature.

7. To provide school books, and generally books of instruction, for the Catholics of the United Kingdom, and of the British Empire, and of the United States.

8. To raise the standard, and systematize the teaching, and encourage the efforts, of the schools already so ably and zealously conducted throughout the country.

9. To give a Catholic tone to society in the great towns.

It is hardly necessary to emphasise the fact that these general aims outlined by Newman assume the twofold character of the university as a professional school and a seat of liberal education. The provision of liberal education for those destined for mercantile pursuits, the higher school of theology, as distinct from practical pastoral training, the creation of literature and the raising of the standard of education and of society, these are all activities of the university as a liberalising influence, as an instrument for the spread of that broad culture that Newman looked upon as the university's primary, though by no means sole aim.

We see that combination of the useful or professional with the more broadly cultural aims also in the next section of the memorandum. Newman was conscious of the fact that at first, and indeed for some years, the number of students would be small, and their requirements limited. In order, therefore, to give the university that wide scope which he felt it should have, he proposed that the professors should at once found certain learned institutions, " large departments of knowledge " as he called them, which would have the double purpose of attracting students and having an intrinsic value, even before the students should come. As instances of such institutions, he mentioned:

1. A school of useful arts, developing and applying the material resources of Ireland; that is, comprising the professorships of engineering, mining, agriculture, etc. etc.

2. An observatory, with the professorships it would involve.

3. An archaeological department, employing itself prin-

cipally on the language, remains, MSS., etc., of ancient Ireland, with a special reference to Catholicity.

4. The medical staff of a hospital, which would be the basis of a professoriate for students in medicine.

There is an interesting note appended to this section, showing that Newman was fully alive to a function of the university which has been strongly stressed in modern times, namely its influence on society in general. He had already intimated this aim earlier in the memorandum by allusion to the creation of literature and the raising of the standard of schools and society in the large towns. He now added the following observation with reference to the setting up of learned institutions:

> Astronomical observers, professors of medical science, the decipherers and editors of ancient writings, chemists and geologists, would in various ways subserve the social interests of Ireland, even though their lecture-rooms at first were but partially filled.

Lest it might be thought that this expression of the social aim of the university was any kind of afterthought, or that the provision of these learned institutions was a mere temporary pragmatic measure forced on Newman by the paucity of students in the early stages of his project, I would remind you of a passage in the *Discourses* which we have already considered, where this social aim is explicitly laid down.

> But a University training is the great ordinary means to a great but ordinary end: it aims at raising the intellectual tone of society, at cultivating the public

mind, at purifying the natural taste, at supplying true principles to popular enthusiasm and fixed aims to popular aspiration, at giving enlargement and sobriety to the ideas of the age, at facilitating the exercise of political power, and refining the intercourse of private life.[5]

In his memorandum Newman outlined fairly definitely the actual years of study which were to be devoted to the various degrees. We will consider them in more detail when we come to the definitive Rules and Regulations. The full course was to cover seven years. The first two years were to be devoted to Arts and Science ending in what was called the degree of Scholar. There were then to be two more years devoted to a more specialised course in Arts or Science or Law, leading to the B.A. (The course in Medicine was not as yet mapped out.) This would be the normal end, but those who wished to go on for the M.A. or Doctorate in one of the higher faculties of theology or medicine would take another three years. It was noted that each course would be complete in itself, to provide for those who would have to leave at various stages.

Referring back to Newman's statement of the general aims of the university I would draw your attention to the remarkable breadth of view which it exhibits, especially when it is recalled that it was composed a century ago. We have already seen that, broadly speaking, the university has always been recognised as a place of higher study, and that this study embraced both professional and liberal knowledge. It was always easy to state a general aim, but often difficult to decide precisely how this aim should be carried into effect. There was always the problem of the means to be taken by the university to secure its ends, or perhaps, to put it more exactly, the problem of what exactly were the fields in which the university should endeavour to exert its influence.

The problem has become exceedingly complicated in modern times, owing to a number of influences, amongst which the chief are the immense strides made in scientific research and technology, the impact of social problems and political aims, and the intricate complications of modern society. There are, however, certain main aims on which at the present day, there is a reasonable amount of unanimity, though there is much controversy as to their relative importance. Broadly speaking, they are the preservation and handing on of traditional culture, preparation for the professions (including the higher branches of industry and commerce), research in every field of knowledge, the development of the individual personality of the student and the raising of the cultural level of society.

These five aims are clearly distinguishable in the pages of Newman's brief memorandum, and we may note that they are all elaborations of, or developments from the two principal aims of the university, liberal and professional knowledge. In his *Discourses* Newman's main object was to stress the former, and he may have at times appeared only to tolerate the latter. But in his practical provisions for the conduct of the university we see that he makes due provision for both.

Before leaving this memorandum of 1854, we may briefly touch on one other section which repeats and emphasises a provision made in the Statement of August 1852.[6] Newman points out that strict local unity would not be possible in an institution comprising the various learned institutions which he proposed. Such unity indeed was, as a rule, not found in the ancient universities such as Paris, Louvain and Oxford, which rather filled the cities where they were placed. The unity which Newman envisaged in his Catholic University was the unity of Catholic dogma and spirit. One valuable means for the preservation of that unity would be a university church, which would be the place for public ceremonies where the university would be visibly represented. " No one," he declared, " can overestimate the influence of an instrument of this kind in inculcating a loyal and generous devotion to the Church in the breasts of the young." [7] But an even more obvious way of securing Catholic unity in the whole institution would be the plan suggested in the statement of August 1852, to which Newman recurs in the present memorandum, namely the separation of the students into small communities of twenty or so, each having a Dean who would exercise the necessary discipline and serve the chapel, and also two or three tutors, young men of a few years' academic standing, who would assist the students in preparing for the lectures of the professors. Once again we see clearly that, though Newman held that the university in the abstract concerned itself with religion as a liberal science rather than with its practical application to the lives of the students, he had no doubt whatever that in the university in the concrete due provision must be made for that practical application, as being a part of the total education of the students.

4

As we have seen, Newman was formally installed as Rector of the Catholic University of Ireland on 4 June 1854. There were many difficulties in his way, but he faced them with characteristic courage and energy. He collected a body of some fifteen professors and lecturers, and the university opened its doors on 3 November 1854. Some twenty young men had passed the entrance examination and were enrolled as the first students. The numbers doubled during the academic year, and in the following autumn the medical school opened with forty-three students. The faculty of science was not fully established until after Newman's departure in 1858, but this was not due to any lack of effort on his part. He appointed professors of physics and chemistry, who lectured in the faculty of medicine and gave public lectures on their own subjects, and he gave every facility to them to establish well equipped laboratories. The breadth of view of both himself and his professors may be judged by the report of the latter drawn up during the year 1857-8 and published in 1858. This document urged the immediate establishment of Chairs of Botany and Zoology, and of Geology and Mineralogy, and the expenditure of a sum of £20,000, a very large figure in those days, on the scientific laboratories.[8] Newman considered this report to be of such importance that he issued no other formal report for the year 1857-8, but presented the professors' recommendations to the bishops, expressing his " full concurrence " [9] with them. The school of engineering was opened in 1855, the first year comprising mathematics, descriptive geometry, natural philosophy (the term then applied to physics) and drawing.

The entire course covered five years, with a licentiate at the end of the fourth year and mastership at the end of the fifth.

Newman carried out to a considerable extent his plan of a residential university, three Collegiate Houses being established: St Patrick's or University House, no. 86, St Stephen's Green, where the lectures were given in Arts and Science; St Mary's, no. 6 Harcourt Street, over which Newman himself presided; and St Lawrence's, no 16, Harcourt Street. In 1857 a Hall for medical students was opened.

In 1855 the Rectorial Council, proposed in the first report of October 1851, commenced its weekly meetings. It consisted of the Vice-Rector and the Dean of Faculties, and during that academic year 1855-56, the second of the University's existence, its main task was the drawing up of the Rules and Regulations. It took as basis the report of the sub-committee of 1851, the decrees of the synodal meeting of May 1854 and the memorandum addressed by Newman to that meeting, all of which we have considered. In May the provisional Rules and Regulations were printed and issued to the officials of the University for their consideration. They were approved by the Rectorial Council almost without change and continued in force until 1869, eleven years after Newman's departure, when they were republished, with minor alterations, as the definitive *Constitution and Statutes of the Catholic University of Ireland*, with the approbation of the bishops.

5

The *Rules and Regulations* [10] is the most detailed document at our disposal for the understanding of the actual working of the university. It is a remarkable revelation of Newman's power of combining broad aims with practical details. Its four sections deal with the Constitution of the University, Discipline, the Academic Course and Examinations. Most of its main provisions are drawn from the three documents which we have already mentioned. We will confine our attention to certain notable additions, concerning mainly the detailed courses of study.

One important feature in the government of the university makes its appearance, the Academic Senate, which was convoked for the first time on 14 July 1856, and which, following the mediaeval custom, recently revived by Louvain, held its meetings in the University Church. However, as its functions do not bear directly on our main theme, which is the intellectual and moral formation given to the students, we may merely remark in passing that all legislative functions were vested in it, and that, in addition to the officials and teachers of the university, it comprised Fellows, those namely who had attained to what would correspond to the doctorate in other universities. For reasons to be seen the title of Doctor was avoided. By this last provision Newman aimed at avoiding the danger which had appeared in Oxford of the preponderating influence of a resident oligarchy.

Turning to the matter of studies, we find the various stages in the academic life of the students given in more detail than in the memorandum of 1854, and bearing new titles. These were: Student (on passing entrance); Scholar (on passing the first public examination at the end of the second year, which entitled to entrance into any of the other faculties); Inceptor (on passing the second examination at the end of the third year, i.e., presuming that the student did not enter another faculty, but continued in that of philosophy and letters); Licentiate (at the end of the fourth year); Fellow (when, after a total course of seven years, the requisite examination was passed). The reason for the substitution of the titles of Licentiate and Fellow for the customary B.A. and either M.A. or Doctorate was that it was known that the government at the time was not willing to grant a charter to the university, and it was doubtful whether regular degrees could be legally granted without a charter.

For the primary (scholar's) degree after two years candidates were obliged to offer three subjects, of which one must be Latin and a second must be a choice of the following: philosophy, criticism, geography, chronology, mathematics, logic or physical science. For the third subject they had their choice of Greek or a modern language. In addition, they were to be examined on the matter of the four Gospels and an advanced Catechism, and they were also required to show a general knowledge of ancient history and geography and the principles of composition. It is not clear whether these requirements were to be tested by formal examination or in some other way. Newman gives a number of specimen combinations for these various subjects to show, as he says, " that the list can be adapted to the classical student, the ecclesiastic, or those who are intended for engineering, for business, etc." [11] It is interesting to note here Newman's pliability. While wishing that this initial course should give a liberal education to all his students, he was ready, even at this stage, to permit a slight degree of specialisation, as long as it did not frustrate his primary purpose.

For the Licentiate—and this we may look on as the key

degree, corresponding to the usual primary degree of B.A. or B.Sc. in our modern universities—the candidates could attain to either " Satisfactory Proficiency " or " Meritorious Proficiency." These rather cumbrous terms were obviously employed to avoid the terms " Pass " and " Honours," associated with a formal degree, about the granting of which, as we have seen, there was some legal uncertainty. The examination was divided into two, and the first portion taken at the end of the third year, giving successful candidates the rank of " Inceptor." This examination constituted a part of the Licentiate only for those who would aim only at " Satisfactory Proficiency," but was merely a qualifying examination for the " Meritorious Proficiency " candidates, who had a completely new examination in the fourth year. We may note here that Newman's system was a compromise between the two well-known types of examinations, that prevailing in American and Scottish universities, in which the examination may be completed by parts, and the more common European form in which the final examination covers the whole course. Newman permitted the former for his Pass candidates, but insisted on the latter for Honours.

In both examinations the subject-matter was divided under four heads: (1) Christian Knowledge; (2) Philosophy; (3) Literature; (4) History. For " Satisfactory Proficiency " the matter under these heads was as follows:

(1) Knowledge of the Four Gospels and the Acts of the Apostles; of the History of the Old Testament and an advanced Catechism.

(2) Logic; six books of Euclid; algebra to quadratics.

(3) One Greek and one Latin historian or orator, i.e., a sufficient portion of their works.

(4) One out of the six tercentenaries of profane history under the Christian era, from A.D. to 1800. Of them, all but the Greek author and profane history were taken in the third year, and the candidates for " Satisfactory Proficiency " had to present only these two for this first examination for the Licentiate. For the " Meritorious " licentiate, candidates were obliged to present a minimum of four subjects, one from each of the following groups:

1. CHRISTIAN KNOWLEDGE:

    i The Church
    ii Holy Scripture
    iii Literature of Religion
    iv Philosophy of Religion

2. PHILOSOPHY:

    v Logic
    vi Metaphysics
    vii Ethics
    viii Schools of Philosophy, Ancient and Modern
    ix Politics and Law of Nations
    x Political Economy
    xi Political Geography
    xii Ethnology
    xiii Polite Criticism and Science of Taste
    xiv Philology
    xv Geometry

3. LITERATURE:

    xvi Latin Classics
    xvii Greek Classics
    xviii Celtic Language and Literature
    xix English Language and Literature
    xx Two Foreign Languages
    xxi Hebrew

4. HISTORY:

    xxii Ancient History, Greek
    xxiii Ancient History, Roman
    xxiv Mediaeval History, Eastern
    xxv Mediaeval History, Western
    xxvi Modern History
    xxvii Ecclesiastical History

It is thus seen that even for the purely literary degree, a wide extent of subjects was provided, indeed as wide as it could possibly be, and yet that Newman was alive to the necessity of a considerable degree of specialisation for honours candidates. We note that the general type of honours degree consisted of one language, one area of history, one branch of philosophy, economics, politics or mathematics, and one branch of Christian Knowledge; and we can hardly deny that as a minimum field for an honours student such a type of degree was calculated to give an excellent general training. The same could be said of the Pass Degree with the classics as its core, history to emphasise the humane element, and logic and mathematics to stimulate abstract learning.

Newman himself never attempted any detailed syllabus for the courses in science, medicine or law. He rightly left these to specialists. For the benefit of the curious it may be mentioned that interesting, though rather scattered indications of the courses in chemistry, physics and medicine are to be found in various reports and examination papers which are preserved in Dublin.

One curious point may be mentioned, which cannot be fully explained. It will have been clear from all that has been said that Newman boldly faced the problem that has troubled every organiser of university curricula in modern times, the problem of the reconciliation of the liberal ideal with the exigencies of professional specialisation. He faced it, doubtless, with all the more determination since he was so convinced of the need of preserving the liberal ideal, and had defended it so eloquently as the principal, though not the only aim of university education. His solution was the provision of a preliminary liberal course for all students. It may be remarked that this is one of the two obvious courses that can be taken. The other is to insist on a certain modicum of liberal study concurrently with the professional studies, at least with the first few years. There are objections to both courses. Insistence on a preliminary course lengthens the whole course excessively, and may lead to the exclusion of some students for economic reasons. There is also the temptation to turn part of this preliminary course into a specialised pre-professional course, thus lengthening the professional course in a concealed manner, and defeating the original aim of the preliminary course. I think it is universally conceded that both of these weaknesses are observable in the American system, which on the other hand, makes a more formal attempt than any other existing system to provide this preliminary liberal education of which we are speaking.

The objection to running liberal courses concomitantly with the professional courses is the tendency on the part of the student to devote the absolute minimum of time to the liberal.

Newman's system avoided this weakness of the concomitant system, and to some extent he precluded the two weaknesses which we have seen to be inherent in the preliminary system, by confining his course to two years. Nevertheless, it cannot be denied that even a two-year course would impose a very long total course on most of our professional students. Newman got out of the difficulty by taking his students very young. In the memorandum of 1854 he assumed that the ordinary age of entrance would be sixteen.[12] I have never found any explanation of why he put the age so low. I can only conclude that he found it to be the normal age at which Irish boys at that time completed their secondary course. The Oxford of his day offered no precedent, as the normal age of entrance at that time was, as it is today, about eighteen. Owing to the increased content and higher standard required today in so many subjects of the secondary course, for instance, in history, mathematics, and science, Newman's entrance age would be out of the question. It must, therefore, be acknowledged that we get no help from Newman's organisation of studies in solving the problem of providing liberal education for professional students without either unduly lengthening or unduly burdening the courses.

6

Before concluding this survey of Newman's practical organisation of the university, we may refer to his views on a topic which is still a very living one, the relative positions of teaching and research. This is a point on which Newman has been misunderstood by two eminent modern writers whose views have received wide publicity, so it is important for us to know what his real teaching was. First of all Newman undoubtedly held that the aim of teaching came before that of research in the university. He states his reasons for this view clearly and succinctly in the preface to his *Discourses*. Their simplicity and brevity has perhaps been the cause why his critics have not understood their full import. Firstly, he states that the object of the university " is the diffusion and extension of knowledge rather than the advancement." And his proof of this assertion is as follows: " If its object were scientific and philosophic discovery, I do not see why a university should have students." [13] I would suggest that Newman's argument is almost too concise, and needs some elaboration to be completely cogent. It certainly proves that teaching is one of the ends of a university, but in itself does not prove that it is the primary end. This, however, would appear to follow from the fact that, from the time of their foundation to the present day, the predominant characteristic of the universities has been that they should be assemblages of professors and students, the latter pursuing knowledge under the guidance of the former. That these professors should themselves continue their search for knowledge appears to be a consequent characteristic, needed for the health of the university, but not for its bare existence. However, we are here only concerned to ascertain Newman's thought, and we give his argument as he gave it.

His second argument is that " to discover and to teach

are distinct functions: they are also distinct gifts, and are not commonly found united in the same person." [14] Furthermore, the task of teaching is so laborious that it precludes the isolation and quiet commonly needed for research. However, it may be noted that Newman does not create a hard and fast distinction between the two functions. You will observe that his words are carefully qualified. "I think," he says, "it must be allowed on the whole that, while teaching involves external engagement, the natural home for experiment and speculation is retirement." [15] And in a well-known passage in the essay on *Christianity and Scientific Investigation*, a lecture written later for the School of Science in the Catholic University, now included in what is commonly called Part II of *The Idea of a University*, Newman clearly states that the university should exercise a directive power in the region of research.

> What an empire is in political history, such is a University in the sphere of philosophy and research. It is, as I have said, the high protecting power of all knowledge and science, of fact and principle, of inquiry and discovery, of experiment and speculation. [16]

However, there is no need to rely only on these passages in the *Discourses* to ascertain what Newman's views were about research. It will be recalled that in the memorandum of 1854 he recommended the setting up of learned institutions within the university which would have value in themselves even before they had students. [17] And in the Rules and Regulations there is an illuminating passage on the duties of the professors, in which Newman demands that a professor is not to be overburdened with lectures, so that he may have time for the steady pursuit and thorough mastery of the department of science or learning which he has undertaken.[18]

I have mentioned that Newman has been taken to task on this point of research by two well-known modern writers. One of them is Mr Bruce Truscot. He declares that he differs fundamentally from the position of Newman that the object of the university is " the diffusion and extension of knowledge rather than the advancement."[19] This is fair enough, but Mr Truscot gives no indication that he has read Newman's reasons for his view, as stated in the preface to the *Discourses*, from which Mr Truscott is actually quoting, and he offers no comment on these reasons. It may also be said that Mr Truscot himself attaches an exaggerated importance to the value of formal research, and suggests that ordinary teaching is of little value in the training of the mind in independent thought. But Mr Truscot's second criticism is a mere travesty of Newman's views. " Few perhaps," he says, " would take Newman's extreme view, and exclude research from the university altogether."[20] From all that we have seen, it is clear that this criticism needs no answer, since it is directed against a view never preached or practised by Newman.

The second critic of Newman in this matter of research is the late Professor Harrold in the introduction to the 1947 edition of the *Idea of a University*, to which we have already alluded in our fifth lecture. Professor Harrold, like Mr Truscot, merely records his dissent from Newman's view that the university is primarily a teaching institution, makes no allusion to Newman's clearly expressed reasons for this view, offers no refutation of them, and makes with Mr Truscot the completely unfounded statement that Newman " denies research any place in university education." [21]

It may freely be granted, as both Mr Truscot and Professor Harrold emphasise, that Newman considered that the main body of research should be carried on in separate research institutions. There is much to be said for this view and much against it. On the whole, such institutions have flourished more on the continent of Europe than in either England or America. But let it be noted, firstly, that even when great research departments form part of a university, they really constitute separate bodies. Their professors must inevitably devote more and more time to research and less to teaching. Their students are advanced students and act more as collaborators than as pupils. The ordinary work of instructing the rank and file of the student body has inevitably to be entrusted, at least in great part, to men devoted to such work. Newman's principle that " to discover and to teach are distinct functions " asserts itself, in spite of the fact that the two functions are carried on by the one institution. And furthermore, as we have seen, Newman was never guilty of the absurdity of dividing the two functions, in practice, into water-tight compartments, but rather, both in his teaching and in his practice, required that the two should go hand in hand, properly regulated and kept within bounds, that zeal for research should never cause neglect of the primary purpose of teaching, and that research should keep that teaching alive and stimulating.

We may remark, in passing, that on this point, so eminent a modern thinker as M. Maritain is in full accord with

Newman. In his *Education at the Crossroads*, published in 1943, he says:

> It is no doubt normal that any instruction given in the University will result in some original work and the advancement of knowledge, especially in science. Yet this is in a way an overflow of the teaching science. In the nature of things the object of the University is the teaching of youth, and not producing books and articles and endless contributions, or making some scientific, philosophical or artistic discovery.[22]

In the same passage in which Professor Harrold criticises Newman's supposed views on research, he attributes to Newman views on the subject of physical science in general to which we have already referred in our fifth Lecture, but which now must seem even more clearly erroneous in the light of what we have seen of the curriculum drawn up by Newman for the Catholic University.

> To the end of his life Newman regarded scientific experiment as a private and individual activity. True to the spirit of pre-scientific Oxford, he writes that " the great discoveries in chemistry and electricity were not made in universities. . . . " Thus in many ways *The Idea of a University* bears the marks of that clerical and humanistic Oxford which, more or less, came to an end with the publication of the Royal Commission's Report (1852) . . . Newman's book appeared at an opportune time for him to vindicate . . . the theological and humanistic culture which the Oxford of Newman and Pusey and Copleston had symbolized for so many years.[23]

The meaning which this passage would inevitably convey to the ordinary reader would be that Newman not merely considered that scientific research should be carried on in special research institutions, a perfectly tenable theory, but that he thought very little of such research and even of any study of science. This impression is heightened rather than lessened, by the grudging concession made by Professor Harrold in a footnote:

> However, we must note that in Newman's practical plans for the Catholic University there was place for a chemical laboratory and an astronomical observatory. Some advancement of knowledge would after all have been inevitable.[24]

Elsewhere in the introduction with which we are dealing, Professor Harrold makes it clear that he was acquainted with *My Campaign in Ireland*. There he would have found not only that there was a place in Newman's plans for a chemical laboratory and astronomical observatory, but also for a full faculty of science with all its subdivisions. In a paper entitled " What I aimed at," also to be found in *My Campaign in Ireland*, he stated: "The establishment of a good School of Science was one of the foremost objects I had in view."[25] And in his report for 1856-7 Newman quotes with approbation the report of W. K. Sullivan, his Professor of Chemistry, on the wide provision made for scientific research in the laboratory.

> It has been fitted up, as the Professor of Chemistry tells me, upon the plan of those established in connection with several of the German universities, and is designed

to meet the wants of three classes of students: 1. those who propose to study chemistry for purely scientific purposes, among which may be named chemico-physiological investigations; 2. those who require a knowledge of chemistry for practical purposes, as agriculture, mining, metallurgy, the various chemical manufactures, bleaching, dying, tanning, brewing, distilling, sugar-boiling, paper-making, etc., and civil engineering; 3. students of medicine, who are required to attend one or more courses of lectures in practical chemistry during the summer months.[26]

We may recall also that Newman set up a complete and most successful Medical School and a School of Engineering, and I would draw your attention to a remark he makes in the Rules and Regulations showing that he even contemplated the possibility of a School of Agriculture, as he intimates that in the case of students of this school a possible exception might be made to his stipulation of a two years' liberal course for all students.[27] When we consider all this, it is apparent that Professor Harrold's insinuation that Newman was little interested in science is an example of a pre-conceived notion prevailing over the facts of the case.

8

PERENNIAL PROBLEMS

WITH REGARD to the construction of this lecture I feel that I owe my hearers a word of explanation. My original idea was to take a fairly wide glance at educational thought since Newman's day, and indicate the extent to which his views had prevailed, and what were the main departures from them. I found, however, that such a treatment of the subject would require far more than one lecture, and that no compression would be possible, since the differences to be indicated were so many and so subtle, and the issues involved often so complicated. Accordingly, I have contented myself with picking out a very few well-known educational writings for comparative treatment. Apart from the exigencies of time I have this justification for such selective treatment, that the great issues involved recur again and again in educational history, though under different forms and with different ramifications, so that the detailed discussion of them as they appear in one work means that one has cleared very much of the ground for their consideration in others.

Moreover, I trust that, though the works selected may appear to have been rather arbitrarily chosen, it will be found that the issues discussed in them are all closely allied to the general subject of our lectures, and will help to elucidate it further.

I

In 1860 Herbert Spencer published a reprint of four Review articles under the title, *Education, Intellectual, Moral, and Physical.* This little book had a remarkable vogue and was translated, according to the author's note to the 1884 edition, into thirteen languages. Its popularity was probably due more to the author's name than to its intrinsic worth, for many of the ideas propounded in it are superficial to the verge of naïveté. However, it does raise one important issue which is closely connected with our main topic. It is indicated by the title of the first article, *What Knowledge is of Most Worth?*

It is curious to note that Spencer had apparently never heard of either Newman's *Discourses* or the Oxford-Edinburgh controversy, for he complains that " the comparative worths of different kinds of knowledge have been as yet scarcely even discussed." [1] He grants that there have been occasional discussions as to the relative merits of classics and mathematics, but rightly holds that this forms only a part of the larger question of the relative worth of all the various branches of knowledge. Spencer makes a distinction between the value of these branches in themselves and their value as intellectual disciplines. Considering first their value in themselves, he rightly states that the aim of education is " to prepare us for complete living." [2] His enumeration of the various activities involved by " complete living " is incomplete inasmuch as it omits all discussion of man's reference to his Creator or to his final end, but it is correct as far as it goes. Education, he says should show us in what way to treat the body; in which way to treat the mind; in what way to manage our affairs; in which way to bring up a family; in what way to behave as a citizen; in what way to utilize those sources of happiness which nature supplies;—how to use all our faculties to the greatest advantage of ourselves and others.[3]

He then goes on to a detailed discussion of the various subjects which equip men for their various activities of life, elementary physiology, mathematics, mechanics, the physical sciences, history, sociology, literature and the fine arts. He next passes to the consideration of these subjects as instruments of mental discipline, and concludes very briefly that as they are the best in themselves, the best for regulating conduct to produce complete living, it follows that they must be the " best fitted for strengthening the faculties," since " it would be utterly contrary to the beautiful economy of Nature, if one kind of culture were needed for the gaining of information and another kind were needed as a mental gymnastic." [4]

In criticising this exposition of Spencer's, we may abstract from the constant assertion made all through that the study of physical science underlies all other subjects, and that it is therefore the most important of all, both for the regulation of conduct and as an intellectual discipline. We have come across a very similar assertion in Peel's Tamworth address, and have considered Newman's criticism of it. What here interests us is Spencer's attempt to systematize the whole field of knowledge.

Our first step must obviously be to classify, in the order of their importance, the leading kinds of activity which constitute human life. They may be naturally arranged into (1) those activities which directly minister to self-preservation; (2) those activities which by securing the necessities of life, indirectly minister to self-preservation; (3) those activities which have for their end the rearing and discipline of offspring; (4) those activities which are involved in the maintenance of proper social and political relations; (5) those miscellaneous activities which fill up the leisure part of life, devoted to the gratification of the tastes and feelings.[5]

Now in fairness to Spencer it must be granted that he holds that in practice education should maintain what he calls " a due proportion " [6] between the studies which direct all the various human activities; and it cannot be denied that this view is correct. What is, however, to be criticised, is his claim that because there is in human life what we may call a chronological order of precedence amongst these activities, they have therefore the same order of importance in themselves, and hence the studies which promote each of them must have that same order of importance. "Knowledge immediately conducive to self-preservation," he says, " is of primary importance " . . . Knowledge needful for self-maintenance " is second in value to none save knowledge needful for immediate self-preservation," [7] and so on. Now, if this merely means that before a man can study anything, he must know how to keep himself alive, it is simply a truism. But Spencer's words imply that this chronological order also connotes an ontological order, an order of excellence, and if this be his meaning, it is quite unproven. A knowledge of elementary hygiene may be necessary to keep a man in proper health so that he may study sociology, but one cannot conclude from that that the study of hygiene has more value in itself than that of sociology.

2

In discussing this question of what is commonly called a hierarchy of values in education, it would appear that there are really two aspects to be considered. First of all, can we establish any universal hierarchy, an order of importance which will hold in any system of education? Secondly, does it follow that this hierarchical order necessarily determines the curriculum in concrete cases? As regards the first aspect, it appears obvious that there is a fixed hierarchy dividing the branches of human knowledge according to the onto-logical value of the truths which they impart. Amidst the vast field of human knowledge, there are discernible certain great and clearly marked divisions. There is theology, which deals with man's relations with his Creator; philosophy in all its branches, which deals with the ultimate nature of being and of man in particular; than a group comprising history and literature which chronicles in different ways the thoughts, desires, passions and imaginings of man; then the physical sciences which reveal the nature and laws of the organic and inorganic worlds, and the arts and crafts which enshrine the action of man's intellect, imagination and mechanical skill when brought to bear on organic and inorganic objects. There are some subjects like mathematics, economics, medicine and law, which may be held to belong in part to more than one of these groups, or of which there may be some debate as to where they should be placed, and there may be some doubt as to the relative ranking of the sciences and the arts. But in general there is discernible in this enumeration a clear hierarchy of values, because it corresponds to a hierarchy in objective existence. God is greater than man—infinitely greater; and man is finitely greater than the rest of the creation. Therefore the know-ledge of man's relation to God is greater than all man's other knowledge about himself or his fellow-men; that knowledge of the ultimate aspects of being which is given by philosophy is greater than the particular aspects of man or the non-human creation revealed in history, literature or science; all knowledge of man is greater than the knowledge of lesser beings revealed by the physical sciences, whilst the artistic or technical achievements, however great they be, of the hands of man, derive their chief value from the various branches of man's knowledge that inspire them.

We must however be careful not to claim for this established hierarchy of knowledge more than is warranted. And this brings us to the second question, its import to the individual curriculum. This hierarchy merely tells us what truths are in themselves of a higher or lower order. It does not, however, provide us with any rule of thumb by which a particular curriculum is to be formed. We can, indeed, always be sure of a few major facts. We can be sure that theology, because of its transcendent importance, cannot be neglected at any stage in man's mental development; and it may be granted, from all that has been said on the subject, that an education which neglects over long periods the humane subjects, is a mutilated and dangerous one. But beyond that, the choice of studies will be regulated, not by their strict ontological value, but by many other considerations, such as the capacity of the students, and their immediate or ultimate aims. Our hierarchy of values, however, does enable us all along to understand what we are doing, to know when we omit one branch, or restrict another, or emphasise a third, what precisely is the loss or gain to the student, how far the mental picture of the universe which we are presenting to him conforms to or departs from the full reality.

This distinction, simple as it is, may, I venture to suggest, help to clear up the confusion that is sometimes found in discussions on the ideal curriculum. In a certain very true sense, the only ideal curriculum would be one which would lead on by gradual stages to a complete mastery of all branches whatsoever of human knowledge, so perfectly balanced as to mirror in the human mind the entire universe, both created and uncreated, and the relative importance of its constituents. Such a curriculum could, of course, only be mastered by a mind of vaster power than is known to man. In practice it has to be scaled down to suit the private capabilities and aims of human minds of various degrees of intelligence, and over the scaling-down process there can be infinite difference of opinion even among those who accept the same fundamental hierarchy of values.

Turning now to Newman, we find that if this hierarchy of values is not formally set out in his *Discourses*, it is at least very clearly implied. In his *Third Discourse* he issues the warning that " it is not every science which equally . . . enlightens the mind," and thus " they differ in importance." [8] The great divisions of these sciences are indicated in the *Ninth Discourse* in which he points out that "there are three great subjects on which Human Reason employs itself: God, Nature and Man," [9] which are the subjects of study respectively of theology, science and literature in its widest sense. In our Sixth Lecture we considered the many passages in which Newman claims for theology the highest place among the branches of human knowledge, and in our Fifth those in which he vindicates the superiority of the philosophical-historical-literary group over the physical sciences. More than this we do not find on this particular aspect of the hierarchy of subjects.

3

Let us return now to the second aspect discussed by Spencer, the relative value of these subjects as instruments of mental training. I confess that I find myself quite incapable of following his reasoning that " the acquirement of those classes of facts which are most useful for regulating conduct, involves a mental exercise best fitted for strengthening the faculties." [10] If we accept Spencer's hierarchy of values, this would mean that a knowledge of elementary hygiene would develop the mind better than a knowledge of economics, and that a knowledge of economics would be superior to the study of literature. But even if we accept our own hierarchy of values, I do not see that the mere fact that one subject deals with a higher order of truths than another thereby makes it a better instrument for mental training. Could it, for instance, be held with confidence that theology is a better instrument for mental training than philosophy, or that biology is better than chemistry?

It seems to me that Newman here puts his finger on the

real truth with his insistence on the power of developing the reasoning faculty as the distinguishing mark of liberal knowledge, and therefore as the criterion of excellence in mental training. When we examine our hierarchy of subjects we find that, in fact, they do more or less constitute also a hierarchy of liberal exercises, but the correspondence is not complete, as the examples we have just given go to show. It would seem then that Spencer's theory of the exact correspondence of ontological value and mental training value cannot be sustained, and that the claims of each subject to exercise the reasoning powers must be considered independently.

It is interesting to note, in confirmation of the view just expressed, that M. Maritain in his *Education at the Cross-Roads*, published in 1943, though quoting Spencer's dictum with approbation, states that he accepts it " from quite another philosophical point of view," [11] which seems to coincide with that of Newman. Here is M. Maritain's gloss on Spencer.

The knowledge which is " of most worth,"—I don't mean which has the most practical value, I mean which makes the mind penetrate into those things which are the richest in truth and intellegibility—such knowledge affords by itself the best mental training, for it is by grasping the object and having itself seized and vitalized by truth that the human mind gains both its strength and its freedom. It is not by the gymnastics of its faculties, it is by truth that it is set free, when truth is really known, that is vitally assimilated by the insatiable activity which is rooted in the depths of self.[12]

We may note that in introducing this topic M. Maritain wisely prescinds from the vexed question of the transfer of abilities, and we may do the same. Whatever be the truth about it, we are on safe ground when we follow Newman's simple rule and take care that our curriculum at every stage gives due prominence to those studies which enrich the mind with knowledge " impregnated by reason."

4

In 1867 John Stuart Mill, on his installation as Rector of the University of St Andrews, delivered the usual Inaugural Address, taking as his subject the nature of University Education. This address is familiar enough to students of the history and theory of education, and I need only stress one or two points in which it either differs from or concurs with Newman's *Idea*. The plan is a simple one. Mill takes in turn all the great divisions of human knowledge, literature, mathematics, the physical sciences, philosophy, theology and the fine arts, and gives a masterly, if not always completely accurate exposition of their effect on the human mind. I will postpone consideration of his views on theology to our next lecture, and will pass over one curious, and I think, rather aprioristic contention, namely that modern languages, history and geography should find no place in the curriculum of a university—even, it would appear, in that of a secondary school—but should be the subject of private study.

The first point of interest that strikes us is Mill's forthright claim that a university is not a place of professional education at all.

Universities are not intended to teach the knowledge required to fit men for some special mode of gaining their livelihood. Their object is not to make skilful lawyers, or physicians, or engineers, but capable and cultivated human beings.[13]

It is just arguable that this is merely a rhetorical exaggeration intended to emphasise, as Newman did, the paramount importance of liberal as compared with professional education. But the words are strong, and are confirmed by the concession which Mill shortly makes that " there is something to be said for having them (professional schools) in the same localities, and under the same general superintendence, as the establishments devoted to education properly so-called."[14] This obviously implies that, in Mill's opinion, there is also something to be said for having them completely separate.

Whatever way we look at it, this contention that a university is not a professional school is a curious one. First of all, historically it is palpably untrue. The mediaeval universities were all professional schools, even though the faculty of arts came to play such a predominant rôle in them, and they have been the general model for universities ever since. It is this historical aspect that we must always insist on when we approach the question of what is the essence of a university. A university is a human institution, set up by the free purpose of men. It is not an *a priori* concept, nor is it a creation whose essence is determined by the constitution of nature. We must, therefore, ask ourselves not what we think a university must be, but what in point of fact it has been and is.

Again, if Mill were ignoring the historical question, and declaring what he thought should be the consitituion of the ideal university, it is strange that he should propose in such a casual manner a change so radical as the separation of the two traditional fields of education. It is obvious that, in practice, no absolutely hard and fast division can be made between liberal and professional studies, and that there is a great deal to be said for the commingling of their boundaries and for the close association of their respective exponents. Newman, for all his insistence on the liberal ideal, and in spite of the fact that his treatise is called *The Idea of a University*, is not at all so extreme in his views. For him the liberal mind is " the special fruit " of the education provided at a university; such education is " the main purpose "[15] of a university. He obviously however admits professional training as a secondary aim. We recall in fact how in his *Seventh Discourse* he actually claims, as against Mill, that the work of professors of Law, Medicine or other professional subjects is more effective in a university than outside it,[16] and how in his constitution of the Catholic University he followed the traditional mediaeval model of a combined liberal and professional school.

5

With regard to the aims and effects of liberal education we find that Mill is in complete agreement with Newman. Speaking of professional pursuits, he says:

> Whether those whose speciality they are, will learn them as a branch of intelligence or as a mere trade, and whether, having learnt them, they will make a wise and

conscientious use of them or the reverse, depends less on the manner in which they are taught their profession, than upon what sort of minds they bring to it—what kind of intelligence and of conscience the general system of education has developed in them. Men are men before they are lawyers, or physicians or merchants or manufacturers; and if you make them capable and sensible men, they will make themselves capable and sensible lawyers or physicians. What professional men should carry away with them from a University, is not professional knowledge, but that which should direct the use of their professional knowledge, and bring the light of general culture to illuminate the technicalities of a special pursuit.[17]

Mill is at one also with Newman in detecting as the characteristic of liberal knowledge its development of the power of reason. His vindication of classical studies is a famous passage, and every page of it echoes this theme. Grammar is to be studied because " the structure of every sentence is a lesson in logic," and the grammar of the ancient languages has a peculiar value because it has the most definite rules and provides distinct forms for the greatest number of distinctions in thought.[18] The classical languages are the best model of style because their secret is " the perfection of good sense."[19] Their content is to be prized because it contains

the wisdom of life: the rich store of experience of human nature and conduct, which the acute and observing minds of those ages, aided in their observations by the greater simplicity of manners and life, consigned to their writings, and most of which retains all its value.[20]

When we come to Mill's consideration of the value of the physical sciences, we find again this insistence on their power of developing and exercising the human reason. Much that he says is excellent, and he develops more fully ideas that are only mentioned in passing by Newman. But he is guilty of certain fallacies and exaggerations. He claims quite rightly that the proper occupation of the intellect is the pursuit of truth, and that the two processes by which we attain to truth are observation and reasoning. But he then claims that these two processes " have been carried to their greatest known perfection in the physical sciences." [21]

> Mathematics and its application to astronomy and natural philosophy, are the most complete example of the discovery of truths by reasoning; experimental science of their discovery by direct observation. [22]

And observe the reason he gives.

> In all these cases we know that we can trust the operation, because the conclusions to which it has led have been found true by subsequent trial. It is by the study of these, then, that we may hope to qualify ourselves for distinguishing truth, in cases where there do not exist the same ready means of verification.[23]

There is a grave fallacy involved in this statement. The fact that we can establish by experimental means the truth of a conclusion does not give us the slightest guarantee that the process of reasoning by which we arrived at it was correct. False reasoning can lead to a correct result, as any schoolmaster knows who has corrected mathematical exercises. Experiment may give us greater certainty of the result, but it is by the addition of a different motive for certainty, and not by any strengthening of the motive provided by reason. Hence, the fact that we have confirmed the results of reasoning by experiment in certain problems does not assist us in the least in approaching problems which do not admit of experimental verification.

Again, there is at least a grave exaggeration in Mill's claim that

it is chiefly from mathematics we realize the fact that there actually is a road to truth by means of reasoning; that anything real, and which will be found true when tried, can be arrived at by a mere operation of the mind.[24]

You can see that there is here again the assumption that the validity of reasoning can be tested by experimental confirmation of the result, but there is also a quite insupportable dismissal of the innumerable instances of reasoning in other studies, not to speak of everyday life, by which we can attain to absolute truth.

We are not surprised to find in the following lines a reference to

the flagrant abuse of mere reasoning in the days of the schoolmen, when men argued confidently to supposed facts of outward nature without properly establishing their premises, or checking the conclusions by observation,

and a statement that this abuse created a prejudice in the modern mind against deductive reasoning " until the

prodigious applications of mathematics to physical science
. . . slowly and tardily restored the reasoning process to
the place which belongs to it as a source of real knowledge."[25]
If we take the term " schoolmen " to apply to the late age of
scholasticism, it may be granted that there is some truth in
the charge that excessive apriorism led to a reaction, but
we detect in Mill's words an ignorance of the great edifice
of true scholasticism and its perennial vindication of reason.
To hold, as he does, that " mathematics, pure and applied,
are still the great conclusive example of what can be done
by reasoning," [26] is to close one's eyes to the whole domain
of theology and philosophy, and gravely to belittle such
fields of intellectual activity as historical, philological or
archaeological research.

These qualifications being made, it may be said that
Mill's analysis of the effects of mathematical reasoning on
the mind is profound and accurate, as is also his exposition
of the value of scientific observation and deduction. What
he has to say about the enlarging effect on the mind of logic,
politics and political economy, psychology and metaphysics
is all very true and stimulating, if we prescind from the
underlying assumption that certainty cannot be attained in
these sciences, or at least that they afford a lesser degree of
certainty than can be reached by either mathematical
reasoning or experimental observation.

6

We now go forward almost a century in educational
history, to find the topics discussed by the *Edinburgh
Reviewers*, Copleston, Davison, Newman, Spencer and Mill

as actual and provocative as ever. We will first direct our attention to beyond the Atlantic, and consider one of the most thoughtful documents produced there in our day on the combined problems of secondary and university education.

In the spring of 1943 a Committee was set up by the President of Harvard University, James Bryant Conant, consisting of twelve members of the Faculties of Arts and Sciences and of Education in that university, to consider the Objectives of a General Education in a Free Society. The report of the Committee, which was published in 1945, dealt with the subject of General Education in both High School and College. Its main purpose is to attack the peculiarly American problem of diversity in the curriculum, and to establish the principles on which any form of unity should or could be founded.

This problem arises from somewhat different causes at the different levels. In the High Schools it arises from the attempt to give to all young people up to the age of seventeen, or in some States eighteen, a formal education which will be suited to their greatly varying abilities and needs. This aim, as the Report points out, is not merely a practical one, simply to fit young people for various kinds of jobs.

Its justification is quite as much one of method; to meet students on their own ground, to draw on their experience, to appeal to their hopes, and, by recognising the influence of circumstance, to mitigate it. Manual training, business training, work in mechanics and agriculture, courses in health and home economics— these and a thousand more functional adaptations of the older disciplines, such as general mathematics instead of algebra and geometry, discussion courses instead of composition and literature, study of work and government in the United States instead of formal history—all reflect in part at least the search for the right means of influencing the great mass of students who, through bent or background or both, learn little from the conventional studies. This search will continue and will almost certainly produce a yet greater diversity, . . . The present diversity of instruction in the high school reflects dimly like a clouded mirror the diversity of our society itself, and it will not be adequate until it catches the image more exactly.[27]

This diversity of aim is exaggerated by the course-unit system, a unit representing a year's work in a subject, and sixteen units being normally required for graduation. The choice of these units is governed by the type of diploma for which the student is studying, and this has the double effect of dividing the high school into a number of lesser schools, each virtually sealed off from the others, and of encouraging the student to regard his studies as a series of blocks, each a unit complete in itself.

In the colleges the main cause of diversity is the influence of vocationalism. Many of them have an openly vocational character which differentiates them from one another. Thus, besides the traditional four years liberal college, we find the agricultural college, the business college, the engineering college, the teachers' college; and even within the colleges there are forces of division. The so-called free election system, sponsored by President Eliot of Harvard in the seventies and eighties of the last century, was based on the principle that all subjects are of the same value. But, to counteract the inevitable incoherence to which it led, the system of majoring or concentrating in some field or cognate fields has arisen. The object of it was to substitute a common form of discipline for the common curriculum that had disappeared, but in practice it has tended to degenerate into higher vocational training—not indeed a thing to be condemned out of hand, but certainly tending to lead the student body further away from the possession of any common heritage of learning.

7

The aim of this Harvard Committee, therefore, is to investigate to what extent some common core of studies can be established, which, while giving due consideration to the undoubted need for diversity, will yet restore to both high school and college studies a unifying purpose and idea. It is interesting to note that the Report starts from this idea of unity, which appears to dominate American educational thought, and which may well be due to the consciousness in the American mind of the colossal task of welding great masses of immigrants and descendants of immigrants into one nation. In a more homogeneous nation the problem would rather present itself first of establishing a common core of studies calculated to benefit every type of student, its unifying effect being an immediate and most desirable consequence.

It is obvious too that when the Report speaks of a common core or a unifying element, it does not immediately envisage a curriculum of subjects, though this problem has ultimately to be faced, if any real solution is to be found. It seeks first of all to establish the purpose, the general character of this core or element, and we recognise at once that this purpose and this character are identical with those of Liberal Education as propounded by Newman. The Harvard Report prefers the term " General Education," mainly to avoid the false impressions to which we have earlier alluded, that liberal education is restricted to a literary or classical education, or that it is the preserve of the privileged few. But when the definitions or descriptions of General Education are given, we recognise them at once. It is " that part of a student's whole education which looks first of all to his life as a responsible human being and citizen." [28] " If one cling to the root meaning of liberal as that which befits or helps to make free men, then general and liberal education have identical goals." [29]

The Report claims that this General Education is of particular value to a democratic society because it makes a man truly free in the sense that he can judge and plan for himself, so that he can truly govern himself, is " universal in his motives and sympathies," and thus is a truly civilised man, " a citizen of the entire universe." [30] In the introduction to the Report by President Conant the identity of General Education and the liberal tradition is deliberately stated.

Neither the mere acquisition of information nor the development of special skills and talents can give the broad basis of understanding which is essential if our civilization is to be preserved . . . Unless the educative process includes at *each level of maturity* some continuing contact with those fields in which value judgments are of prime importance, it must fall far short of the ideal. The student in high school, in college, and in graduate school, must be concerned, in part at least, with the words " right " and " wrong " in both the ethical and the mathematical sense. Unless he feels the impact of those general ideas and aspirations which have been a deep moving force in the lives of men, he runs the risk of partial blindness.[31]

In all these passages we hear the echoes of the words of Newman and before him of Davison and Copleston, and realise how perennial is the ideal which they express.

8

It is obvious that we cannot follow in detail the suggestions made by this Report for the drawing up of general courses whether in high school or college. We can only pick out a few stages in the reasoning followed, and show how the root problems dealt with by Newman keep constantly recurring. For instance, at the outset the Report establishes a fundamental difference between the natural sciences and what it calls the humanities, evidently including in this latter term not only literature but also philosophy. The natural sciences, it says, " describe, analyze and explain "; the humanities " appraise, judge and criticize. In the first, a statement is judged as true or false; in the second a result is judged as good or bad."[32] We recall at once Davison's words endorsed, though he does not quote them exactly, by Newman in his *Seventh Discourse*, that the literary-historical-philosophical group of subjects " are all under the control of the same power of moral reasoning. There is a better and a worse in the execution of them." [33] The Harvard Report introduces two interesting distinctions. It points out correctly that formal logic and mathematics occupy a kind of intermediate position. They help in reducing to abstract terms the concrete data of the physical sciences. Yet in essence, they belong to the scientific group. Their task is to ascertain, not to evaluate. The Report also claims, again it would seem correctly, that what are commonly called in America the Social Studies, history, economics and politics, partake of the nature of both groups, since the scientific method must be largely employed to quarry out the facts on which they are based, and yet these facts are such as to call for that assessment of better and worse which so peculiarly develops the liberal point of view.

Yet, while claiming for the humanities in the wide sense this special liberating power, the Report points out that this does not mean that physical science is incapable of liberal treatment. It says:

> In his altogether unjustified humility the scientist wrongly interprets the distinction between liberal and illiberal in terms of the distinction between the humanities and the sciences. Plato and Cicero would have been very much surprised to hear that geometry, astronomy, and the sciences of nature in general are excluded from the humanities. [34]

While noting that the Report here uses the term humanities in a rather confusing way as equivalent to liberal studies of all kinds, whereas it has just used it to denote non-scientific

studies, we may agree with this dictum, and recall also
that the traditional Seven Liberal Arts, the Trivium and
Quadrivium, included Mathematics and Astronomy.

Again, the abilities which should be developed by
General Education are thus summarised by the Report:
" to think effectively, to communicate thought, to make
relevant judgments, to discriminate among values." [35] When
we examine the detailed description given of these abilities,
we find that they are all among those enumerated by
Newman as the fruit of that philosophical knowledge which
he defines as " knowledge impregnated by reason," [36] the
" digestion of what we receive into the substance of our
previous state of thought," " the knowledge, not only of
things, but of their mutual and true relations." [37]

Thus " effective " or " logical " thinking involves, according
to the Report " the ability to discern a pattern of relation-
ships—on the one hand to analyse a problem into its
component elements, and on the other to recombine these
. . . so as to reach a solution." [38] The " effective thinker
. . . is not satisfied merely with noting facts, but his mind
ever soars to implications." [39]

> The making of relevant judgments involves the ability
> of the student to bring to bear the whole range of ideas
> upon the area of experience. It is not now a question of
> apprehending more relationships within ideas, but of
> applying these to actual facts. [40]

The discrimination among values " covers not only awareness
of different kinds of value but of their relations, including
a sense of relative importance and of the mutual dependence
of means and ends." [41] The word " value " is one that is much

overworked in modern pedagogical writings, and for a scholastically trained mind it is much more satisfying to substitute the term " good," or in some cases " the criterion of goodness," or again " the power to discern and appraise the good." The Harvard Report rightly points out that values or " good " may be of different kinds. Its classification is rather more popular than scientific.

There are the obvious values of character, like fair play, courage, self-control, the impulse of beneficence and humanity; there are the intellectual values, like the love of truth and the respect for intellectual enterprise in all its forms; there are the aesthetic values, like good taste and the appreciation of beauty,[42]

and later it speaks of moral values in the strict sense of ethical standards.

At the close of this section there occurs a statement which we should at first be inclined to reject, and which, indeed, seems to be in contradiction with the basic distinction set up by the Report itself between the natural sciences and the humanities. " Discrimination in values," it is stated, " is developed by the study of all the three areas of learning," [43] these areas being the physical sciences, the social sciences and the humanities. It will certainly be granted that the other abilities enumerated, to think effectively, to communicate thought, and to make relevant judgments, could be developed by scientific studies, and we recall that Newman allowed that physical science could develop such qualities of the liberal mind. But the method of physical sciences excludes the appraisal of the good. However, it is apparent that what the Report means is that, in fact, science should be taught with reference to its results to man, though this really is to cross the boundary from science into economics or even ethics.

In the natural sciences facts are studied in abstraction from values. But this separation, while pragmatically valid, leads to disaster if treated as final. Values are rooted in facts, and human ideals are somehow a part of nature.[44]

Similarly, in the case of the social sciences, facts are not the whole truth.

The historian or social scientist as *teacher* should probably go further and present to the student the human past and human institutions not merely as facts but as attempted embodiments of the good life in its various phases.[45]

9

Into the detailed proposals of the Harvard Report for the provision of General Education, it is needless for us to go. In general, it may be said that the Report favours both in High School and College a core course for all students including the three large areas of physical science, the social sciences and the humanities. In the High School study in these areas should occupy half the student's time and be spread over the entire four year course. The Report, however, rightly points out that there must be elasticity in the planning of courses, and emphasises the fact that, while it is easy to provide for the needs of gifted pupils, it is exceedingly difficult to provide for the less gifted, who form the large majority. This difficulty is so frankly acknowledged, and so clearly set out that it must raise serious doubts as to the possibility of providing General Education by formal schooling for all children up to seventeen or eighteen, and hence as to the desirability of compulsory formal schooling for them at all. For the Colleges it is proposed that in the first two years there should be six courses in General Education, of which one must be taken from each of the three great areas. The Report does not in any way envisage the abolition of specialisation, realising both its value and its inevitability, but hopes to counteract it by these general courses.

A minor point of interest is the proposal that the humanities in the General Course should be studied by the so-called Great Texts system, which I believe obtains in some other American Colleges, the aim of such a course being according to the Report, " the fullest understanding of the work read rather than of men or periods represented, craftsmanship evinced, historic or literary development shown or anything else." [46] Among the optional courses for General Education it is proposed that there should be Philosophy which, the Report states, may be for some students " one of the most vital of intellectual experiences," [47] though this recommendation is tempered by the fact that the Report acknowledges, and does not feel called on to combat, the prevailing doubt as to the objectivity of any philosophy.

However, what interests us is not so much the practical proposals of this Harvard Report, which are necessarily conditioned by special circumstances, as the general principles on which they are based. Whether the writings of Newman actually inspired these principles, I cannot tell. But it is certainly remarkable to find how exactly the Report agrees with him in its emphasis on the value of general or liberal education, in its analysis of the nature of that education and of the mental gifts which it produces, and in its insistence on the special, though not exclusive power of the literary-historical-philosophical group of subjects to impart it.

We recall too how insistent Newman was on the fact that his advocacy of liberal education implied no disrespect to the professions, no blindness to the fact that a university is a professional school, but only an awareness of the difference between the two aims, and of the dangerous limitations of professional training. The Harvard Report utters this same warning.

> We are living in an age of specialism, in which the avenue to success for the student often lies in his choice of a specialized career, whether as a chemist, or an engineer, or a doctor, or a specialist in some form of business or of manual or technical work . . . Specialism is the means for advancement in our mobile social structure; yet we must envisage the fact that a society controlled wholly by specialists is not a wisely ordered society. We cannot, however, turn away from specialism. The problem is how to save general education and its values within a system where specialism is necessary.[48]

The Report points out that specialism not only enhances what it well calls " the centrifugal forces in society "[49] but that even from the point of view of economic success, it has its limitations.

> Specializing in a vocation makes for inflexibility in a world of fluid possibilities. Business demands minds

capable of adjusting themselves to varying situations
and of managing complex human institutions. Given the
pace of economic progress, techniques alter speedily;
and even the work in which a student has been trained
may no longer be useful when he is ready to earn a
living or soon after.[50]

The Report makes the further pertinent observation that
general education helps men to develop the power of
summing up the abilities of others on whom they must rely
in matters of which they have themselves no knowledge,
and quotes the remark of William James that " an educated
person knows a good man when he sees one." Such a power
is of particular value in a democratic form of society, where
so much depends on the election of reliable representatives.

10

One of the ablest of the many Reports published under
the aegis of the English Ministry, formerly Board, of Education is the *Report of the Consultative Committee on Secondary
Education with special reference to Grammar Schools and Technical
High Schools*, published in 1938 and commonly known as
the Spens Report. The second Appendix to this Report,
contributed by the Secretary, Dr R. F. Young, is a lucid,
and on the whole reliable sketch of the development of the
idea of liberal studies. We will refer more fully later on to
this Appendix, but we may note at once that, in a footnote
on page 411, it refers both to T. H. Huxley's definition of
a liberally educated man and to Newman's exposition of
liberal education in *The Idea of a University*. Excuse is made
for not dealing more fully with either, since they apply

properly to liberal education at the university stage. The note however adds: " It is probable, however, that these and similar descriptions of general academic culture exercised some influence on the development of the conception of liberal education at the grammar-school age."

The question whether Newman's ideas actually influenced grammar-school curricula in England is one that would be exceedingly difficult to answer, but what is quite certain is that the principles which he laid down are undoubtedly valid for education at any stage. It may be granted that they are of much greater importance at the university stage, since it is there that the problems of specialisation and vocationalism become acute. But even in the elementary school, and to a greater extent in the secondary school, the fundamental problem arises of the nature of the various types of knowledge imparted, those which, in the main, convey factual knowledge, and those which also tend to develop the reasoning power. In the elementary school, the problem is only inchoate, because the bulk of the work consists in the mastering of the processes of reading and writing, which are largely mechanical, and because other subjects such as mathematics, history and geography must have, at this stage, a largely factual character. The child must be given matter on which to reason, even though he is all the time being led on to reason. But in the secondary stage the reasoning process is being rapidly developed, and as this stage progresses, the problem of balancing the acquisition of facts with the acquiring of the power of reasoning becomes ever more urgent and difficult, according as the task of preparation for a vocation becomes more immediate.

It will, in fact, be seen that the question of liberal and non-liberal subjects does crop up frequently in the pages of this valuable report. Thus, at the outset of its consideration of the curriculum of the Grammar School, the Report records that the first definite outline of this curriculum in modern times in England was given by the Board of Education in its Regulations for Secondary Schools in 1904. It was there stated that provision must be made for a " general education of a kind and amount suited to an age range at least from 12 to 17." The Spens Report rightly remarks that the term " general education " is a loose and unsatisfactory one. It is sometimes used to denote the study of a wide range of subjects. Again, it may mean a training which is considered suitable for every future occupation as opposed to a training which specifically prepares for a single calling, and it may also mean a training which aims at the development in the pupil of certain attributes, habits, skills, sentiments and attitudes of mind, as well as the possession and use of knowledge.[51] From our study of Newman we are familiar with all these meanings, and we recognise that they express different aspects of liberal education. The wide curriculum, as we have seen, is not essential, but *ceteris paribus* is a help, and we know that liberal education is suitable for every future occupation precisely because it develops certain attributes of mind. The Spens Report contents itself with saying that, to prevent confusion, it will avoid the use of the term " general education," but we shall find that in its prescriptions it always has in view a type of knowledge which we recognise as liberal knowledge in Newman's sense.

Thus it sets down rightly a general aim for the Grammar School, the training of the pupil, " first as a person with a body, a mind and a spirit, second as a future citizen of a democratic country, and third as one who will have work of some kind or other to do for a livelihood." [52] We may grant that we find nothing about bodily training in Newman's *Discourses*. It is a question which decreases in importance as the student grows older, and which may be almost entirely left to himself at the university stage. In any case, let me again remind you that Newman never intended his *Discourses* to be a complete treatise on education. Even with regard to university education we know that we have to go to his other writings and to his practice as Rector of the Catholic University to get his full teaching. It is not, however, necessary to stress the fact that the other aims set out by the Spens Report, the training of the individual in himself and with reference to his fellow men, and his preparation for a definite vocation, are, in very broad outline, the plan of the whole series of Newman's *Discourses*.

There is also a very interesting comment on the importance of the curriculum. The Report rightly says that the total education of the child depends on many other imponderable factors, the influence of the parents, the teachers, even, in the background, of the State, and numerous extracurricular activities. But, it adds, " the curriculum, in the narrow sense of the world, must always retain its central place." [53] This contention certainly seems sound. It would I imagine, be a task quite beyond the power of the human intellect to assess the relative effects on the student of the various influences that mould his total being, but we can quite safely say that both the form and content of the formal curriculum, to which he devotes so much time, and which is the constant instrument of his formation, must play a very great part. The point is too large to permit of more than an indication here, but I venture to say that in this consideration we find at least a partial answer to those critics of Newman who have found his exposition of liberal education excessively intellectual. Once again, let us recall that he was not writing a treatise on the total education of men, but an exposition of the difference between two great types of knowledge and the part they play in that total education. His insistence, therefore, on the power of the curriculum is a perfectly just one, but indicates no disregard for the innumerable other influences, spiritual, psychological and corporal, that go to produce the whole man.

We cannot do more here than glance briefly at the other passages in this Report which are germane to our subject. We find, for instance, a very reasoned plea that stress should be laid on the study of the national language, history and artistic traditions. This plea, however, is not based on any kind of nationalistic exclusiveness, but on the ground that it is in their own national traditions that English boys and girls will first become aware of the common Western European tradition.[54] We recall how eloquently that tradition was defended by Newman in his Address on Christianity and Letters. The Spens Report does not enter into any detailed defence of it, but assumes rightly that it is a heritage worthy of preservation, and one on which liberal education is largely, though not exclusively based.

Again, we hear the echoes of a great many familiar thoughts in a passage in which the Report sets out what should be aimed at in the teaching of those subjects in which the intellect is more intimately concerned.

Education means far more than the acquisition of a number of disconnected fragments of information with such power of observation, clear thought and expression as may have been picked up on the way. The value of information has been grossly exaggerated in all systems of education and is grossly exaggerated in popular esteem . . . The accumulation of facts leads too often to a surfeit of inert, uncodified knowledge leading nowhere. It is unfortunate that it is a tendency of school examinations to attach a far greater value to a knowledge of facts than to the ability to use them. As Henri Poincaré once said: " Science is built up with facts as a house is built up with stones, but a collection of facts is no more a science than a heap of stones is a house," and this statement is not without its application to other subjects. We do not wish to depreciate the value of information, but unless facts are utilisable and intended to be used, they serve no purpose . . . The educative effects of any branch of study consist in its suitability and usefulness in providing material for thought, for the perception of relations, for matter on which the pupil may strengthen his powers of reasoning; in its invitation to the pupil to form interests or sentiments about a subject; in its assistance in the building up of such habits as perseverance, sanity of judgment and initiative.[55]

We would, however, have to disagree, I think, with the next sentence which states: " But these values inhere, not in particular subjects, but in the spirit of study." This statement would be true if it merely meant that every intellectual subject is capable of liberal treatment, but we have seen that it cannot be accepted if it implies that all subjects lend themselves equally to such treatment.

Among the courses which the Report recommends for study by all Grammar School pupils at some stage is one in general science, and in this the liberal or philosophical approach is recommended. The Report suggests the following three main aims of such a course:

(i) It should give pupils some knowledge of the natural laws which operate in the universe, and of their application. This is an appeal to wonder and interest, as well as to utility. (We recall here how Newman chooses the marvels of the physical world as one instance of the type of knowledge which produces enlargement of mind).

(ii) As a complement to historical studies, it should reveal the influence of scientific thought and achievement in the evolution of our present-day civilisation and perhaps even more important, it should indicate its possibilities, for good and evil alike, in the future of the human race. The appeal here is to social interest and social utility.

(iii) It should give children an introduction to scientific methods of thought and investigation. This appeal is essentially one to the intellect and, in so far as it is achieved, science takes the place of the mediaeval study of logic. [56]

The Report points out that most existing science courses lay too much stress on the third aim, which has mainly a value for the pupil who is to pursue a scientific career. It also recommends that science should be taught to every child—a debatable opinion, but one with which I personally agree. For these children the value of the course will be not utilitarian but liberal. It will be to the individual pupil, as the Report puts it, " an element in his own life and useful to him as the indispensable background of much current thought." [57] It will, therefore, rightly stress those elements of personal and social interest which mark the first two aims set forth by the Report.

II

I have already referred to the second Appendix to this Report [58] as giving an able and lucid history of the concept of liberal education. It traces the evolution of the traditional Seven Liberal Arts, which for the Greeks were the handmaids of philosophy, for the Romans the successive stages leading to perfection in Rhetoric, and for the mediaeval schools the foundation for the three great professional faculties of Theology, Law and Medicine. It points out, probably correctly, that the confusion sometimes found between liberal and classical education may be traced back to the Renaissance scholars who regarded the technique of style (*eloquentia*) in Latin or the vernacular, and the miscellaneous learning required for understanding the classical author (*eruditio*) as the main objects of collegiate education. In practice in the grammar-schools the old Trivium was restricted to grammar and rhetoric; dialectic and all the subjects of the Quadrivium being gathered under the general heading of *eruditio*, which was the mark of an advanced scholar. In England this purely linguistic character of the grammar-schools, and the consequent confusion between a liberal and a classical education became more marked owing to the revived interest in Greek in the second half of the eighteenth century.

At the close of this Appendix [59] there occurs a curious confusion of thought which goes to show that our efforts to form clear and accurate ideas on the subject of liberal education have not been unnecessary. A number of quotations is given, with apparent approbation, sustaining the view that the distinction between liberal and technical, or vocational education is a fallacious one, that all liberal education is technical and all technical education liberal. The most extreme of them is, as we might expect, from John Dewey, in his *Democracy and Education* (1922) page 305. Here are a few lines.

Of all the segregations of educational values . . . that between culture and utility is probably the most fundamental. While the distinction is often thought to be intrinsic and absolute, it is really historical and social. It originated, so far as conscious formulation is concerned, in Greece, and was based upon the fact that the truly human life was lived only by a few who subsisted upon the results of the labour of others. This fact affected the psychological doctrine of the relation of intelligence and desire, theory and practice.

It was embodied in a political theory of a permanent division of human beings into those capable of a life of reason and hence having their own ends, and those capable only of desire and work, and needing to have their ends provided by others. The two distinctions, psychological and political, translated into educational terms, effected a division between a liberal education, having to do with the self-sufficing life of leisure devoted to knowing for its own sake, and a useful, practical training for mechanical occupations, devoid of intellectual and aesthetic content . . . The problem of education in a democratic society is to do away with the dualism . . .

Our studies enable us to make two criticisms of this and the other quotations. Firstly, we have seen that the historical origin of the idea of liberal education has nothing whatever to do with the question whether such a thing actually exists. Even if the Greeks based it on their aristocratic concept of society—and this is open to question—what we want to know is whether it can be discerned even in the most democratic form of education. And secondly, we have seen that, in practice, all liberal knowledge can be called technical in the sense that it may be used for the benefit of mankind, and that even the most mechanical pursuits are accompanied by some form of reasoning which gives them at least an inchoately liberal character. But the distinction must be recognised, and is in fact recognised even by those writers who claim to abolish it, between those pursuits which demand and develop—to use Newman's splendid term— " knowledge impregnated by reason," and those in which such knowledge is reduced to an inconsiderable minimum. We would say that the problem of education in a democratic society is not to do away with the dualism, but to give to each student that combination of both types of knowledge which is best suited to his abilities and his aims.

9

THE RESTORATION OF ORDER

I

IN THIS LECTURE we propose to consider the bearing of Newman's teaching concerning the place of religion in education on our present-day educational problems, especially at the university level. Let us ask ourselves first what has happened since Newman's day, to what extent do the problems he envisaged still exist and what new ones have arisen.

Obviously, the root problem which he discussed in his *Discourses*, the exclusion of religion from education, is just as alive as ever. The old liberal view, that religion is a private affair and therefore irrelevant to the pursuit of other branches of knowledge, is even more confidently and far more widely held than in the days when Newman belaboured it in the Dublin Rotunda. Side by side with it we find that more pragmatic form of liberalism, professed in Newman's day by the founders of London University, which passes no judgment on the intrinsic merits of religious thought as an intellectual study—is sometimes, indeed, favourable to it—but holds that there is no way of making public provision for its teaching which does not infringe upon the rights of some section of the community. The more militant form of liberalism, that which rejects religion as something non-intellectual and therefore to be wholly opposed, has certainly gained ground. Newman gives in his *Ninth Discourse* a skilful analysis of its causes, but his whole approach to his subject implies that he considered the more tolerant form of liberalism to be the prevalent school of thought in the England of his day. How far positive antagonism to religion has grown since then, it is difficult to say, but that it has grown is undeniable. Its growth is a direct result of the spread of materialism in its various forms, and it received a powerful impetus in modern times in certain countries from the emergence of the peculiar form of materialism that is manifested in the various brands of totalitarianism.

But in addition to these older forms of hostility to religion, we find a much more subtle phenomenon, one which is therefore even more dangerous, namely the denial of all objective values in education, including of course religious values. This denial is found in somewhat different forms in the two main schools of thought that have dominated education during the past fifty years, naturalism and pragmatism. It is more implicit in naturalism, the theory that educational aims should be derived from a study of the person to be educated, with its consequent emphasis on biological influences in the life of the child, on the study of the psychological processes involved in the act of learning, on the power of environment and on methods of study whereby, in various ways, the child tends to assume the functions of the teacher. It is more explicit in pragmatism, whose veteran exponent, John Dewey, defines education as " the formation of right mental and moral habitudes in respect to the difficulties of contemporary social life," [1] and who holds as a corollary that "we cannot establish a hierarchy of values among studies . . . the only ultimate value which can be set up is just the process of living itself." [2]

It is noteworthy that these two schools of thought have exercised their fullest influence on elementary education, and their least on university education. One can only guess at the reasons for this, but one cannot help suspecting that the inherent contradictions of these systems become clearer according as the minds of those to whom they are applied become more mature and independent. I would venture to say that the tenets of naturalism simply drop out of sight in the university, except in the department of education, and even there they are unconsciously treated as sauce for the young goose rather than for the adult gander. Pragmatism, however, though less heard of in the universities as a formally accepted principle, is greatly in evidence in that informal guise which is commonly called the technological bias.

This bias has been admirably described and criticised in a very recent work, *The Crisis in the University*,[3] by Sir Walter Moberly, Chairman of the University Grants Committee, and I feel that I cannot improve on his analysis.[4] He points out how the traditional Christo-Hellenic tradition, which inspired the older English universities, and indeed most of the universities of the world a century ago, yielded to the liberal tradition with its insistence on the value of learning for learning's sake, on the independence of learning from Church or State or commerce or industry, on openness of mind and detachment, on the liberty and initiative of the student. In this liberal tradition we see at least a certain impatience with objective standards, and in some cases, a repudiation of them, as in that extreme form of liberalism that flourished, and to some extent still flourishes in the American universities under the title of the elective system. Today, however, the liberal tradition has been largely ousted by the technological tradition, which is less a philosophy than a practical urge, brought about by the fact that the growth and achievements of applied science have forced the universities to devote far more of their time and energies to the training of workers in this field, and also by the fact that this branch of study treats of what is of vital interest to the common run of men. Applied science is distinctive both in its aims and methods. Its aim is frankly to material welfare of man, its methods are empirical, analytic and selective. It distrusts abstract reasoning, and it tends to confine itself to those fields which yield practical results.

The fruits of this technological tradition are many and disastrous. There has been bred a shrinking from the contentious issues of politics and religion. The effect of this was not so noticeable up to the end of the last century, because fixed ways of thinking actually persevered, even when their rational basis was denied or doubted. But today the very fundamentals of right and wrong living are being denied, and clamour for reassertion. The neutrality that is affected in academic circles is a false one, concealing marked prejudices and assumptions in the fields of politics, religion and ethics. This neutrality has helped to produce a fragmentation of studies, which begins even before the university, and brings the student there, in the apt wording of Sir Walter Moberly, " with his mind already set in an attitude of incuriousness outside his own restricted field." [4]   To describe what he finds in the university, Sir Walter quotes the description given of it by Archbishop William Temple as "a place where a multitude of studies are conducted, with no relation between them except those of simultaneity and juxtaposition." [5] He does not learn there the power of seeing life as a whole. He develops no sense of responsibility, because life appears to him only as a set of experiences— precisely the pragmatism of Dewey, though accepted more as an assumption or a working method than as a philosophy. He is the victim of unfaced, and therefore unproved and often false presuppositions. He is encouraged to amass knowledge of facts, but not knowledge of their value to himself or his fellow-men.

To remedy this fragmentation, which is a direct result of the abandonment of fixed values, certain remedies have been proposed, of which the most modern and most influential, because it appears to deal with the actual needs of the day, is scientific humanism.

> Today many of the younger teachers and older students find their inspiration in a blend of Francis Bacon and Karl Marx . . . The universities must be planned, and the plan must be based on the practical needs of a changing world. The criteria used in assessing these needs must be social welfare and social justice instead of the stability of a class-society. In place of the present chaos the universities must again diffuse a general culture; but that should be, not the classical culture of the ancient world, but the scientific culture of the world of to-day. [6]

This involves a thorough-going rationalism. The critical methods of the physical sciences must be applied over the whole field of knowledge. Neutrality must be abandoned. The universities must be allied with all forces making for social progress.

This programme has some attractive features. It exposes the existing lack of aim, and draws on the intellectual stimulus that comes from linking the university with what is most vital in intellectual culture. But it has also great and fatal defects. It underestimates the value of intellectual culture in itself. It subordinates the university to the social reformer. Its extreme utilitarianism defeats itself. Preoccupation with immediate problems prevents wider and deeper research. Scientific humanism fails to take account of the fact that the primary problem in social welfare is not to produce more, but to induce in man the disposition to make what is available go round.

The scientific humanists shirk three problems: the problem of values, the problem of power and the problem of the transcendental. The first two of these are closely interconnected. Scientists are now realising that scientific inventions are capable of doing great harm as well as great good, and so they can no longer plead that they can prescind from the use to be made of them. Scientists have overnight become moralists and must overhaul their equipment. They find themselves inadequate to the task, because the mere application of scientific method to psychology and sociology is not a remedy, since the conclusions come to may differ widely. Nor is the mere zeal for truth of the scientific mind a sufficient force to overcome the immense power of human antagonisms. Even if it were granted that the true scientist could always be trusted to use his knowledge for the betterment of mankind, this would not be true of the wider public that greedily avails itself of scientific achievements merely as an instrument to power.

> There is little in his (the scientist's) teachings, though there is a good deal in his practice and his implicit assumptions, to deter his pupils from becoming adventurers or Kommissars. But in crises like the present, unformulated and uncriticized assumptions are not enough; to build on them is to build on sand.[7]

The root problem is the recognition of some kind of superior " Law," that is binding because it is intrinsically right and reasonable. Together with this goes the recognition of the value of the individual, and the fact that he is not a mere subject for " conditioning."

The final challenge which scientific humanism shirks is the challenge of the supernatural. It is all-important to decide whether or not it is necessary for man to be in right relations to God in order that he may be in a healthy state. This issue is regarded as simply unimportant by the scientific humanist. He may not attack religion, but he thinks he can succeed in spite of ignoring it. The Christian feels the utter temerity of the scientific humanist in tackling the task of conditioning man to perfection.

From this very able analysis of the aims and defects of scientific humanism it will be seen that its radical defect is the incomplete assessing of intellectual and moral values. It does, indeed, go further than the teachings of what we may call the crude technologist, but the values it recognises are incomplete and insufficient.

It may be well, for the sake of clarity, to allude very briefly at this point to another remedy for the fragmentation of studies which is noted by Sir Walter Moberly, namely classical humanism.[8] Its root teaching is that there is a certain good way of life based on a systematic understanding of the structure and functions of the human mind, and that the principles of this way of living were laid down once and for all by the Greeks and Romans and have become part of the common intellectual stock of Europe. As thus enunciated, and as divorced from the teachings of Christianity, it is propounded only by a small and diminishing group of scholars. It fails mainly because it is inadequate to master the volcanic passions of this modern world, and because it understates the power and value of scientific knowledge.

2

Turning now to the question of how far Newman's teaching provides a remedy for the evils just outlined, we must begin by making it clear that we are not claiming any exclusive credit for Newman as an exponent of the truths he propounds. Many of them are simply commonplaces of Christianity. They are to be found in the writings of the Fathers of the Church and of the great scholastics, and they largely determined the constitution of the mediaeval universities. They figure in any modern Catholic textbook of education, indeed they inspired the writings of all Christian educationists of other denominations up to quite recent times, and inspire many of them still. Newman's great virtue was that he propounded them so forcibly, and related them so clearly to the problems of his day, which are largely the problems of ours. Since our particular study is Newman's

Discourses, we shall find it convenient to follow them as they are found there.

We must first observe that Newman did not formally discuss that denial of objective values that is at the bottom of the troubles of our age. He was professedly addressing an audience of Christians, who still assumed certain great fundamental truths, such as the existence and nature of God and the relations between God and his creation, especially man. They were, moreover, men who assumed the validity of human knowledge and therefore the objectivity of the order which they perceived in the universe. Hence they had fairly unanimous views as to the purpose of man, and had no doubts that the various sciences actually did convey to him knowledge which would help him, to a greater or less extent, in the achievement of that purpose. Newman's main aim was to bring home to them that the various sciences are of their nature fragmentary, and that they require the help of one another to perfect the mind of man, whilst even within their own bounds their influence will be more or less great according to the wider or narrower field of truth which they explore.

Nevertheless, the line of his argument is most helpful in approaching this problem of objective values. Newman, it is true, simply assumed that such values existed. He could confidently ask his hearers to grant that

all that exists, as contemplated by the human mind, forms one large system or complex fact, and this of course resolves itself into an indefinite number of particular facts, which, as being portions of one whole, have countless relations of every kind, one towards another. Knowledge is the apprehension of these facts, whether in themselves, or in their mutual positions and bearings.[9]

He could also assume, as we have seen, the hierarchy of values in these facts

from the internal mysteries of the Divine Essence down to our own sensations and consciousness, from the most solemn appointments of the Lord of all down to what may be called the accident of the hour, from the most glorious seraphim down to the vilest and most noxious of reptiles.[10]

When speaking of the study of man, he could assume that man has relations which are more or less important, " whether his relation to God, or to his king, or to his children, or to his own component parts," [11] which more or less important relations form the subject-matter of the sciences of theology and moral philosophy, of politics, of economics and of physiology. You recall in the *Ninth Discourse* his great division of human knowledge into the three subjects: God, Man and Nature, and his claims for the primacy of theology and the superiority of humane studies to the natural sciences.

It is, of course, obvious that if Newman were propounding such a concept of truth today, it would be necessary for him, as it is for us, to adopt a more apologetic tone, and to vindicate much of what he could assume in 1852, beginning, perhaps, with the validity of knowledge. But the main line of his approach is still the right one. If there is any correct ordering of human thought, any possible establishment of a correct scale of intellectual values, it must be based on this conviction that knowledge is a valid grasp of the objective order of the world and of the relative value of its components. The definitions of education are very numerous. They vary, not only according to the philosophies of the formulators of them, but also according to the views that happen to be uppermost in their minds. All, however, agree that education is some sort of formation or perfection of man to fit him for some sort of task. That task involves inevitably the consideration of the creation that surrounds him, and if he has no certainty as to what it is, or what is the relative value of its components, then the task of education becomes impossible because it is meaningless.

Again, in assessing the causes of the present confusion and fragmentation of studies, there is much to be learned from Newman's demonstration in his *Fourth Discourse* of the tendency of the mind of man to set up some set of values which, if not corresponding to those that exist objectively, must by definition be false. You recall how he traces this tendency to the natural working of the intellect in throwing into system the objects conveyed to it by the senses, and how he notes that it shows itself in ordinary life by the common phenomenon of hasty generalisation, and in matters of research and speculation by the exaltation of one science into the key to all knowledge. There is a passage in the original *Fifth Discourse* which foreshadows remarkably the fragmentation, the emergence of false values, and the resulting scepticism, that are so typical of our day.

It seems that the human mind is ever seeking to systematize its knowledge, to base it upon principle, and to find a science comprehensive of all sciences.

And sooner than forego the gratification of this moral
appetency, it starts with whatever knowledge or science
it happens to have, and makes that knowledge serve as
a rule or measure of the universe, for want of a better,
preferring the completeness and precision of bigotry
to a fluctuating and homeless scepticism. What a singular
contrast is here between nature and theory. We see
the intellect in this instance as soon as it moves at all,
moving straight against its own conceits and falsities, and
upsetting them spontaneously, without effort, and at once.
It witnesses to a great truth in spite of its own professions
and engagements. It had promised, in the name of the
patrons of our modern Colleges and Universities, that
there need not be, and that there should not be, any
system or philosophy in knowledge and its transmission,
but that Liberal Education henceforth should be a mere
fortuitous heap of acquisitions and accomplishments;
however, here, as it so often happens elsewhere, nature is
too strong for art. She bursts violently and dangerously
through the artificial trammels laid upon her, and exercises her just rights wrongly, since she cannot rightly.
Usurpers and tyrants are the successors to legitimate
rulers sent into exile. Forthwith Private Judgment moves
forward with the implements of this or that science, to
do a work imperative indeed, but beyond its powers. It
owns the need of general principles and constituent ideas,
by taking false ones, and thus is ever impeding and
preventing unity, while it is ever attempting and thereby
witnessing to it. From the many voices crying " Order "
and " Silence," noise and tumult follow. From the very
multiplicity and diversity of the efforts after unity on

every side, this practical age has thrown up the notion of it altogether.[12]

3

When we consider Newman's exposition of the place of theology in this objective order on which intellectual order must be based, it would seem that his method of approach is of peculiar value to Catholics, and to all who share with them the fundamental beliefs of Christianity, in the struggle to restore that order to education. Roughly speaking, the difficulty that meets us is this. It is taken for granted by all outside the Catholic Church that a Catholic subordinates everything to his religion. Hence any statement that he makes concerning the restoration of order to education is regarded as being merely a concealed effort to propagate religion by means of education. We find this assumption, for instance, in a very recent work which is uniformly friendly towards Catholicism, *Glaucon, An Inquiry into the Aims of Education*, by Professor M. V. C. Jeffreys of Birmingham University.[13] " The Roman Catholics," says Professor Jeffreys, " have been most uncompromising in their maintenance of the principle of the denominational school, but their object has perhaps been to spread Catholicism rather than to improve education." If this be the impression of a friendly writer who is an earnest Christian, it is understandable that our motives must be much more suspect to those who are indifferent or hostile to religion.

Now we know that in a sense the assumption is a true one. In that objective order of truth which we believe to be the guiding norm of education, the truths of religion occupy an essential and primary place. Catholics believe that they are in possession of a large body of religious teaching which corresponds to the objective relations between God and man. It is, therefore, utterly impossible for them to promote what they believe to be true education without at the same time promoting that teaching. The main difficulty lies in the word " subordination." For those who do not believe in religion such subordination means falsification. For Catholics and for all who share their views, it means propounding all other branches of knowledge in their correct relation to religion, and therefore in accordance with objective truth.

In the task of disarming hostility to this view and securing for it at least reasonable consideration, Newman's approach to the problem of the place of religion in education is eminently helpful. We have in his *Second Discourse* what we may call the establishment of the minimum claim of religion, namely that if it be granted that it is a science, then viewed merely as one among many sciences, it has at least as much right to a place in the curriculum as any other. That established, he proceeds to the proof that it is a science, and in the *Third Discourse* that it is a science which is of unique extent and has a unique hearing on all others. That careful gradation of the question would appear to be exceedingly necessary today. If we commence by assuming that theology is all-important, we are apt to meet with an immediate assumption of our prejudice. If we start with the qualified statement that its claims at least merit serious consideration, it is unlikely that any man, unless he be hopelessly biassed, can refuse further consideration of the question. " It can be plausibly argued," says Sir Walter Moberly in the work to which we have already alluded,

" that the religious view is false, but it cannot be plausibly argued that, if true, it is less than all-important." [14]

Furthermore, if we cannot secure assent to the next stage of the argument, namely that theology is a science, and one of supreme importance, we shall have at least made it clear that we believe this claim to be forced upon us by objective fact, and have shown those who differ from us that our approach to the problem is the same as theirs. We do not start with a presupposition that theology is supreme among the sciences, and then determine our view of all others in that light. We approach the whole field of knowledge with an open mind, but believe that such an open mind reveals to us both the existence of theology as one of the sciences, and its supremacy amongst them.

A further help in the demonstration of the objective nature of our approach to the problem of religion in education is to be found in Newman's teaching as to what constitutes the " form " or " soul " of liberal education. It may be granted that this precise terminology is rarely, if ever, heard of today. But the issue involved does arise when a search is being made for some unifying principle in education, and when the claim is made that religion provides that principle. Thus, in a well-known Catholic text book, *A Catholic Philosophy of Education* by those two veterans in the field of American education, Dr John D. Redden and Dr Francis A. Ryan, of Fordham University, we find this typical statement: " Religion must, of necessity, permeate all life and education. Its teachings constitute the very core and foundation upon which all education . . . must be founded." [15] And in the Harvard Report, which we considered in our Eighth Lecture, the same teaching is recorded with respect, if not with complete approbation. Speaking of the search for some principle which will give to education the " clear, coherent meaning " which it has lost, the Report says:

> Sectarian, particularly Roman Catholic colleges, know of course their solution, which was generally shared by American colleges until less than a century ago: namely, the conviction that Christianity gives meaning and ultimate unity to all parts of the curriculum, indeed to the whole life of the college.[16]

It would appear that what Newman has to say about " the form " or " soul " of education throws light on the exact sense in which those statements are true, and also suggests a helpful line of approach in propounding them to those to whom any such claim for the primacy of theology suggests an intellectual tyranny.

We recall from our Sixth Lecture that the difference of opinion about the use of the term " form " or " soul " of education really resolves itself into a question of the suitability of a metaphor. A " form," as we recall, is a principle postulated by scholastic philosophy in the composition of matter, or in the composition of the human substance, and it cannot possibly be attributed literally to a body of knowledge. The point at issue, therefore, is whether there is one feature of the whole body of knowledge which may be fairly compared to a " form " or " soul," because it confers unity on that body. We have seen that in the papal documents of Newman's time the claim was made that the title might fairly be applied to one branch of knowledge, namely theology, on account of its supreme place, and its vital relations with every other science. The argument implied was that if theology is omitted from the total scheme of sciences, the damage done to every other science is universal and irreparable. Newman, on the other hand, claimed the title of " form " for that comprehensive quality of Liberal Knowledge that makes it approximate to objective reality with all its relations. It is obviously quite an open question which of these two claims is the more just, and it is clear that either application of the term " form " or " soul " may be used without prejudice to the other. But in our task of trying to restore order and unity, it would seem wiser, with Newman, not to emphasise in the first place that unity which theology gives to the curriculum. I have acknowledged that I think Newman was mistaken in attributing to the papal documents any suggestion that theology in some way affects the intrinsic principles of the other sciences—an error, which, as we have seen, is rejected by the Vatican Council—but it may be granted that to present the claims of theology to minds not previously prepared, might well give rise to such a misinterpretation.

Such a preparation is provided by Newman's insistence on the comprehensive nature of liberal knowledge as being its " form " or " soul " in the sense of giving to it its unity; for this insistence once again emphasises the purely objective nature of the Catholic approach to the problem of knowledge. Each branch of knowledge, including theology, is assessed at its own value. None can be omitted, or overstressed or understressed without destroying the harmonious unity of the whole. It is only when this objective grasp has been accomplished that the preponderating claims of theology are recognised, and then we may more fittingly and cogently urge its claims as being the " form " or " soul " of knowledge, or hold that " its teachings constitute the very core and foundation upon which all education must be founded " or that it " gives meaning and ultimate unity to all parts of the curriculum."

4

It must be emphasised, moreover, that Newman's insistence on the unifying effect of the philosophical comprehensiveness of liberal knowledge, and his choice of metaphor to describe it, do not in any way imply a denial to theology of its primary and its unifying power. The very objectivity of his approach emphasises all the more what he has to say about the essential and universal relation of theology to all other sciences.

And here we need do no more than recall his magnificent exposition in the *Third Discourse*, which we considered in our Sixth Lecture, of that truth which he sums up in the one brief question: " What science will not find one part or other of its provinces traversed by its path? (i.e. that of theology)? "[17] There is, moreover, a secondary consideration brought forward by Newman, to which we have already referred, but which we now see to be of great value in our endeavour to secure for theology its proper place in the hierarchy of knowledge. This consideration is what Newman describes as " the wide reception " of theology.

(Theology) has had a place, if not possession, in the intellectual world from time immemorial; it has been received by minds the most various, and in systems of religion the most hostile to each other . . . It occupies our language, it meets us at every turn in our literature, it is the secret assumption, too axiomatic to be distinctly professed, of all our writers; nor can we help assuming it ourselves, except by the most unnatural vigilance . . . When was the world without it? Have the systems of Atheism or Pantheism, as sciences, prevailed in the literature of nations, or received a formation or attained a completeness such as Monotheism? We find it in old Greece, and even in Rome, as well as in Judea and the East. We find it in popular literature, in philosophy, in poetry, as a positive and settled teaching, differing not at all in the appearance it presents, whether in Protestant England, or in schismatical Russia, or in the Mahometan populations, or in the Catholic Church. If ever there was a subject of thought, which had earned by prescription to be received among the studies of a University, and which could not be rejected except on the score of convicted imposture, as astrology or alchemy; if there be a science anywhere, which at least could claim not to be ignored but to be entertained, and either distinctly accepted or distinctly reprobated, or rather, which cannot be passed over in a scheme of universal instruction, without involving a positive denial of its truth, it is this ancient, this far-spreading philosophy.[18]

Newman, as we recollect, was addressing himself to men who accepted the objective truth of religious belief, and hence the dilemma which he proposed to them was completely cogent, that religion is either false or all-important. Today the number has greatly grown in the world of those who will unhesitatingly deny that there is a dilemma at all.

But even to those who reject the objective value of religious belief, its universal character is a challenge. Even if it be a delusion, there can be no adequate account of the world's history that does not accept its existence and chronicle its persistence and varied manifestations, nor can there be any serious study of human psychology that takes no notice of it.

Furthermore, whilst Newman is insistent on the fact that theology cannot determine the intrinsic principles of other sciences, he is just as insistent that they cannot trespass on theology's proper province. And here again it seems that his approach is the most effective one, for it is based not on the supremacy of theology, but merely on its nature as a science in itself, dealing with a set of truths specifically different from those dealt with by other sciences. The claim he makes in the *Fourth Discourse* that, if one science is dropped out of the circle of knowledge, another will usurp its place is, indeed, developed at length with reference to theology, but he is careful to emphasise the fact that this phenomenon is also observable with reference to secular studies, and that the usurpation in that case is just as indefensible. If, he says, " ethics were sent into banishment, its territory would soon disappear, under a treaty of partition, as it may be called, between law, political economy, and physiology." And what again, he asks " would become of the province of experimental science, if handed over to the Antiquarian Society; or of history, if surrendered out and out to Metaphysicians? "[19] The claim that theology should be undisturbed in its own province has more hope of being listened to if it is realised that this claim is based on a principle which is universally recognised with regard to other sciences, for then the issue is reduced to proving that theology is a true science with its own province and principles.

Now it is true that to present this latter claim in all its fullness involves the proof of the truth of religious belief, and this vast subject is excluded *ex professo* from Newman's *Discourses*. Yet it is obvious that the presentation of this claim will be facilitated by the examination which he makes of the nature of theology as it is conceived by all who accept its validity. This examination should go far to assure the sceptic that theology, even if it be a delusion, is at any rate a self-contained delusion, and that belief in its tenets is no barrier to the pursuit of other branches of knowledge.

We have already touched on several of the passages in which Newman thus clarifies the scope of theology. There is, for instance, in the *Third Discourse* that magnificent passage in which Newman answers his own question: " What is Theology? ", and the lengthy analysis in the *Fourth Discourse* of the precise manner in which certain secular subjects may be said to intrude on the domain of theology when they abandon their own domain. There is in the *Ninth Discourse* the examination of the causes of apparent hostility between secular knowledge and theology.

However, an even more apposite passage is to be found in the Lecture on *Christianity and Physical Science*, given by Newman in the School of Medicine in the Catholic University of Ireland in November 1855, and now included in the collection of papers commonly known as the Second Part of the *Idea of a University*. You recall that in our Sixth Lecture we made reference to a passage in another of these papers, that on *Christianity and Scientific Investigation*, in which Newman expresses the confidence of the instructed

Catholic that no real contradiction can ever occur between faith and science. The passage from the Lecture on *Christianity and Physical Science*, to which we are now turning our attention, establishes the grounds for that confidence by contrasting the scope and method of theology with that of secular knowledges, more particularly of physical science which is considered to clash more frequently with theology. To be fair to Newman we must quote at some length, for the merit of the passage, as is so often the case in his writings, derives from the painstaking and persuasive elaboration of a simple yet fundamental truth.

Let us begin with a first approximation to the real state of the case, or a broad view, which though it may require corrections, will serve at once to illustrate and to start the subject. We may divide knowledge, then, into natural and supernatural. Some knowledge, of course, is both at once; for the moment let us put this circumstance aside, and view these two fields of knowledge in themselves, and as distinct from each other in idea. By nature is meant, I suppose, that vast system of things, taken as a whole, of which we are cognizant by means of our natural powers. By the supernatural world is meant that still more marvellous and awful universe, of which the Creator Himself is the fullness, and which becomes known to us, not through our natural faculties, but by superadded and direct communication from Him. These two great circles of knowledge, as I have said, intersect; first, as far as supernatural knowledge includes truths and facts of the natural world, and secondly, as far as truths and facts of the natural world are on the other hand data for inferences about the supernatural. Still, allowing this interference to the full, it will be found, on the whole, that the two worlds and the two kinds of knowledge respectively are separated off from each other; and that, therefore, as being separate, they cannot on the whole contradict each other. That is, in other words, a person who has the fullest knowledge of one of these worlds, may be nevertheless, on the whole, as ignorant as the rest of mankind, as unequal to form a judgment, of the facts and truths of the other. He who knows all that can possibly be known about physics, about politics, about geography, ethnology and ethics, will have made no approximation whatever to decide the question whether or not there are angels, and how many are their orders; and on the other hand, the most learned of dogmatic and mystical divines—St. Augustine, St. Thomas—will not on that score know more than a peasant about the laws of motion, or the wealth of nations. I do not mean that there may not be speculations and guesses on this side and that, but I speak of any conclusion which merits to be called, I will not say knowledge, but even opinion. If, then, Theology be the philosophy of the supernatural world, and science the philosophy of the natural, Theology and Science, whether in their respective ideas, or again in their own actual fields, on the whole are incommunicable, incapable of collision, and needing, at most, to be connected, never to be reconciled . . .

But if there be so substantial a truth even in this very broad statement concerning the independence of the fields of Theology and general Science severally, and the consequent impossibility of collision between them, how much more true is that statement, from the very nature of the case, when we contrast Theology, not with Science generally, but definitely with Physics.[20] In Physics is comprised that family of sciences which is concerned with the sensible world, with the phenomena which we see, hear, and handle, or, in other words, with matter. It is the philosophy of matter. Its basis of operations, what it starts from, what it falls back on, is the phenomena which meet the senses. Those phenomena it ascertains, catalogues, compares, combines, arranges, and then uses for determining something beyond themselves, viz., the order to which they are subservient, or what we commonly call the laws of nature. It never travels beyond the examination of cause and effect. Its object is to resolve the complexity of phenomena into simple elements and principles; but when it has reached those first elements, principles, and laws, its mission is at an end; it keeps within that material system with which it began, . . . with matter it began, with matter it will end; it will never trespass into the province of mind . . .

The physical philosopher has nothing whatever to do with first causes, and will get into inextricable confusion, if he introduces them into his investigations . . . Within the limits of those phenomena (of the material world) he may speculate and prove; he may trace the operation of the laws of matter through periods of time; he may penetrate into the past, and anticipate the future; he may recount the changes which they have effected on matter, and the rise, growth and decay of phenomena; and so in a certain sense he may write the history of the material world as far as he can; still he will always advance from phenomena, and conclude upon the internal evidence which they supply. He will not come near the questions, what that ultimate element is, which we call matter, how it came to be, whether it can cease to be, whether it ever was not, whether it will ever come to nought, in what its laws really consist, whether they can cease to be, whether they can be suspended, what causation is, what time is, what the relations of time to cause and effect, and a hundred other questions of a similar character.

Such is Physical Science, and Theology, as is obvious, is just what Science is not. Theology begins, as its name denotes, not with any sensible facts, phenomena or results, not with nature at all, but with the Author of nature—with the one invisible, unapproachable Cause and Source of all things. It begins at the other end of knowledge, and is occupied, not with the finite, but the Infinite. It unfolds and systematizes what He Himself has told us of Himself; of His nature, His attributes, His will, and His acts. As far as it approaches towards Physics, it takes just the counterpart of the questions which occupy the Physical Philosopher. He contemplates facts before him; the Theologian gives the reasons of those facts. The Physicist treats of efficient causes; the Theologian of final. The Physicist tells us of laws; the Theologian of the Author, Maintainer, and Controller of them; of their scope, of their suspension, if so be; of their beginning and their end. This is how the two schools stand related to each other, at that point when they approach the nearest; but for the most part they are absolutely divergent. What Physical Science is engaged in I have already said; as to

Theology, it contemplates the world, not of matter, but of mind; the Supreme Intelligence; souls and their destiny; conscience and duty; the past, present, and future dealings of the Creator with the creature.[21]

5

Whilst the dichotomy which Newman establishes between theology and physical science is undoubtedly as complete as he depicts it to be, we may perhaps add some slight qualifications to that which he establishes between theology and secular knowledge in general. They do not, however, lessen in any degree the force of his argument.

If we include, as we should, philosophy under the heading of secular knowledge, it may be granted that there are two branches of it which, in a sense, overlap the field of theology, namely natural theology or theodicy, and ethics. But they overlap only as to their subject-matter, the nature of God and the morals of man, for which we have two sources of knowledge, reason and revelation. Theology, therefore, exercises a closer guidance over them than over any other subjects, because it provides a definite check on all their chief findings. It does not, however, affect their internal principle which is that of reason. The same is true, though in a more indirect way, of the other branches of philosophy, ontology, psychology, cosmology and epistemology, insofar as revelation implies certain conclusions which fall within the province of these sciences. Another allied group of sciences, politics, economics and sociology, come into close contact with that branch of theology which is known as moral. But if these contacts be closely examined, it will be found that they never imply a clash between the principles of theology and those of these sciences, but only a determination of the point at which some finding of the latter, valid in its own sphere, involves a decision in the moral order, which properly belongs not to them, but to theology.

These reservations—and they are rather explanations than reservations—being made, Newman's exposition of the complete independence of theology and the secular sciences in their respective spheres is accurate and cogent. Its line of argument should be of the greatest value in approaching the task of assuring those who differ from us in the matter of religious belief that we have this in common with them, that we seek to restore order in education, not by imposing irrational prejudices, but by endeavouring to determine that order in the objective universe, conformity to which can alone produce order in the universe of the intellect.

For we must face the issue squarely—and we shall consider it in detail in our final lecture—that the problem in education is precisely that problem that concerns us all so intimately, the nature of man and his destiny. We have seen that there is today widespread dissatisfaction amongst earnest men, whether they have religious beliefs or not, about the present confusion of education, and the perils to civilisation which that confusion creates. When it comes to the practical task of reducing that confusion to order, the question propounded by Herbert Spencer at once arises: " What knowledge is of most worth? " And out of that question arises another: " What is the meaning of worth? " Obviously, worth is the value that knowledge has in helping man to accomplish something. And again, a third question arises: " Is that something to secure for himself and others the greatest possible degree of material comfort in this life, the least possible suffering, or is there some greater, spiritual destiny to be aimed at?" Unless this question is fairly faced and answered, all efforts to restore order in education, and to give it a direction which will preserve and foster, instead of destroying our civilisation, are, by the very nature of the case, doomed to failure.

10

ENDURING PRINCIPLES

I

WE HAVE NOW to conclude our survey of the principles contained in Newman's great and seminal work. I would commence by once more stressing a note which I have already sounded, namely that no claim can be made that Newman gives us a complete treatise on education, even on university education. He had, as we have seen, the specific purpose of demonstrating the illogicality of education divorced from religious teaching, and his main attention is devoted to that purpose. The general argument which he used, that true knowledge is philosophically comprehensive, enabled him to pass on to his secondary theme, that the imparting of such comprehensive knowledge is the principal aim of a university education. Out of this twofold theme, or rather these two aspects of the same theme, arise many other considerations. They cover, indeed, most of the important problems of education, but if we find any untouched, or if any appear to be inadequately stressed, it is only fair to ask ourselves whether or not they are essential to the treatment of the main theme.

Newman, indeed, would have been the last man to hold that his *Discourses* contained everything that was to be said on the subject of education, or even on his own proper subject of university education. In my Fourth and Seventh Lectures I mentioned my belief that there are certain defects in the composition of the *Discourses* which were due to the pressure under which they were written. The first five were delivered at intervals of a week, and it is obvious from Newman's correspondence that they were being composed as he went along. Moreover, he had hanging over him the prospect of the trial for libel brought against him by the ex-priest Achilli, which took place a few weeks after his Fifth Lecture, and involved him in most complicated business concerning the bringing of witnesses from abroad. In a letter of 15 June 1852 to the Rev. C. Newsham, President of Ushaw College, he writes:

> As to my Lectures, they have cost me no one knows how much thought and anxiety—and again and again I stopped, utterly unable to get on with my subject, and nothing but the intercession of the Blessed Virgin kept me up to my work . . . For three days I sat at my desk nearly from morning to night, and put aside as worthless at night what I had been doing all day . . . I am ashamed so to speak, as if I were achieving any great thing, but at my age I do not work out things as easily as I once did.[1]

Apart from such special considerations which would make Newman unwilling to claim perfection for his work, it may be remarked that all his educational writings display a marked moderation of tone, which on the one hand warns the reader not to expect too much from them, and on the other inspires confidence in opinions expressed with such caution and objectivity. Perhaps in no field is doctrinaire dogmatising so rife as in that of education. Newman is one of the rare figures in that field who is completely free from it. He is, indeed, inflexible in laying down his principles, but shows a marked reserve in suggesting what should be their detailed application. In his own words, he conceives education to involve " questions not simply of immutable truth, but of practice and expedience." [2] If then we find that he refrains at times from descending to particulars, we may attribute this not to any inability to apply his doctrines—this ability is convincingly displayed in his provisions for the conduct of the Catholic University of Ireland—but to his grasp of the fact that they can be equally well applied in a number of different ways.

But whatever qualifications we may make, it remains certain that Newman's *Discourses* contain very much that is extraordinarily applicable to all our present day educational problems. All we need do is to emphasise certain parts of his teaching, since the evils they deal with have grown in extent and have become more dangerous. Thus it is true that though Newman indicates the confusion that is certain to arise from any mutilation of the scheme of knowledge, he was more concerned in his day to demonstrate the illogicality of the great mutilation that was being actually proposed, the omission of all religious teaching, and to try to prevent it. Today we are faced not only with that mutilation as a long-established fact, but also with confusion as an equally well-established fact, and one which is fraught with immense danger owing to the possibility of unprincipled men taking advantage of it to propagate ideas disastrous to mankind. To put it in another way, the problem today is not so much the restoration of religious teaching to its proper place in the curriculum, as the saving of all other intellectual culture from becoming self-destructive.

2

But the solution which Newman proposed for his problem is, of course, the solution for that of today, namely the restoration of a complete, ordered view of the universe. In no other way can intellectual order be restored. The mind cannot create order, but must discover it, if its knowledge is to be a reflection of objective reality and therefore true knowledge. Furthermore, as is assumed by Newman, there must be acknowledged in that order a hierarchy of values. There are truths of greater or less importance in themselves and hence of greater or less importance to man. The clearer the discernment of this order, the more perfect, or to use Newman's terms, the more comprehensive, philosophical, scientific, or liberal will knowledge be, the more stamped with the imprint of reason, the more universally beneficial to man.

It is perfectly true that these great principles will not give a detailed answer to every particular problem of university organisation, but they will keep that organisation on general safe lines. They show for instance why and how far the technological bias of today is to be resisted. There is no question of a mere conservative opposition to scientific progress, no question of a mere anti-technological bias. Technology, that is specialised scientific knowledge applied to problems of material welfare, must be recognised as a good in itself. As we saw in our Fourth Lecture, all knowledge is a perfection of the mind, and technological knowledge is such a perfection. But it is a very limited perfection, and one that leaves the mind peculiarly vulnerable to misdirection, a misdirection that is all the more dangerous as the technological knowledge becomes more perfect. It is a remarkable tribute to Newman's prescience that, writing as he did in the early years of an era of unprecedented scientific discovery, he was able, on the one hand, to appreciate to the full the value of scientific studies, yet on the other to put his finger unerringly on the two dangerous tendencies that were so soon to develop in them, specialisation and utilitarianism.

Again, these wide principles will not dictate the curriculum for every type of student at every age, but they do point very definitely to the desirability for every student of every type of some contact with the humanities in the wide sense, the literary-historical-philosophical group of studies. It is not, as we have seen, that a claim is made for these studies that they give a culture that is specifically different from that given by scientific pursuits. We have seen that Newman readily granted that the latter also could be instruments of liberal education. But there is an immense difference in degree between the liberalising influence of the two groups; and that of the scientific group is steadily diminishing under the two influences of specialisation and utilitarianism. We are thus provided with an answer to the indignant protest that a scientist is surely a man of culture. We can readily grant that he is, but we hold that his purely scientific culture is a limited one, which of its very nature does not blend with other cultures, and hence, on the one hand, is no encouragement to what is good in them, and, on the other, is peculiarly vulnerable to false pretensions on their part.

Furthermore, these principles render us perfectly clear about the grounds on which we defend the peculiar and universal value of humane studies. The claim is often made that they are to be valued because they represent the European tradition. This is perfectly true, but the statement must be fully understood and carefully qualified. It may be granted that the vast bulk of literature that concerns us is European literature, that the history that throws most light on our problems of today is mainly European history, and that practically all the philosophy that is worth knowing comes to us from European sources. It may also be granted that European culture has a peculiar value for us precisely because it is European, that there is a special message for us in the study of the thought of those generations out of whose strivings our own nations have arisen, and that our own culture, whatever it may add, will be most profitably based on that of men whose circumstances and whose problems were not so very different from ours.

Nevertheless, it must be recognised that this is only one argument for the value of humane studies, and one that could to some extent be applied also to scientific studies, at least in their historical aspect. There is, however, a more fundamental argument for the value of the humanities, one which we have already considered at length, and that is, that, irrespective of their place of origin, they constitute the study of man. The facts that they reveal to us are facts concerned with all his higher activities, sentient, volitional, emotional, aesthetic, psychological, ethical, religious. The bearings of these facts on one another and on all other facts are of paramount value, and therefore, according to our broad principles, peculiarly liberal, because their subject-matter stands high in the hierarchy of values, because it raises issues of supreme importance to man, and because it demands the greatest efforts on the part of his reason.

We may note here that the claim made for the value of humane studies is, of course, enormously strengthened if they are taken, as they should be, to include theology. It is here that we, with Newman, part company with the classical humanists, who, as against materialists and pragmatists, assume the superiority of man's intellectual and volitional life to his biological life, but who ignore or minimise the question of his relation to God. They thereby gravely weaken their own position. Among the intellectual activities of man his ethical persuasions are of peculiar significance, and have influenced deeply all his other activities and thereby the course of his history. It may be argued that a study of these ethical persuasions merely as mental phenomena is a valuable contribution to culture, but it must be acknowledged that this study will be of incomparably greater value if these persuasions are regarded as permanent valid norms of right conduct. The classical humanist, indeed, usually accepts them as such, but experience shows how ineffectual is such an acceptance unless it is based on the supreme ethical fact of man's relationship to God. Moreover, going back to our broad principles, it is clear that the inclusion of this relationship gives to humane studies a new and high—indeed supremely high significance, which correspondingly enhances the claim of these studies to be deemed peculiarly liberal. It may be added that the belief in the eternal destiny of man which logically follows from belief in God imparts another wide range of significance to the study of man's intellectual and volitional life as found in the humanities.

3

Granted, then, that the principles we have established enable us to determine with a considerable degree of confidence the aim and content of the ideal curricula of higher studies, a practical problem at once presents itself. Is it better that we, as Catholics, attempt to secure the realisation of this aim and content by founding and supporting our own Catholic universities, or should we content ourselves with working to secure its realisation—whether as teachers or students—in the existing institutions of higher learning, which have now become largely undenominational? Here once again it cannot be claimed that our principles will dictate the final verdict in every case, but their guidance will be of paramount importance in forming that verdict.

To avoid misunderstanding two preliminary points should be made clear. Let us first remember that, as we have already seen in our Sixth Lecture, a Catholic university is not necessarily one conducted by clerics, though, for historical reasons, almost all the existing Catholic universities are clerical foundations. The one essential characteristic of a Catholic university is that, by its constitution, its teaching should be in harmony with the tenets of the Catholic faith. In practice this demands that at least the large majority of its academic staff should be Catholics. Secondly, it must be freely acknowledged that in many countries this problem simply does not arise. It is only a practical one where, as in the United States, the wealth of the Catholic body enables it to support its own universities, or where, as in Holland, state subvention is available alike to denominational and non-denominational institutions.

From all that we have seen in these lectures, it must be clear that, accepting Newman's definition of liberal knowledge as a comprehensive view of the objective universe and the manifold interrelations of its components, for a Catholic the logical conclusion is that only a Catholic university can consistently and completely provide this knowledge. Such a belief may seem to others to be presumptuous or intolerant, but we have traced, mainly in the writings of Newman, the ineluctable reasoning process that leads to it. The Catholic believes that the science of the relations between God and man enters in a most intimate way into the entire scheme of knowledge, and delimits in most important respects the provinces of all other branches of knowledge. He believes that the Catholic Church alone is a divinely-guaranteed source of this science in its fullness, and he sees that, in point of fact, her teachings on a large number of vital religious issues are not held outside her own ranks. The conclusion to him is obvious, that in schemes of knowledge proposed without her guidance, there must be gaps, there must be deformities, of greater or less extent.

Now let us make a few very necessary qualifications. Obviously, no claim can be made that the perfection of their philosophy automatically guarantees efficiency to Catholic scholars. That will depend, as it does for all men, on their talent, their industry, their opportunities. Consequently, it cannot be claimed that the organisation and curriculum of a Catholic university will be, in every particular, superior to those of other universities. They may in many particulars be greatly inferior. The great lines of religious belief and the great philosophical principles connected with religious belief will keep the Catholic university on sound lines in general, but there will be no guarantee, for instance, that the detailed gradation of its studies, or the combination of subjects which it offers for degrees, will be the best possible.

Nor is there any question of underrating the ability of scholars who profess other faiths, or who have no definite beliefs. Many of them may, by the virtue of their beliefs, if they have them, or of their natural rational conclusions, or by tradition, be guided by principles identical with ours, or at any rate arrive at conclusions identical with ours, and hence their teachings will, in fact, have that characteristic of harmony with objective reality which we hold to be the characteristic of true knowledge. This, of course, will be especially true of those few universities which are still controlled by other Christian denominations, or in which the influence of such denominations is still paramount.

Again, we may grant, with Newman, that theological considerations do not affect the intrinsic principles of other sciences, and that there are sciences which, even extrinsically are comparatively little affected by these considerations. There are, therefore, large fields of knowledge in which all minds may meet on equal terms. We may grant that the general influence of many non-denominational universities is still greatly beneficial to mankind, because of the preponderating influence in them of men whose principles are at least effectively Christian. And we can even give full credit to the contributions to knowledge made by men whose principles we believe to be false. We may disagree

with many or all of their conclusions, but may benefit by
the fruits of their erudition, and by the light that they
throw on great problems even by what we hold to be the
wrong approach.

In spite of these qualifications, however, we cannot
exclude the conviction that, without the guidance of the
Catholic faith, it is impossible for an academic institution
to present consistently in its perfection, that comprehensive
view of truth which we believe to constitute liberal knowledge. Amongst the members of non-denominational universities, there is rarely found consistent belief in an objective
order of reality, rarely any consistent standard of intellectual
or ethical values. Indeed, the very idea of a non-denominational institution excludes the possibility of any such
comprehensive view being held by the whole body. And
here we are back to the fundamental theme of Newman's
Discourses, that, without religion, there can be no unity or
order among the various branches of knowledge. We must
recollect, as we have already seen, that undenominational
education is a system of exceedingly modern growth, hardly
more than a century old. In its early days its disruptive
effect on the whole range of human knowledge was not
obvious. For a long period, the majority of university
teachers continued to be Christians, and even when that
majority declined, Christian theological and ethical principles
continued to prevail by the force of tradition and the force
of their appeal to reason. They are, however, today being
ousted by all kinds of formal philosophies and informal
assumptions, and the confusion foretold by Newman is
only too manifest.

The principle of academic freedom is harmless, and even

beneficial when exercised within the proper bounds of each sphere of secular knowledge. It is, however, highly dangerous when it is taken to mean that complete freedom is to be given to each professor to impose his general cultural views on the institution of which he is a member. And if he seeks to impose religious or ethical views, or views on subjects closely related to religion or ethics, it is surely even more dangerous to hold that he should be free from all control. Even the most thorough-going liberals realise that a limit has been reached when a professor's views are, in the general esteem of the society in which he lives, subversive of that society or subversive of public morality. What is not realised is that long before the stage is reached when such obvious danger arises, grave harm may have been done.

But how is the necessary control to be exercised? In a non-denominational university, the governing bodies are precluded by definition from any such control. Even if, in extreme cases, such bodies act to discourage certain teachings, experience shows how difficult it is to secure unanimous action in such a matter. It would seem, therefore, that such control can only be effectively exercised by a body of men who hold the same fundamental religious beliefs, and have therefore more or less the same philosophical and cultural outlook, and who, moreover, are entitled by the constitution of the body to which they belong to make conformity to such beliefs a previous condition of service, in other words, by the members of a denominational university.

In other universities control can only be indirect, by the propagation of the ideals of individuals or groups. Much, indeed, can be done in this way, and it will have our

sympathy and support, whether it be in the form of the open
profession of Christian principles by those who hold them,
or the acceptance by non-Christians of ways of thinking
which are in conformity with Christian principles, and
which also make a strong appeal to natural reason, and are
likely to be accepted by all men of goodwill as antidotes
to our present evils. In the securing of such acceptance,
the great arguments of Newman's *Discourses* should prove
of service on account of their strongly rational basis. It is
certain that very much would be accomplished by the
universal acceptance of his vision of liberal knowledge as
one broad, comprehensive system based on objective truth,
of his insistence on the exercise of reason as the principle
of that knowledge, and of his exposition of the peculiar
merit of humane studies as being a record of man's life at
its highest level.

We have earlier referred to that very able work of Sir
Walter Moberly, *The Crisis in the University*. It is of great
interest to us to note to what extent a sincere Anglican
concurs with us on this issue and how he differs. When
posing the question how order is to be restored amidst the
present chaos of academic thought, Sir Walter discusses the
question whether we should "work today to make the
Christian religion the basis and foundation of the whole
curriculum of the university." [3] He rejects such a solution
of the problem on three grounds. Firstly, it is impracticable,
and secondly it would be inequitable. Seeing that he is
considering the English universities as they at present exist,
"no longer supported only by particular groups or intended
for the use only of particular groups or for the propagation
of particular opinions," [4] his conclusions are doubtless

correct. His third ground for rejecting the Christian solution is that it would not " really further the Christian cause." [5] He argues that the only form of Christianity which would have any hope of general adoption by the university would not be authentic Christianity, but a vague ethos which " implies a belief in truth and goodness and a sustained effort to attain them." As he is again thinking here of the situation in existing universities, his view may be accepted. But we must part company with him when he goes on to argue further that

> while we ourselves are assured that the whole truth is to be found in Christ, we have to recognize that it is not in the possession of Christians, either individually or collectively . . . It follows that an all-Christian university, if we could have it, would be defective . . . In the present state of the world Christians themselves ought not to want an all-Christian university. [6]

We have already granted that an all-Catholic university may, indeed, be defective in certain respects, but we are confident that its general orientation will be sound, and that the eternal principles on which it is founded will infallibly guide it in its task of educating men to be both scholars and " authentic Christians." We cannot, therefore, accept as a general proposition Sir Walter Moberly's belief that " it is a delusion to suppose that the adoption of a Christian platform by the university today would really further the Christian cause." [7] A glance at the Catholic universities of the United States would immediately dispel this belief.

Sir Walter returns to this theme in a later chapter, entitled *Freedom and Integration*, in which he discusses the problem of how to preserve in the university a definite purpose or orientation, whilst giving freedom of expression to individual teachers. At the close of this chapter he gives a summary of his views from which we may quote a few essential passages.

(i) As Christians we hold that nothing short of the Christian faith supplies a basis which does full justice at once to integration and liberty. In our view Christ, as the ultimate source of wisdom and of truth, is the only possible ground for a genuine unity of outlook and aim . . .

(ii) But in present circumstances and in any new future the university's common basis cannot be specific Christianity, and its members should not try to make it so. Yet the university should have a recognizable and conscious orientation. This should take the form of a common moral outlook or *Weltanschauung*, which sees the challenge of our time in personalist rather than technical terms, which, though not specifically Christian, is " christianized " in that it has been deeply influenced by Christianity, and which is a basis on which Christians and large numbers of non-Christians can work cordially together . . .

(iii) We reject the policy of conserving this orientation by any kind of formal " tests " or terms of subscription. But some legitimate regard for it may be had in making appointments, and particularly key appointments. There is a place and a use within the university for a dissenter even in fundamentals, but it is marginal rather than central.[8]

Whilst sympathising with Sir Walter Moberly's fundamental beliefs, and acknowledging that, in the existing
universities nothing more is possible than what he suggests,
it is impossible not to surmise that his proposals will be
less effectual than he hopes. Many questions arise. Who is
to decide on this "common moral outlook," if it is not
"specifically Christian"? Who is to decide between the
comparatively harmless "dissenter" and the "wrecker" to
whom Sir Walter has earlier referred. He holds that
". . . the university's fundamental orientation must be
maintained. The admission to teaching posts of those who
repudiate it in such quantities as to threaten it should be
opposed." [9] Who is to decide when the number of such
men has become dangerous, or for that matter whether the
admission of one particular man may not constitute a major
danger? Those familiar with university life know how
quickly a "marginal" figure may become "central." All
these considerations go to confirm our belief that only in
a purely Christian university can Christian principles of
education be fully and permanently maintained, and for us,
though we recognise and respect the beliefs of other
denominations, a purely Christian university is a Catholic
university.

So much being said regarding the relative merits of the
denominational and non-denominational university, we may
approach more closely the problem of the measure of support
to be given by Catholics to their own universities and to
others. It is well to acknowledge at the outset that no hard
and fast rules can be established. Our principles obviously
dictate the general rule that Catholic universities deserve a
large measure of support from Catholics. However, it is

clear that many circumstances also demand from Catholics co-operation with other universities. We have acknowledged freely that the erudition and industry of the teachers in many of these institutions produces cultural fruits by which Catholics may gratefully benefit, and that not infrequently their cultural outlook is based on principles entirely or almost entirely identical with our own. There is again the obvious consideration that, as students or teachers, Catholics have incomparably better opportunities than they would have as outsiders, to leaven university thought with the philosophy which they believe to be the correct one.

And here we may forestall a common objection, namely that a Catholic should enter a university as a student or a teacher, but not as a propagandist. We have already dealt with this objection, and pointed out that it is impossible for a Catholic to divorce his cultural from his religious views, but we may add that a Catholic is not really different from other men in this. All men have some philosophy of life which inevitably colours their approach to education. All teachers, and, to some degree, even all students are propagandists as well as scholars, in the sense that their general outlook on culture and on life itself must of necessity communicate itself in some degree to the academic community of which they form part. As we have seen, one of the greatest dangers of today is that so many propagandists are found in every university, and often the most effective are those who are least conscious of their power. Even the teachers who disclaim all propaganda, and hold that it is the sole business of each member of the academic body to stick to his own job, are propagandists of one of the most dangerous of all philosophies, laissez-faire. Obviously, a

Catholic, no more than any other man, should not be guilty of intolerance or meddling in what is not his own business, but if he enters a university, he must go in under his own colours, and demand to be accepted for what he is. He must devote himself conscientiously to his own particular task, whether of learning or of teaching, but if he renounces his right to assert his own philosophy of life and to endeavour to make that philosophy effective in the general cultural life of the university, not only is he untrue to his own principles, but he is failing to give to the university of which he forms a part the highest contribution of which he is capable.

With regard to the attendance of Catholic students in non-denominational universities, there is an argument commonly put forward in its favour which requires careful consideration. It is urged that, in view of the circumstances of life today, in which Catholics must live their lives amongst men whose religious views and philosophy of life differ from their own, it is better that they should be educated in non-denominational universities, since there they will become accustomed to hearing the views which they will encounter later on. This will not only equip them better to defend their own position, but will also give them a wider view and hence a better education.

There is a certain amount of truth in this view, but it cannot be accepted without considerable reservation. A completely sheltered existence is as bad for a young mind as it is for a young body. But there must be a limit to the hardening process. It is undoubtedly wise not to coddle a child with scarves and woollen vests at the first sign of the east wind, but it is equally wise not to send him out in a swim-suit when the snow is on the ground. Similarly, it is good for a young man's spiritual and intellectual health to let him come in contact with principles that challenge his own, but it does not follow that he will always survive the sustained onslaught of such principles propounded by far more mature and able minds than his. The provisions of the Canon Law, the official legal code of the Catholic Church, make it clear that there is a danger to be contemplated here. Canon 1374 expresses a general prohibition of the frequentation of non-denominational places of education by Catholics, and states that in cases where the local bishop permits its toleration, certain precautions are to be taken for the safeguarding of faith. The various Rescripts issued by the Holy See concerning the undenominational Queen's Colleges in Ireland, to which we alluded in our Fourth Lecture, declared such institutions to be intrinsically dangerous. This does not mean that they are intrinsically bad—we have already stressed the point that they may at times be productive of very great good—but that there is in them a danger to religious belief arising from their very constitution—from the key fact that their teachers may be men of any philosophy, and fully entitled to propagate it. Whilst, then, the stimulating effect on the student's mind of the interplay and even the clash of various philosophies may be freely admitted, the danger involved must not be underrated, and at times it may be recognised to outweigh whatever advantage is to be gained.

The argument that education imparted by a body of teachers of various religious beliefs and various philosophies is in itself better than education imparted by a body of men of homogeneous beliefs, needs even more qualification.

Such education may possibly be better in some respects, but always for incidental reasons. The knowledge of various religious and philosophical beliefs, gathered at first hand from sincere exponents of them, may help to throw light on the problems with which they are concerned, and give greater clarity to whatever ultimate solution may be come to. It may also happen that certain cultural problems which are only remotely connected with religion or philosophy may be more successfully solved by those whose fundamental principles Catholics do not share. And we have already granted that, within the proper ambit of any secular subject, religion and philosophy are often not involved at all. Clearly then, the wider the pool of teachers from whom choice is made, the more prospect there is of excellence of teaching in that subject.

But in view of all that we have established as to the nature of liberal knowledge, it would be impossible for us to concede that views which we believe to be at variance with objective fact could actually constitute such knowledge. The existence and development of such views could, indeed, form part of its content, but not their acceptance as truth. And even the theoretical study of them cannot be allowed to outweigh or hinder the acquirement of objective truth as far as it can be attained.

This raises a very practical point for the Catholic student of certain subjects such as philosophy, and history and economics insofar as they involve religious and philosophical problems. In a non-denominational university, he is obliged to spend the greater part of his time pursuing these subjects from standpoints which are different from his own, and listening to the exposition of views which, however interesting and able, he does not believe to represent objective fact. Even when his professors are men of liberal mind, and endeavour to deal fairly with every view, the attention allotted to that which he believes to be the one which really matters is necessarily very limited. It may be urged that it is his business to supply what he thinks to be lacking, and that his teachers will often even encourage him to do this. But even in such favourable circumstances, which are not always the rule, the task thereby thrown on him is very heavy, and he may have little or no opportunity to secure extrinsic assistance.

In this regard, the study of philosophy offers particular difficulty. Those who have studied scholastic philosophy, which is the official philosophy of the Catholic Church, and whose main teachings are guaranteed to Catholics by their close connection with theology, know that, in spite of its comparatively fixed and easily recognisable terminology, and its uniform presentation by all Catholic writers, it is a subject which requires not only the closest application, but also that gradual digestion that only time and repetition can give. Once, however, it is mastered as a framework, the study of all other philosophies is comparatively easy. Non-scholastic philosophies, on the other hand, present to the beginner the obstacles of uncertain terminology and variety in their presentation by individual teachers, and the struggle to master their reasonings and conclusions will leave him but little time for supplementing and correcting them by the system which he believes, in the main, to represent things as they really are. One is reminded of the remark attributed to an American undergraduate who was obliged to attend the lectures of certain distinguished non-scholastic philosophers: "Clever guys, but they spend most of the time teaching what ain't."

Instances in which academic men deliberately set out to undermine the existing religious beliefs of their students, though unfortunately not unknown, are comparatively rare. In any case, there is no need to dwell on such an obvious danger. A more subtle one derives from that courteous scepticism which assumes that wisdom consists in a detached survey of opinions, and that to commit oneself to definite convictions is to coarsen one's intellectual fibre. Such an attitude easily communicates itself to the immature mind because of its superficial resemblance to true liberality, and because it saves the trouble of making embarrassing or even painful decisions. It has quite recently been the subject of some witty comments by Mr Christopher Hollis in a review of Mr William Buckley's *God and Man at Yale*.

> The sceptic's position may be an honourable and tenable one, but of its nature it proves either too little or too much. If we cannot possibly know the truth, if one opinion is necessarily as good as another, then what is the point of education? What is the point of spending money on the propagation of knowledge if there is no such thing as knowledge? If there are nothing more than competing ignorances, at least we might as well choose the cheapest.[10]

5

These considerations naturally lead us on to reflect on the strongest claim which a Catholic university has to the adherence of Catholic students, namely the insistence made by it on the fact that education is the training of man for some definite purpose, or in other words the fact that a philosophy of education is identical with a philosophy of life. Observe that I use the word " insistence." It would certainly be presumptuous and false to deny to other educational institutions, or at least to individual members of them, the recognition of this fact.[11] Indeed a distinguished modern Catholic writer on education, Dr de Hovre, devotes the opening chapter of his monumental work *Le Catholicisme, Ses Pédagogues, Sa Pédagogie*, to establishing the thesis that it is recognised by every great educationist from Plato onward. But a Catholic university derives a peculiar advantage from the unanimity of its members as to what the philosophy of life is, and as to the main methods of inculcating it. Even to one who does not agree with the philosophy it propounds, it must be clear that such unanimity imparts a peculiar driving force to the teaching it inspires. But we are here dealing more particularly with the Catholic student, and for him this unanimity must have a peculiar attraction, because it means certain guidance about the most important of all things, the purpose of life and the means to attain it.

The common objection, of course, to such teaching is that it is dogmatic and narrow. We have already seen Newman labouring the point through page after page that dogmatism can never be narrow, because it merely means the inculcation of truth. We are really here back at the fundamental question whether there is an objective order of things and whether man can attain to any certain knowledge of it. If he can, then he is quite entitled to dogmatise. The fact is that everybody dogmatises, even the sceptic about his scepticism, and the pretence of not dogmatising leads to palpable self-contradiction. In our Eighth Lecture we postponed the consideration of John Stuart Mill's views on moral and religious teaching as declared in his Inaugural Address to the University of St Andrews in 1867. These views may well be considered here, since they go to prove that in the matter of propounding a philosophy of life the only choice is between dogmatism and scepticism.

Mill commences with the assertion that "no one can dispense with an education directed expressly to the moral as well as the intellectual part of his being,"[12] and he makes it clear that he is here alluding to religion in general as well as to morality in the strict sense. It may be remarked at once that, if ever there was a dogmatic statement on a most fundamental point, this is one. We may pass over his preliminary remark that it is beyond the power of schools and universities "to educate morally or religiously,"[13] this being the function of the family. As a general proposition this statement is completely contradicted by what follows, but Mill explains that he is here speaking of "training the feelings and the daily habits."[14] Such a definition of "moral and religious training" is certainly an extraordinarily narrow one, and we need not waste time in discussing whether it would be possible to give such training outside the family.

Mill then continues:

What is special to a university on these subjects (morality and religion) belongs chiefly, like the rest of its work, to the intellectual department. A university exists for the purpose of laying open to each succeeding generation, as far as the conditions of the case admit, the accumulated treasure of the thoughts of mankind. As an indispensable part of this, it has to make known to them what mankind at large, their own country, and the best and wisest individual men, have thought on the great subject of morals and religion. There should be, and there is in most universities, professional instruction in moral philosophy; but I could wish that this instruction were of a somewhat different type from what is ordinarily met with. I could wish that it were more expository, less polemical, and above all less dogmatic . . . I do not mean that he (the teacher) should encourage an essentially sceptical eclecticism. While placing every system in the best aspect it admits of, and endeavouring to draw from all of them the most salutary consequences compatible with their nature, I would by no means debar him from enforcing by his best arguments his own preference for some one of the number. They cannot all be true; though those which are false as theories may contain particular truths, indispensable to the completeness of the true theory. But on this subject, even more than on any of those I have previously mentioned, it is not a teacher's business to impose his own judgment, but to inform and discipline that of his pupil.[15]

There are in this passage a number of loose statements and false assumptions, of which it will suffice to pick out the more obvious. First of all, there is Mill's demand that the teaching on moral philosophy is to be *less* dogmatic. No individual statement can be more or less dogmatic. Either it is dogmatic or it is not. Hence, the only meaning that can be attributed to Mill's words is that he will admit some dogmatism, but only a little of it. This interpretation of his meaning is borne out by the next passage in which Mill grants that the teacher is at liberty to express his belief in the certainty of some of his teachings. He seems however to think he has gone a little too far here, and adds the warning that " it is not a teacher's business to impose his own judgment, but to inform and discipline that of his pupil." [16] In this, Catholic teachers, and I should think all teachers of commonsense would agree with Mill. To impose one's own judgment is to demand acceptance of it on the sole ground of one's own authority. Such a demand might conceivably be sometimes made of schoolboys, for the reason that they are as yet incapable of mastering the arguments required to establish certain truths, but it would be a very rash university professor who would act on the principle of, " I am Sir Oracle, and when I speak, let no dog bark." It would appear, indeed, that in issuing this protest against the teacher imposing his own judgment, Mill is merely tilting against windmills, and that the reservation he thereby makes does not in the least modify his previous admission that a teacher may propose at least some of his teachings, not as mere possible opinions, but as certain truths.

Mill then proceeds to the discussion of the teaching of religion, under which title he evidently includes both revealed religion and natural truths of religion which do not come under the precise heading of morality.

I shall not enter into the question which has been debated with so much vehemence in the last and present generation, whether religion ought to be taught at all in universities and public schools, seeing that religion is the subject of all others on which men's opinions are most widely at variance. On neither side of this controversy do the disputants seem to me to have sufficiently freed their minds from the old notion of education, that it consists in the dogmatic inculcation from authority, of what the teacher deems true. Why should it be impossible, that information of the greatest value on subjects connected with religion, should be brought before the student's mind . . . without (his) being taught dogmatically the doctrines of any church or sect . . . ? This diversity (of religious views) should of itself be a warning to a conscientious teacher that he has no right to impose his view authoritatively upon a youthful mind . . . The various Churches . . . are quite competent to the task which is peculiarly theirs, that of teaching each its own doctrines . . . to its own rising generation. The proper task of an University is different; not to tell us from authority what we ought to believe . . . but to help us to form our own belief in a manner worthy of intelligent beings.[17]

This, again, is a very confused passage—and I have purposely omitted some of the more confused parts of it. It contains three main statements which we may examine. Firstly, that there are certain professors who inculcate religious beliefs on their own authority. We have met with this bogey before in connection with the teaching of moral philosophy. No sane teacher will attempt to inculcate religious belief on his own authority, for he does not possess that authority. The most he can do is to give his reasons why he believes one religion to be true. But, secondly, Mill holds that he must not even do this. He must confine himself to explaining the nature of the various religious beliefs. We have already seen that Mill concedes that a teacher of moral philosophy may present one system as that which he believes to be true, and there is absolutely no reason why the same concession should not be made with regard to religion. Thirdly, the churches may teach their doctrine dogmatically, but not the university professor. This any Catholic, and presumably any believer in a church with teaching authority will grant. The church may dogmatise—and it may be observed that she does so in the strict sense of proposing a truth on her authority. The most that the university professor can do is to inform his students of what the church teaches, and to give his reasons why he accepts her authority.

In the course of this criticism of Mill's views, we have enunciated various principles that guide the Catholic teacher of moral philosophy or religion, or indeed any Catholic teacher insofar as his subject involves morality or religion. We may now briefly summarise these principles. It is certainly his duty to expound every system fully and fairly. However, he is fully entitled to express his certain belief in one system, and indeed would be failing in his duty if he did not. He does this dogmatically, in the sense of expressing a firm conviction, but not in the sense of invoking his own authority. If he invokes authority, it is that of the church which he invokes, and he must expound his reasons for accepting it. His dogmatism in either sense, far from being narrow, opens up to the student, by the means of natural certitude or faith, a whole range of knowledge which a mere theoretical treatment of religious beliefs would leave untouched.

We have already made reference to M. Maritain's work,

Education at the Crossroads, containing the substance of lectures delivered at Yale University in 1943. M. Maritain is a Catholic philosopher who cannot be accused of narrowness, and it is therefore interesting to note that his doctrine in these lectures as to the function of a teacher of philosophy is identical with that which we have enunciated. M. Maritain commences by stating his opinion that " a good philosophy should be a true philosophy,"[18] one, namely, which the professor believes to represent objective truth. The question then arises of his aim in teaching. M. Maritain points out that he may have three aims. There is, firstly, the task of acquainting his students with " the common though unformulated heritage of philosophical wisdom which passes through any real teaching of philosophy, whatever may be the system of the teacher."[19] Secondly, there is the task of awakening in the student the power of reasoning. But, continues M. Maritain,

> there is indeed a third point, which is valid only for philosophers as hardened as myself; they may always hope, indeed, that by virtue of its very truth, the philosophy which they think to be true, as I do Aristotelian and Thomistic philosophy, will gain momentum among their fellow-men, at least in the generation to come.[20]

If this may be the legitimate aim of a teacher of scholastic philosophy, presumably M. Maritain would claim it even more strongly for a teacher of Catholic theology, who believes that what he offers to his students has not only the assurance of reason, but also that of divine revelation.

Time now demands that we bring to a conclusion our consideration of Newman's great work and of the numerous issues that arise from it. We do so with the consciousness of how much more could be said, of how much could have been said better. But this is not surprising. Our whole study has brought into clear light the fact that a philosophy of education is essentially a philosophy of life, and is therefore concerned with the most fundamental principles known to man, principles which are capable of endless investigation and of infinitely varying applications.

One great reason for hope that this work of ours will have been of value is the fact that the study of education is for most men the only study of philosophy which they make, and for all men the commonest and that which affects their lives most intimately. There was never an age in which formal education was so widespread, and this has naturally led to widespread discussion as to its value. It will, indeed, be a great boon to mankind if this discussion leads, as it naturally should, to more widespread discussion of the value of life for which education is a preparation. The study of Newman's *Idea of a University*, of his kindred writings, and of his practical application of the principles contained therein, should be of very great value in the encouragement of such a trend of thought. Such a study will reveal the workings of a great mind, deeply versed in almost every field of human knowledge, keenly alive to the most subtle workings of human thought, inspired by the most noble moral ideals, and by a clear vision of man's immortal destiny, a mind which had been purified in the crucible of spiritual struggle and sacrifice, and was thus peculiarly fitted to the task of creating that harmonious synthesis of the relations between God, man and the rest of the universe, which constitutes in essence the philosophy of life and therefore of education.

FOREWORD

1 *The Life of Cardinal Newman*, I, pp. 390-416
2 Since these lectures were delivered, there has appeared the exceptionally able work of Professor A. Dwight Culler, then associate professor of English at the University of Illinois, now professor of English at Yale University, *The Imperial Intellect, A Study of Newman's Educational Ideal*. (Yale University Press, 1955). This book covers most of the ground which I traverse, and in far greater detail. I feel, however, that my lectures may serve as a useful introduction to students commencing their study of Newman. Professor Culler's will provide them with a wider and more profound examination of the themes which I outline.

LECTURE ONE

ACADEMIC FERMENT

1 The original title of these lectures was " The Background of Newman's *Idea of a University*."
2 For the historical sketch which follows, I have relied mainly on two works of recognised reliability; Sir Charles Mallett's *History of the University of Oxford*, vol. III, and D. A. Winstanley's *Early Victorian Cambridge*.
3 *First Discourse*, pp. 3-4. The page references throughout are to the edition edited by Professor Charles Frederick Harrold. (London: 1947).
4 *Seventh Discourse*, p. 139.
5 *Edinburgh Review*, no. xxix, p. 43
6 ibid., p. 44
7 ibid., p. 46
8 ibid., p. 48
9 ibid., p. 49
10 ibid., p. 51
11 Whitehead, *The Aims of Education and other Essays*, 1942 ed., p. 3
12 *Edinburgh Review*, no. xxix, pp. 51-2
13 *Seventh Discourse*, p. 137
14 ibid., p. 139

15 Edward Copleston, *A Reply to the Calumnies of the Edinburgh Review against Oxford, containing an account of the Studies pursued in that University*, Oxford: 1810, pp. 107 *sqq*. My references are to the second edition which is in the Bodleian Library, Oxford. Printed for the Author and fold (sic) by J. Cooke and J. Parker and J. Machinlay.

16 ibid., pp. 111-12. *Seventh Discourse*, pp. 150-1. No source is given by Copleston for this quotation. Newman says (p. 150), "Vid. Milton on Education." The reference is to the *Tractate on Education*, addressed to Mr Samuel Hartlib (1673), Pitt Press Series edition, London: 1890, p. 8.

17 Copleston, op. cit., p. 113.

18 ibid., p. 114

19 ibid., p. 115

20 ibid., pp. 115-16

21 ibid., p. 119

22 ibid.

23 ibid., p. 133

24 ibid., p. 165

25 ibid.

26 ibid., p. 168

27 ibid., p. 167

28 *Edinburgh Review*, vol. XVI, no. XXI, pp. 158-87, Art. VII

29 ibid., p. 179

30 ibid., p. 180

31 ibid., p. 181

32 ibid., pp. 181-2

33 ibid., p. 185

34 *Quarterly Review*, August 1810, p. 203

35 ibid.

36 *Quarterly Review*, October 1811, p. 180. *Seventh Discourse*, p. 154

37 ibid.

38 ibid.

39 ibid.

40 *Quarterly Review*, October 1811, p. 182

41 ibid., p. 181

42 ibid., p. 186

43 ibid., p. 187

44 Not to be confused with his contemporary, Sir William Rowan Hamilton, the famous Irish mathematician and astronomer.

45 *First Discourse*, p. 4

46 "On the State of the English Universities, with more especial reference to Oxford." *Edinburgh Review*, June 1831, vol. LIII, no. CVI, pp. 304-427. December 1831, vol. LIV, no. CVIII, pp. 478-504.

47 ibid., October 1834, vol. LX, no. CXXI, pp. 202-30. January 1835, vol. LX no. CXXII, pp. 422-45.

48 These articles were reprinted in *Discussions on Philosophy and Literature, Education and University Reform*, 1852. My references are to the second edition, 1853. The present reference is p. 479.

49 ibid., p. 482

50 ibid., p. 475

51 ibid., p. 544

52 ibid., p. 500

53 Hamilton, *On a Reform of the English Universities with special reference to Oxford; and limited to the Faculty of Arts*, 1852, p. 763.

54 ibid., p. 824

55 ibid.

56 ibid., p. 782

57 ibid., p. 788

LECTURE TWO

A NEW UNIVERSITY FOR A NEW WORLD

1 Joseph Priestley, *Lectures on History and General Policy; to which is prefixed An Essay on a Course of Liberal Education for civil and active life*, Birmingham, 1786. Cited by H. Hale Bellot in *University College London 1826—1926*, London: 1929, a work on which I have chiefly relied for the historical portion of this lecture.

2 P. A. Bruce, *History of the University of Virginia*, New York: 1920-22, I, p. 222. (Cited Bellot, op. cit., p. 10).

3 Adamson, *A Short History of Education*, Cambridge: 1930, p. 279

4 Cited Bellot, op. cit., p. 64

5 Arthur Penrhyn Stanley, *The Life and Correspondence of Thomas Arnold, D.D.*, II, p. 97

6 *Edinburgh Review*, vol. XLIII, 1826, pp. 316, 340

7 Lady Holland, *A Memoir of Rev. Sydney Smith*, 1869, p. 179. (Cited Bellot, op. cit., p. 177)

8 Bellot, op. cit., p. 180

9 ibid., p. 218

10 ibid., pp. 233-4

11 Anne Mozley, *Letters and Correspondence of John Henry Newman during his Life in the English Church*, II, p. 97

12 The modern period is admirably dealt with in *The Story of the University of London; What and Where it is*, by R. J. S. McDowall, M.D. and D. M. Gurney, B.A., London: 1952.

LECTURE THREE

THE SEED-GROUND OF NEWMAN'S *IDEA*

1 As the audience to which these lectures were addressed was mainly composed of students, I endeavoured, as far as possible, to refer them to such first-hand sources as were easily accessible. Miss Mozley's work has, of course, been repeatedly drawn on by writers who have dealt with Newman's youth, and has more recently been supplemented by other documents contained in the Oratorian archives in Birmingham.

Since these lectures were delivered, the *Autobiographical Memoir* has been reprinted in *John Henry Newman; Autobiographical Writings* by Fr Henry Tristram (London: 1956). My page references, except where otherwise indicated, are to this book which is more easy to obtain than Miss Mozley's original work.

2 Mr J. R. H. Weaver

3 Tristram, op. cit., p. 40

4 ibid., p. 46

5 ibid., pp. 77-8

6 ibid., pp. 65-6

7 *Apologia pro Vita Sua*, part III, p. 109. My references are to the 1913 edition.

8 Tristram, op. cit., p. 66

9 ibid., p. 67

10 Cited by Wilfrid Ward, *The Life of Cardinal Newman*, I, p. 37

11 *Apologia*, III, p. 115

12   Tristram, op. cit., p. 69
13   ibid., p. 90
14   ibid., p. 91
15   ibid., p. 92
16   Maisie Ward, *Young Mr Newman*, London: 1948, p. 180
17   Fergal McGrath, *Newman's University: Idea and Reality*, Dublin: 1951, p. 180
18   Quoted by Maisie Ward, op. cit., p. 156
19   *Apologia*, III, p. 117
20   Anne Mozley, op. cit., I, p. 206
21   *Apologia*, III, p. 117
22   Maisie Ward, op. cit., p. 158
23   They are entitled " The Tamworth Reading Room " and occupy pp. 254-97 of the 1872 edition. I have not thought it necessary to give page references for the quotations given, since they are so easily verifiable, but there are references in the text to the letters in which they will be found.
24   R. W. Church, *The Oxford Movement*, London: 1891, pp. 113-14
25   Wilfrid Ward, op. cit., I, p. 58
26   Newman, *Fifteen Sermons Preached before the University of Oxford*, London: 1843. The present reference is p. 282 of the 1887 edition.
27   ibid., p. 287
28   ibid., pp. 290-1
29   ibid., p. 291. Cf. Lecture One, p. 44, views of Sir William Hamilton.
30   All the older biographies of Newman have dealt with the history of his religious convictions. On the whole their accounts do not differ greatly. More modern writers have had the benefit of access to the immense correspondence of Newman and his friends, and have thus been able to give a fuller and more accurate picture of his mind at various periods. Amongst these modern works three may be specially recommended to the student; *Young Mr Newman* by Maisie Ward, *Newman, His Life and Spirituality*, by Louis Bouyer (English translation by J. Lewis May), and *Newman at Oxford: His Religious Development*, by R. D. Middleton, a sympathetic work from the Anglican standpoint. There are many acute judgements in Seán Ó Faoláin's *Newman's Way*, although the book is mainly concerned with Newman's relations

with his family. For a general view of the events of the period I have never found anything to equal Christopher Dawson's *The Spirit of the Oxford Movement.*

31 Church, op. cit., p. 9
32 Cf Lecture Two, p. 69
33 Wilfrid Ward, op. cit., II, pp. 460-2
34 *Apologia,* III, pp. 107-11; IV, pp. 150-3
35 *Apologia,* IV, pp. 139 *sqq.*
36 ibid., p. 150
37 ibid., p. 176 *sqq.*

LECTURE FOUR

THE SCIENCE OF SCIENCES

1 *Idea of a University,* London: 1947, pp. xxxiii-xxxv
2 *Second Discourse,* pp. 18-19
3 ibid., p. 38
4 Bruce Truscot, *Redbrick University,* London: 1943, p. 175. At the time of writing these lectures the identity of " Bruce Truscot " and the late Professor Alison Peers was a well-guarded secret.
5 *Third Discourse,* pp. 40-1
6 ibid., pp. 42-3
7 *Historical Sketches,* I, 2, p. 294, (London: 1882)
8 *Third Discourse,* pp. 61-2
9 ibid., p. 65
10 *Fifth Discourse,* p. 88
11 *Third Discourse,* p. 46. Cf Lecture One, p. 42, views of Sir William Hamilton.
12 *Fifth Discourse,* p. 90
13 ibid.
14 ibid., p. 91
15 ibid.
16 ibid., p. 92
17 ibid., p. 95
18 ibid., pp. 95-6

19 ibid., p. 97
20 ibid., p. 90
21 ibid., p. 98
22 This original *Fifth Discourse* is reprinted in the 1947 edition of *The Idea of a University*. The reference is p. 394.
23 *Fifth Discourse*, p. 98
24 Cf Lecture One, p. 43, views of Sir William Hamilton.
25 *Fifth Discourse*, pp. 99-100
26 ibid., p. 108
27 *Sixth Discourse*, pp. 118-19
28 ibid., p. 129
29 *Seventh Discourse*, pp. 145-6
30 ibid., pp. 146-7
31 ibid., p. 156
32 ibid., pp. 157-8

LECTURE FIVE

THE STUDY OF MAN

1 *Idea of a University*, appendix, p. 394
2 *Fifth Discourse*, pp. 89-90
3 The classical source in English on this topic is Rashdall's *The Universities of Europe in the Middle Ages*, (Oxford: 1895; revised edition, Oxford: 1936) especially vol. I ch. 2, What is a University? Rashdall may also be consulted for the constitution of the individual mediaeval universities, whilst on both mediaeval and modern universities a wealth of information is to be found in Stephen d'Irsay, *Histoire des Universités Françaises et Etrangères des Origines á nos Jours*, Paris: 1933.
4 d'Irsay, op. cit., I, pp. 292-3
5 *Second Discourse*, p. 19
6 T. H. Huxley, *Science and Education, Essays*, New York: 1894, p. 191
7 Truscot, op. cit., p. 47

8 ibid.
9 *Seventh Discourse*, p. 142
10 *Third Discourse*, p. 42
11 *Seventh Discourse*, p. 154
12 *Ninth Discourse*, p. 201
13 Sir Richard Livingstone, *A Defence of Classical Education*, London: 1917, p. 33 *sqq.*
14 *Third Discourse*, pp. 41, 42, 44
15 *Sixth Discourse*, pp. 116-17
16 *Ninth Discourse*, p. 194
17 *Fifth Discourse*, p. 96
18 *Seventh Discourse*, p. 147
19 *Idea of a University*, pp. xx-xxi
20 *Fifth Discourse*, p. 95
21 *Seventh Discourse*, p. 144
22 *Lecture on Christianity and Letters*, p. 230
23 Christopher Dawson, *Understanding Europe*, London: 1953, p. 5
24 ibid., p. 7
25 ibid., p. 20

LECTURE SIX

SACRED AND SECULAR KNOWLEDGE

1 *Second Discourse*, p. 39
2 ibid., p. 23
3 ibid.
4 ibid., p. 24
5 ibid., pp. 25, 26
6 ibid., p. 27
7 ibid., p. 33
8 *Third Discourse*, pp. 54-9
9 ibid., pp. 57-8
10 ibid., p. 59
11 ibid.
12 ibid., p. 60

13 ibid., pp. 61-2
14 ibid., p. 64
15 *Fifth Discourse*, p. 96
16 *Ninth Discourse*, p. 191
17 ibid., pp. 194-201
18 ibid., p. 201
19 ibid., p. 207
20 *My Campaign in Ireland*. This book was published for private cir-
    culation by Father William Neville of the Oratory, Birmingham,
    in 1896. It contains numerous documents relating to the Catholic
    University of Ireland, Newman's annual reports, papal documents,
    rules and regulations of the University, etc. The original *Fifth
    Discourse* was reprinted in Harrold's edition of *The Idea of a University*
    and the page references are to this source, except where otherwise
    noted.
21 *Idea of a University*, pp. 389-406
22 ibid., pp. 390-1
23 ibid., p. 393
24 ibid., p. 391
25 ibid., p. 394
26 ibid., p. 396
27 ibid., p. 398
28 ibid., pp. 398-9
29 It is remarkable that Newman devotes so much attention to a
    system which was rarely adopted in his day. The nearest approach
    to it which is commonly found is the "simple Bible reading
    without comment" prescribed in the Lancasterian schools in
    England and in the National Schools in Ireland. It is possible
    that Newman's interest in this question arose from the attempts
    made by Whately, who, as Protestant Archbishop of Dublin,
    was a prominent member of the National Board in Ireland, to
    have some form of common religious teaching introduced into
    the Irish schools. He actually composed for this purpose a text-
    book, *Introductory Lessons on Christian Evidence* (1837), revised
    (1849) as *Lessons on the Truth of Christianity*, and endeavoured
    unsuccessfully to have it adopted in the schools. (Cf McGrath,
    op. cit., pp. 36-7).
30 *Idea of a University*, pp. 399-400
31 ibid., p. 400

32 ibid., pp. 401-2
33 *My Campaign in Ireland*, pp. lxxix—lxxxii
34 This memorandum was published in 1956 by Father Henry Tristram in *John Henry Newman: Autobiographical Writings*. The present reference is pp. 322-3
35 *Idea of a University*, p. 399
36 Detailed quotations may be found in McGrath, op. cit., p. 277
37 Tristram, op. cit., p. 322
38 *Collectio Lacensis; Acta et Decreta sacrorum Conciliorum recentium*, vol. VII, Col. 75.
39 It is found in *Idea of a University*, pp. 333-53.
40 ibid., p. 349
41 ibid., pp. 342-3
42 Cf McGrath, op. cit., pp. 168-74
43 *Historical Sketches*, III, 1, p. 183
44 ibid., pp. 183, 181

LECTURE SEVEN

THE *IDEA* IN PRACTICE

1 *My Campaign in Ireland*, pp. 77-81. As this book is now so difficult to obtain, I have throughout this chapter added references to my own work *Newman's University: Idea and Reality*, which contains numerous important excerpts. These references appear in parenthesis. The present reference is pp. 115-22.
2 ibid., pp. 271-8 (193-4)
3 ibid., pp. 88-91 (294-5)
4 ibid., pp. 93-100 (297-313)
5 *Seventh Discourse*, p. 157
6 *My Campaign in Ireland*, pp. 97-8 (298)
7 ibid., p. 98
8 McGrath, op. cit., p. 372. This report is not included in *My Campaign in Ireland*, but is referred to on p. 207.

9 *My Campaign in Ireland*, pp. xxxvii-xxxviii
10 ibid., pp. 101-45 (383-9, summary)
11 ibid., p. 138 (388)
12 ibid., p. 99 (299)
13 *Idea of a University*, p. xxvii
14 ibid., p. xxx
15 ibid., p. xxxi
16 ibid., pp. 335-6
17 *My Campaign in Ireland*, pp. 96-7 (298)
18 ibid., 110-11 (386)
19 Truscot, op. cit., p. 47
20 ibid., p. 106
21 ibid., p. xx
22 Jacques Maritain, *Education at the Crossroads*, New Haven and London: 1943, p. 84
23 *Idea of a University*, pp. xx-xxi
24 ibid., p. xx
25 *My Campaign in Ireland*, p. 298 (330)
26 ibid., pp. 177-8 (420-1)
27 ibid., p. 139

LECTURE EIGHT

PERENNIAL PROBLEMS

1 Herbert Spencer, *Education, Intellectual, Moral and Spiritual*, London: 1929, p. 4
2 ibid., p. 7
3 ibid.
4 ibid., p. 53
5 ibid., p. 8
6 ibid., p. 10
7 ibid., p. 9
8 *Third Discourse*, p. 42
9 *Ninth Discourse*, p. 194

10 Spencer, op. cit., p. 43
11 Maritain, op. cit., p. 51
12 ibid.
13 F. A. Cavenagh (ed.), *James and John Stuart Mill on Education*, Cambridge: 1931, p. 133
14 ibid., p. 134
15 *Fifth Discourse*, p. 90
16 *Seventh Discourse*, p. 147. Cf. Lecture Five, pp. 152-3
17 Cavenagh, op. cit., p. 134
18 ibid., p. 150
19 ibid., p. 154
20 ibid., p. 151
21 ibid., p. 160
22 ibid., pp. 160-1
23 ibid., p. 161
24 ibid.
25 ibid., p. 162
26 ibid.
27 *Objectives of a General Education in a Free Society*, Cambridge, Mass.: 1945, pp. 11-12
28 ibid., p. 51
29 ibid., p. 52
30 ibid., p. 53
31 ibid., pp. viii-ix
32 ibid., p. 59
33 *Seventh Discourse*, pp. 154-5
34 *Objectives of a General Education*, p. 55
35 ibid., p. 65
36 *Fifth Discourse*, p. 99
37 *Sixth Discourse*, p. 119
38 *Objectives of a General Education*, p. 65
39 ibid., p. 66
40 ibid., pp. 69-70
41 ibid., p. 71
42 ibid., pp. 71-2
43 ibid., p. 73
44 ibid.
45 ibid.
46 ibid., p. 205

47 ibid., p. 209
48 ibid., p. 53
49 ibid.
50 ibid., p. 54
51 *Report of the Consultative Committee on Secondary Education with special reference to Grammar Schools and Technical High Schools*, London: 1938, p. 141.
52 ibid., pp. 145-6
53 ibid., p. 147
54 ibid., p. 153
55 ibid., pp. 172-3
56 ibid., pp. 244-5
57 ibid., p. 245
58 ibid., pp. 403 *sqq.*
59 ibid., pp. 412-14

LECTURE NINE

THE RESTORATION OF ORDER

1 John Dewey, *Democracy and Education*, 1942, p. 386
2 ibid., p. 281
3 Sir Walter Moberly, *The Crisis in the University*, London: 1947
4 ibid., especially chapters 2-4
5 ibid., p. 59
6 ibid., p. 71
7 ibid., p. 85
8 ibid., pp. 93-9
9 *Third Discourse*, pp. 40-1
10 ibid., p. 41
11 ibid., p. 43
12 *Fifth Discourse*, pp. 392-3
13 M. V. C. Jeffreys, *Glaucon, An Enquiry into the Aims of Education*, London: 1950, p. 150
14 Moberly, op. cit., p. 89

15 John D. Redden and Francis A. Ryan, *A Catholic Philosophy of Education*, p. 192
16 *Objectives of a General Education*, p. 39
17 *Third Discourse*, p. 59
18 ibid., pp. 60-1
19 *Fourth Discourse*, p. 65
20 As is seen from the following sentence, Newman is here using the term " Physics " to designate Physical Science in general. In his day, " Natural Philosophy " was the name for that branch of science now called " Physics."
21 *Idea of a University*, pp. 309-13

LECTURE TEN

ENDURING PRINCIPLES

1 Ward, op. cit., p. 316. McGrath, op. cit., p. 162
2 *First Discourse*, p. 9. These words were added to the second edition.
3 Moberly, op. cit., p. 99
4 ibid., p. 102
5 ibid., p. 103
6 ibid., pp. 104-5
7 ibid., p. 103
8 ibid., pp. 160-1
9 ibid., p. 159
10 *The Tablet*, 5 April 1952
11 Cf. *Christian Education* (the Bampton Lectures 1944) by the late Right Rev. Spencer Leeson, Bishop of Peterborough, former headmaster of Winchester: " This (the Christian) faith, in the souls of those who hold it, is exclusive of all others—there is no room for compromise or modification, and an education founded on that faith must differ entirely in purpose and method from an education founded on another faith, or on no faith, if indeed that is possible . . . This . . . may sound dogmatic. It is dogmatic, and it is meant to be. There can be no practice

of any kind, educational or other, that is not founded on dogma, either express or implied." (p. 115).

12 Cavenagh, op. cit., p. 182
13 ibid.
14 ibid.
15 ibid., pp. 183-4
16 ibid., p. 184
17 ibid., pp. 185-6
18 Maritain, op. cit., p. 72
19 ibid., pp. 72-3
20 ibid., p. 73

INDEX OF NAMES